NiNGEN'S
NiGHTMARES®

To my wife.

—*J. P. Kalonji*

NINGEN'S NIGHTMARES®

Written and illustrated by
J. P. Kalonji

Cover colors by
Dan Jackson

DARK HORSE BOOKS®

Publisher
Mike Richardson

Editor
Philip R. Simon

Assistant Editor
Everett Patterson

Designers
Kat Larson with Heather Doornink

Digital Production and Retouch
Ryan Jorgensen

Published by Dark Horse Books
A division of Dark Horse Comics, Inc.
10956 SE Main Street
Milwaukie, OR 97222

DarkHorse.com | KalonjiArt.com

To find a comics shop in your area, call the Comic
Shop Locator Service toll-free at 1-888-266-4226.

NINGEN'S NIGHTMARES

Special thanks to Siu-Anne Marie Gill, Dan Jackson, and Kait Zuidema

First edition: April 2013
ISBN 978-1-59582-859-0

1 3 5 7 9 10 8 6 4 2
PRINTED IN THE UNITED STATES OF AMERICA

HAGAKURE

It's nice to think of the world as a dream.

When you wake up from a nightmare, you tell yourself it was a bad dream.

They say the world we live in isn't very different from a dream.

—Jocho Yamamoto
(1659–1719)

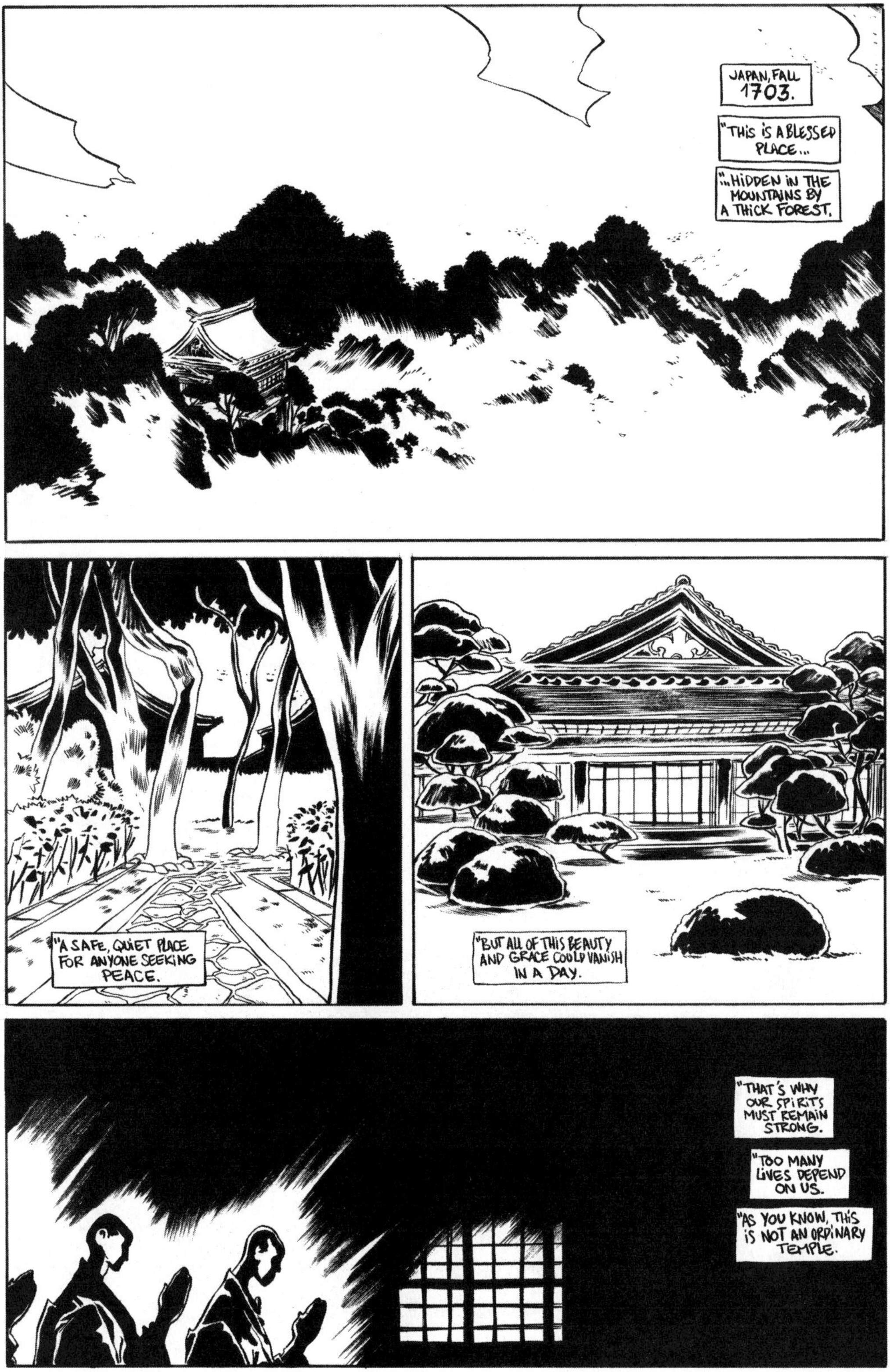
JAPAN, FALL 1703.
"THIS IS A BLESSED PLACE...
"...HIDDEN IN THE MOUNTAINS BY A THICK FOREST.
"A SAFE, QUIET PLACE FOR ANYONE SEEKING PEACE.
"BUT ALL OF THIS BEAUTY AND GRACE COULD VANISH IN A DAY.
"THAT'S WHY OUR SPIRITS MUST REMAIN STRONG.
"TOO MANY LIVES DEPEND ON US.
"AS YOU KNOW, THIS IS NOT AN ORDINARY TEMPLE.

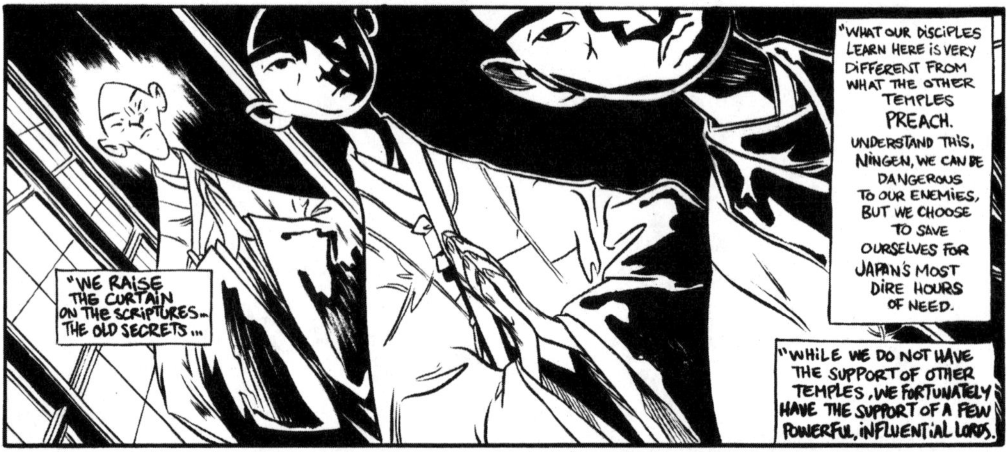
"WE RAISE THE CURTAIN ON THE SCRIPTURES... THE OLD SECRETS...
"WHAT OUR DISCIPLES LEARN HERE IS VERY DIFFERENT FROM WHAT THE OTHER TEMPLES PREACH.
UNDERSTAND THIS, NINGEN, WE CAN BE DANGEROUS TO OUR ENEMIES, BUT WE CHOOSE TO SAVE OURSELVES FOR JAPAN'S MOST DIRE HOURS OF NEED.
"WHILE WE DO NOT HAVE THE SUPPORT OF OTHER TEMPLES, WE FORTUNATELY HAVE THE SUPPORT OF A FEW POWERFUL, INFLUENTIAL LORDS.

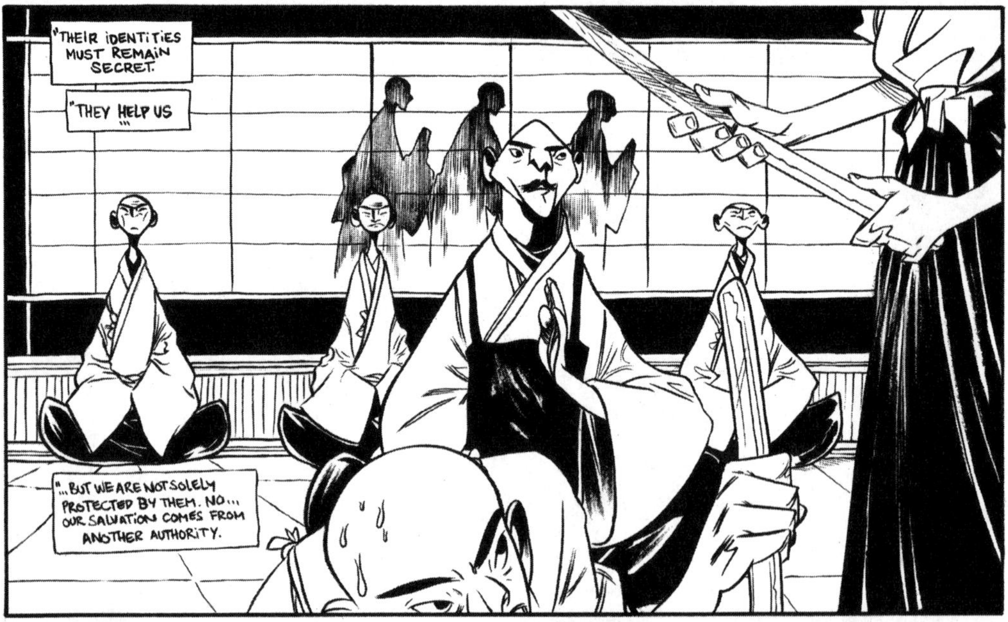
"THEIR IDENTITIES MUST REMAIN SECRET.
"THEY HELP US...
"...BUT WE ARE NOT SOLELY PROTECTED BY THEM. NO... OUR SALVATION COMES FROM ANOTHER AUTHORITY.

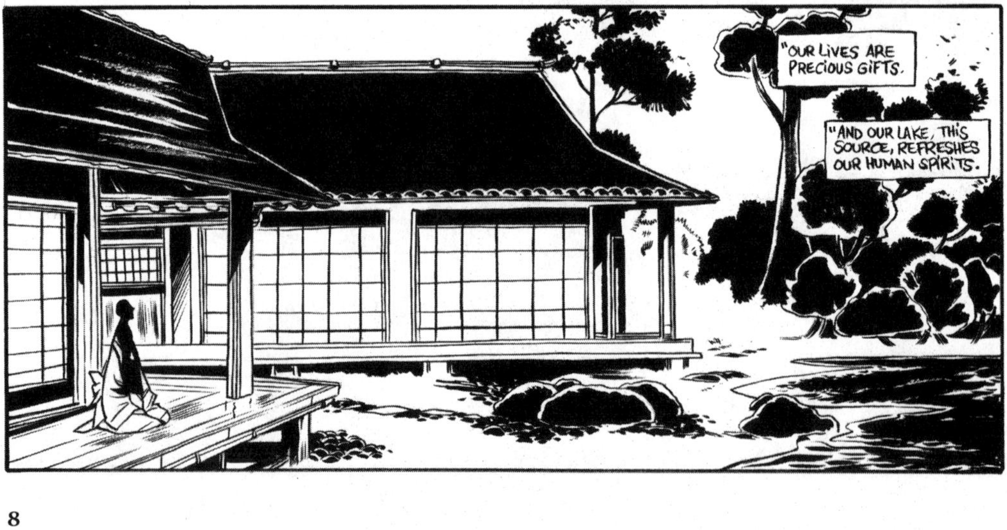
"OUR LIVES ARE PRECIOUS GIFTS.
"AND OUR LAKE, THIS SOURCE, REFRESHES OUR HUMAN SPIRITS.

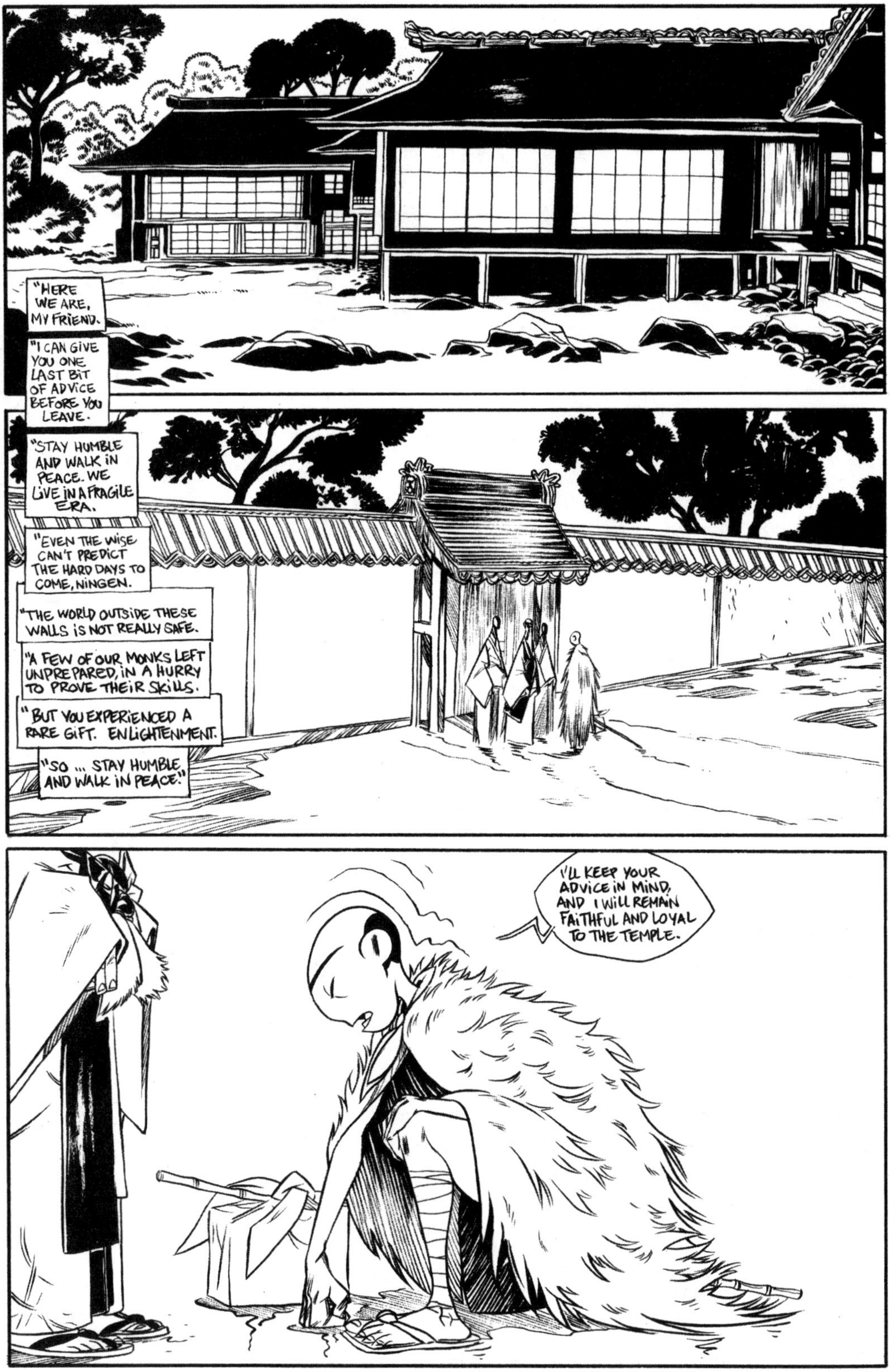
"HERE WE ARE, MY FRIEND.
"I CAN GIVE YOU ONE LAST BIT OF ADVICE BEFORE YOU LEAVE.
"STAY HUMBLE AND WALK IN PEACE. WE LIVE IN A FRAGILE ERA.
"EVEN THE WISE CAN'T PREDICT THE HARD DAYS TO COME, NINGEN.
"THE WORLD OUTSIDE THESE WALLS IS NOT REALLY SAFE.
"A FEW OF OUR MONKS LEFT UNPREPARED, IN A HURRY TO PROVE THEIR SKILLS.
"BUT YOU EXPERIENCED A RARE GIFT. ENLIGHTENMENT.
"SO ... STAY HUMBLE AND WALK IN PEACE."
I'LL KEEP YOUR ADVICE IN MIND, AND I WILL REMAIN FAITHFUL AND LOYAL TO THE TEMPLE.

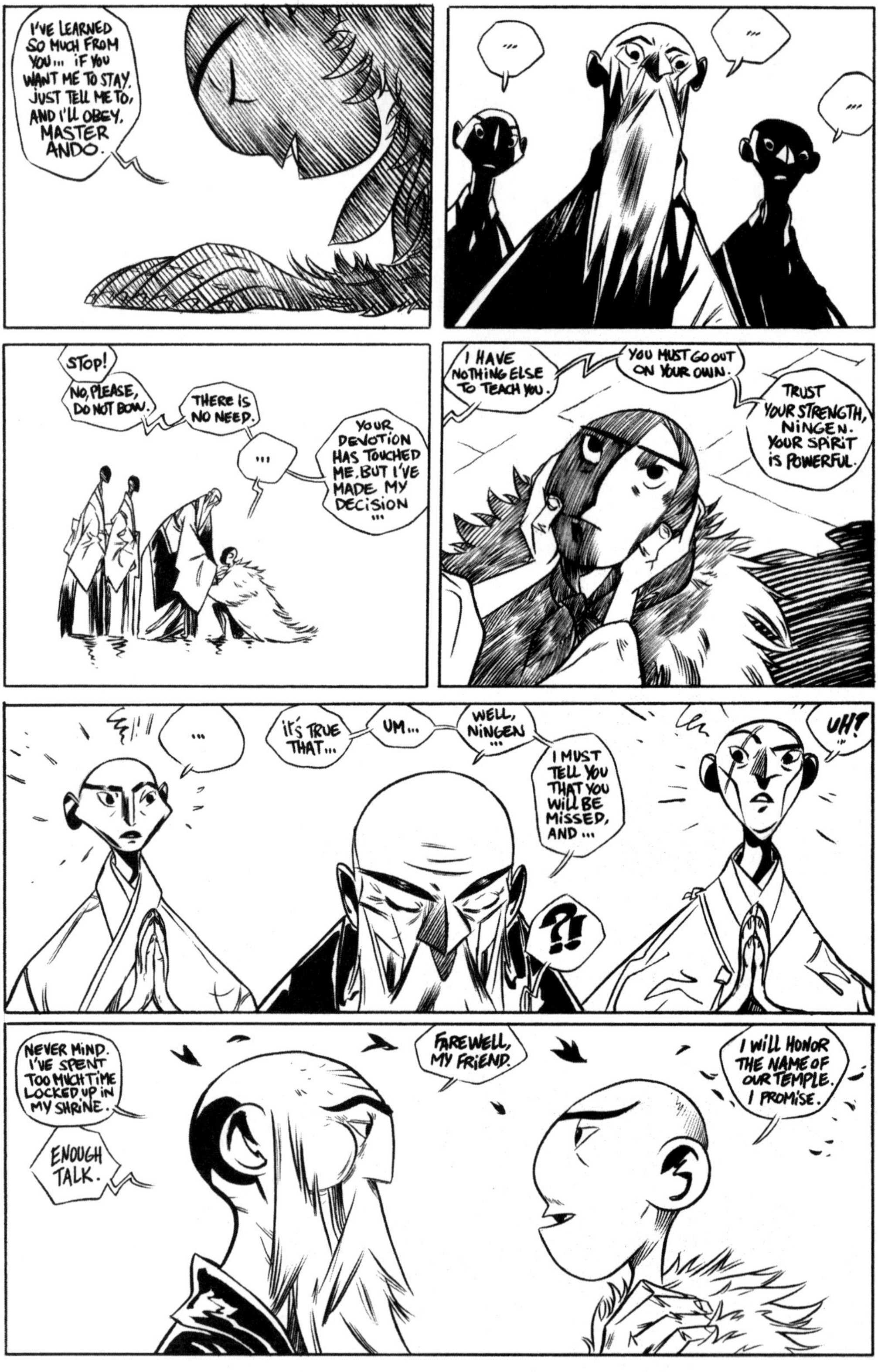
I'VE LEARNED SO MUCH FROM YOU... IF YOU WANT ME TO STAY, JUST TELL ME TO, AND I'LL OBEY, MASTER ANDO.
...
...
...
STOP!
NO, PLEASE, DO NOT BOW.
THERE IS NO NEED.
...
YOUR DEVOTION HAS TOUCHED ME, BUT I'VE MADE MY DECISION ...
I HAVE NOTHING ELSE TO TEACH YOU.
YOU MUST GO OUT ON YOUR OWN.
TRUST YOUR STRENGTH, NINGEN. YOUR SPIRIT IS POWERFUL.
...
IT'S TRUE THAT...
UM...
WELL, NINGEN ...
I MUST TELL YOU THAT YOU WILL BE MISSED, AND ...
UH?
?!
NEVER MIND. I'VE SPENT TOO MUCH TIME LOCKED UP IN MY SHRINE.
ENOUGH TALK.
FAREWELL, MY FRIEND.
I WILL HONOR THE NAME OF OUR TEMPLE. I PROMISE.

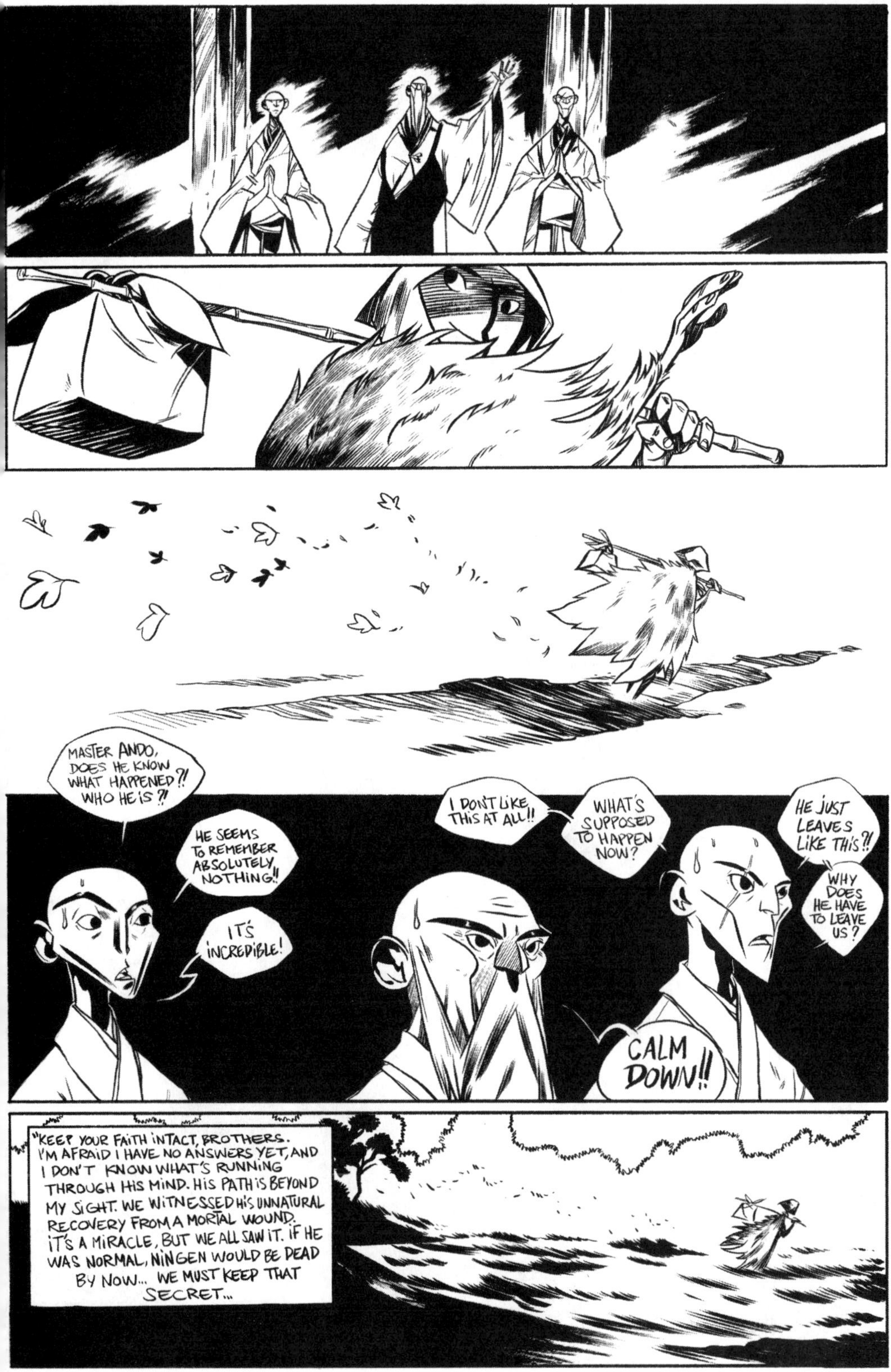
MASTER ANDO, DOES HE KNOW WHAT HAPPENED?! WHO HE IS?!
HE SEEMS TO REMEMBER ABSOLUTELY NOTHING!!
IT'S INCREDIBLE!
I DON'T LIKE THIS AT ALL!!
WHAT'S SUPPOSED TO HAPPEN NOW?
HE JUST LEAVES LIKE THIS?!
WHY DOES HE HAVE TO LEAVE US?
CALM DOWN!!
"KEEP YOUR FAITH INTACT, BROTHERS. I'M AFRAID I HAVE NO ANSWERS YET, AND I DON'T KNOW WHAT'S RUNNING THROUGH HIS MIND. HIS PATH IS BEYOND MY SIGHT. WE WITNESSED HIS UNNATURAL RECOVERY FROM A MORTAL WOUND. IT'S A MIRACLE, BUT WE ALL SAW IT. IF HE WAS NORMAL, NINGEN WOULD BE DEAD BY NOW... WE MUST KEEP THAT SECRET...

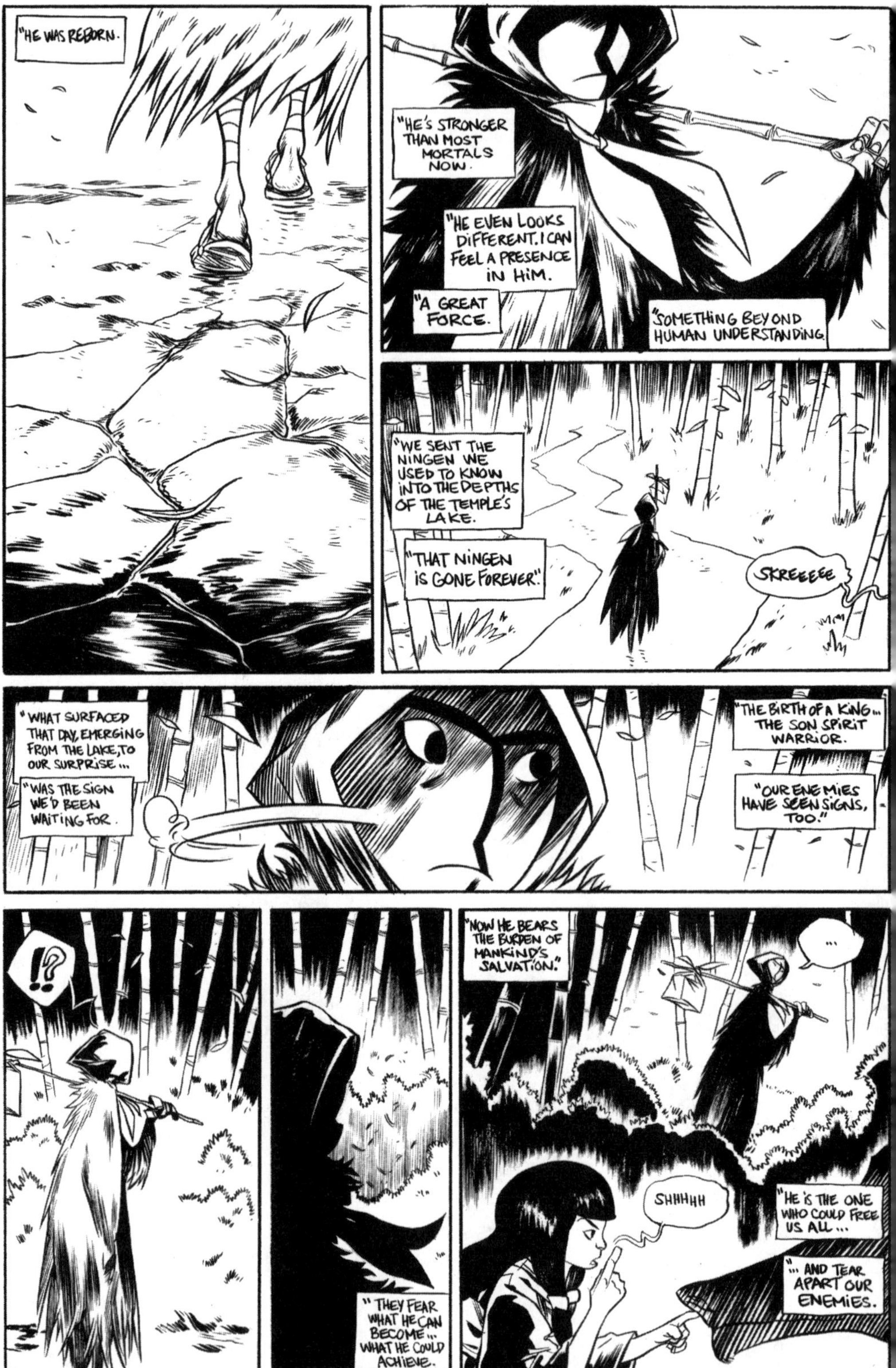
"HE WAS REBORN.
"HE'S STRONGER THAN MOST MORTALS NOW.
"HE EVEN LOOKS DIFFERENT. I CAN FEEL A PRESENCE IN HIM.
"A GREAT FORCE.
"SOMETHING BEYOND HUMAN UNDERSTANDING.
"WE SENT THE NINGEN WE USED TO KNOW INTO THE DEPTHS OF THE TEMPLE'S LAKE.
"THAT NINGEN IS GONE FOREVER."
SKREEEEE
"WHAT SURFACED THAT DAY, EMERGING FROM THE LAKE, TO OUR SURPRISE...
"WAS THE SIGN WE'D BEEN WAITING FOR.
"THE BIRTH OF A KING... THE SON SPIRIT WARRIOR.
"OUR ENEMIES HAVE SEEN SIGNS, TOO."
!?
"THEY FEAR WHAT HE CAN BECOME... WHAT HE COULD ACHIEVE.
"NOW HE BEARS THE BURDEN OF MANKIND'S SALVATION."
...
SHHHHH
"HE IS THE ONE WHO COULD FREE US ALL...
"... AND TEAR APART OUR ENEMIES.

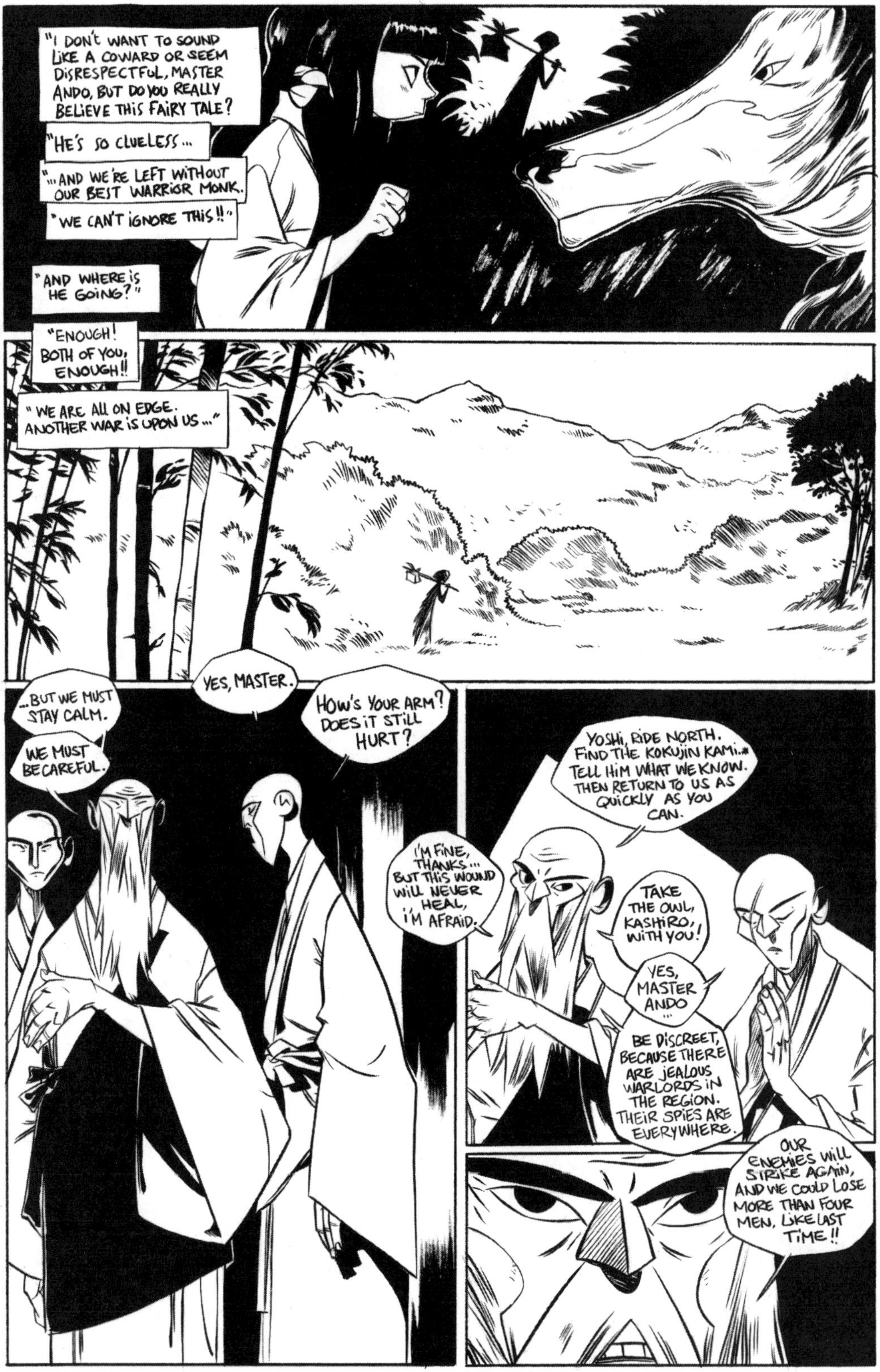
"I DON'T WANT TO SOUND LIKE A COWARD OR SEEM DISRESPECTFUL, MASTER ANDO, BUT DO YOU REALLY BELIEVE THIS FAIRY TALE?
"HE'S SO CLUELESS...
"...AND WE'RE LEFT WITHOUT OUR BEST WARRIOR MONK.
"WE CAN'T IGNORE THIS!!"
"AND WHERE IS HE GOING?"
"ENOUGH! BOTH OF YOU, ENOUGH!!
"WE ARE ALL ON EDGE. ANOTHER WAR IS UPON US..."
...BUT WE MUST STAY CALM.
WE MUST BE CAREFUL.
YES, MASTER.
HOW'S YOUR ARM? DOES IT STILL HURT?
I'M FINE, THANKS... BUT THIS WOUND WILL NEVER HEAL, I'M AFRAID.
YOSHI, RIDE NORTH. FIND THE KOKUJIN KAMI.* TELL HIM WHAT WE KNOW. THEN RETURN TO US AS QUICKLY AS YOU CAN.
TAKE THE OWL, KASHIRO, WITH YOU!
YES, MASTER ANDO...
BE DISCREET, BECAUSE THERE ARE JEALOUS WARLORDS IN THE REGION. THEIR SPIES ARE EVERYWHERE.
OUR ENEMIES WILL STRIKE AGAIN, AND WE COULD LOSE MORE THAN FOUR MEN, LIKE LAST TIME!!

* BLACK MAN-GOD

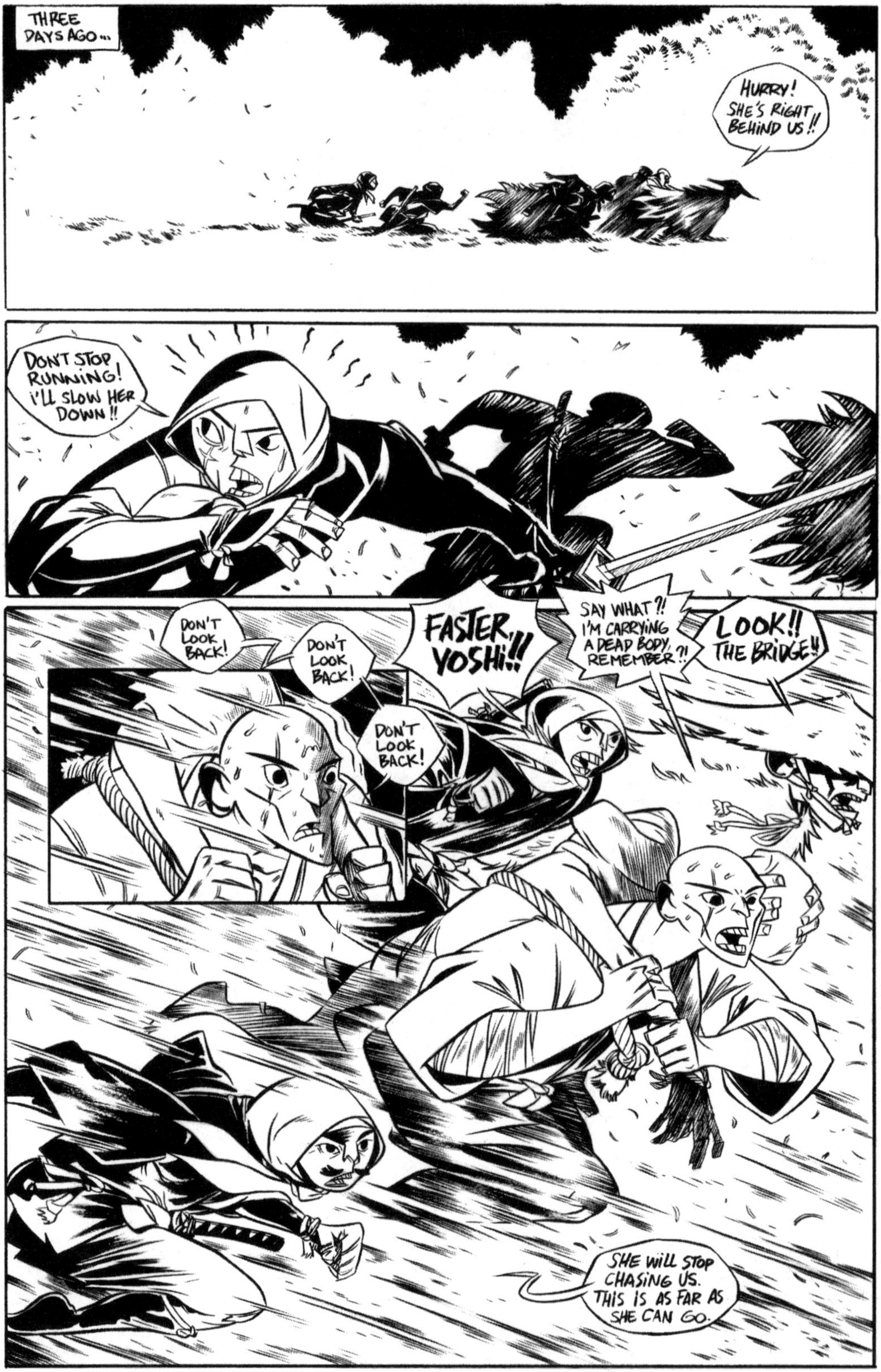
THREE DAYS AGO...
HURRY! SHE'S RIGHT BEHIND US!!
DON'T STOP RUNNING! I'LL SLOW HER DOWN!!
DON'T LOOK BACK!
DON'T LOOK BACK!
DON'T LOOK BACK!
FASTER, YOSHI!!
SAY WHAT?! I'M CARRYING A DEAD BODY, REMEMBER?!
LOOK!! THE BRIDGE!!
SHE WILL STOP CHASING US. THIS IS AS FAR AS SHE CAN GO.

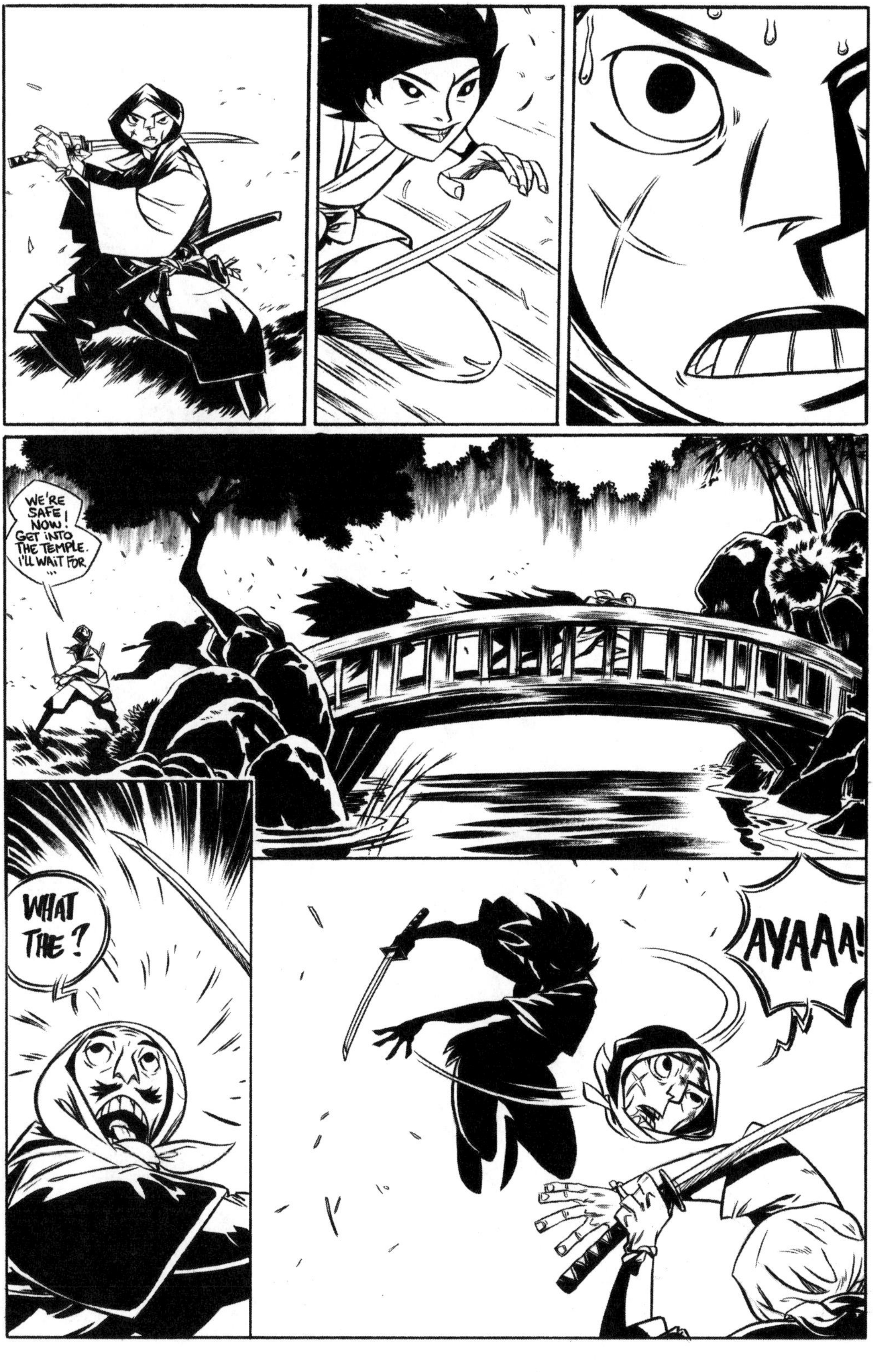

WE'RE SAFE! NOW! GET INTO THE TEMPLE. I'LL WAIT FOR ...
WHAT THE?
AYAAA!

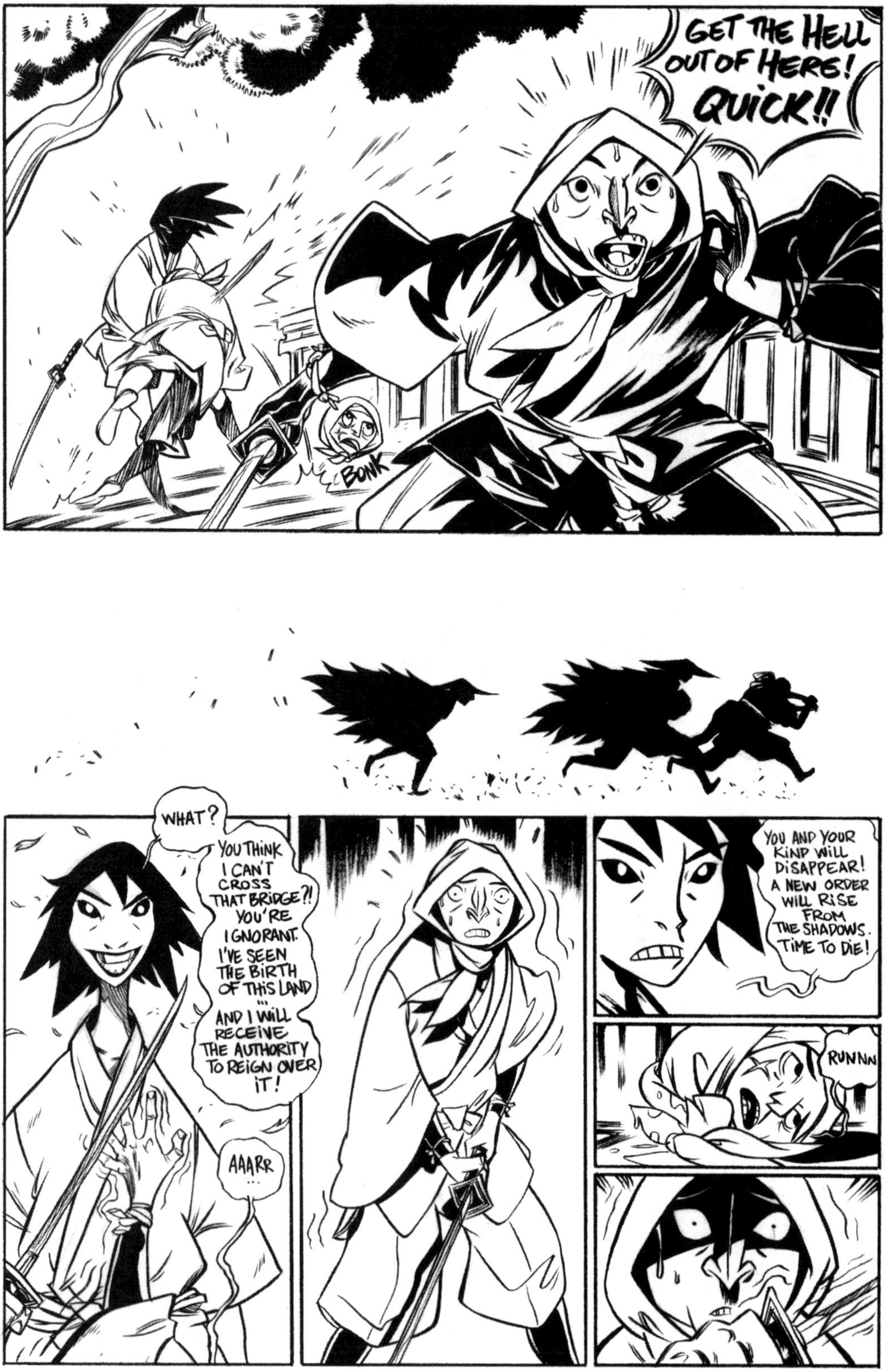

GET THE HELL OUT OF HERE! QUICK!!
BONK
WHAT?
YOU THINK I CAN'T CROSS THAT BRIDGE?! YOU'RE IGNORANT. I'VE SEEN THE BIRTH OF THIS LAND ... AND I WILL RECEIVE THE AUTHORITY TO REIGN OVER IT!
AAARR ...
YOU AND YOUR KIND WILL DISAPPEAR! A NEW ORDER WILL RISE FROM THE SHADOWS. TIME TO DIE!
RUNNN

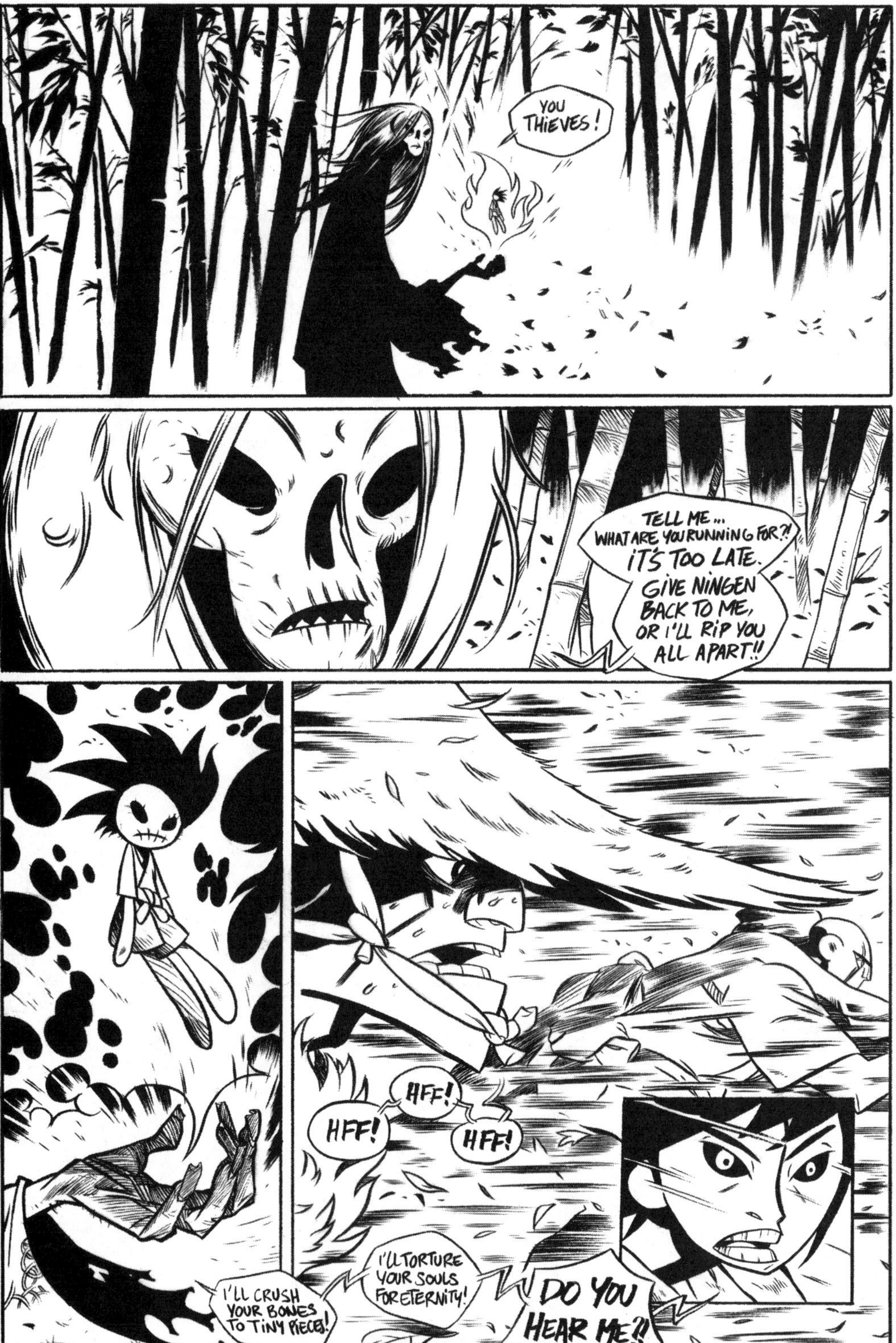
YOU THIEVES!
TELL ME... WHAT ARE YOU RUNNING FOR?! IT'S TOO LATE. GIVE NINGEN BACK TO ME, OR I'LL RIP YOU ALL APART!!
HFF!
HFF!
HFF!
I'LL CRUSH YOUR BONES TO TINY PIECES!
I'LL TORTURE YOUR SOULS FOR ETERNITY!
DO YOU HEAR ME?!!

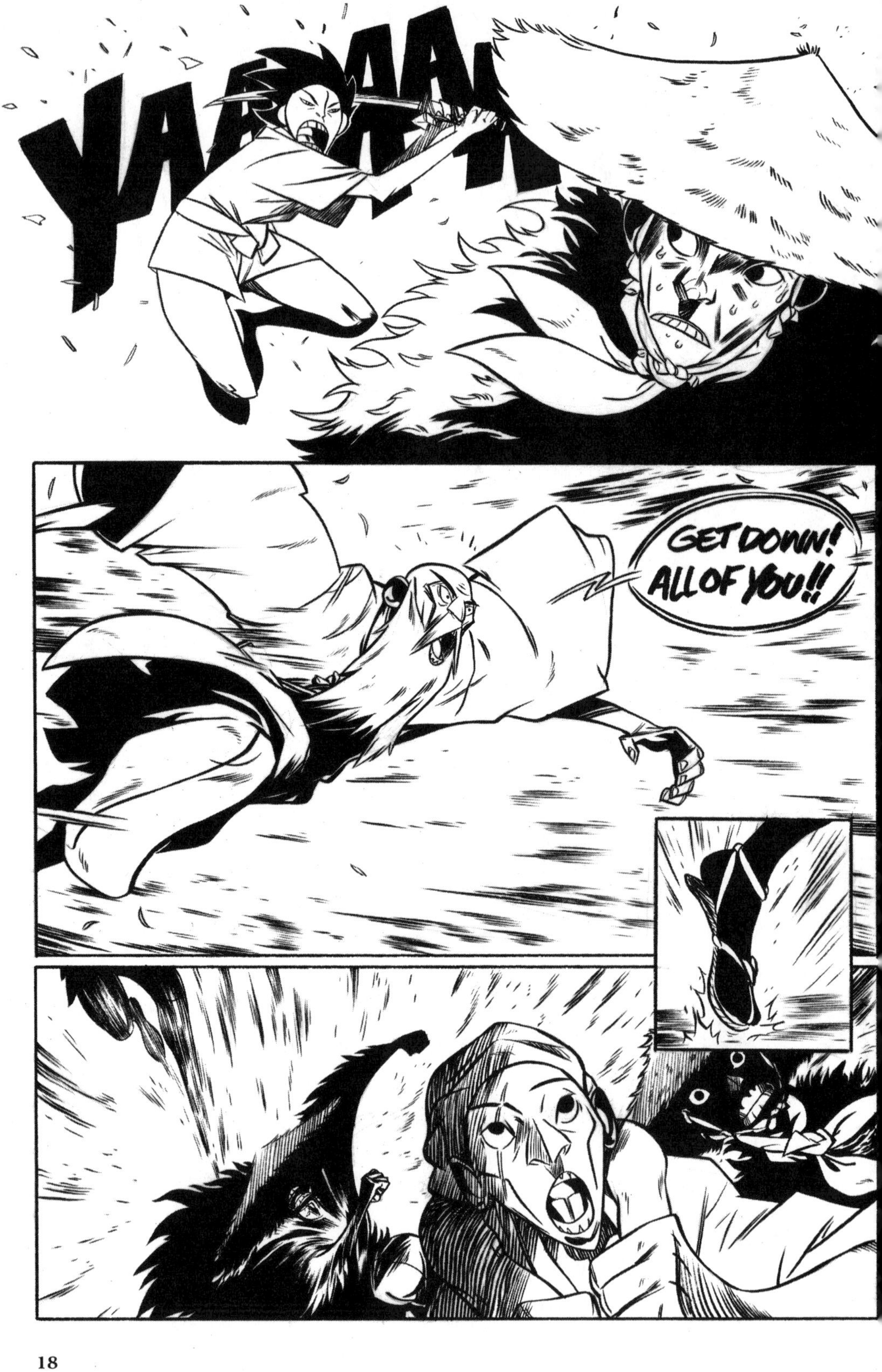
YAAAAH
GET DOWN! ALL OF YOU!!

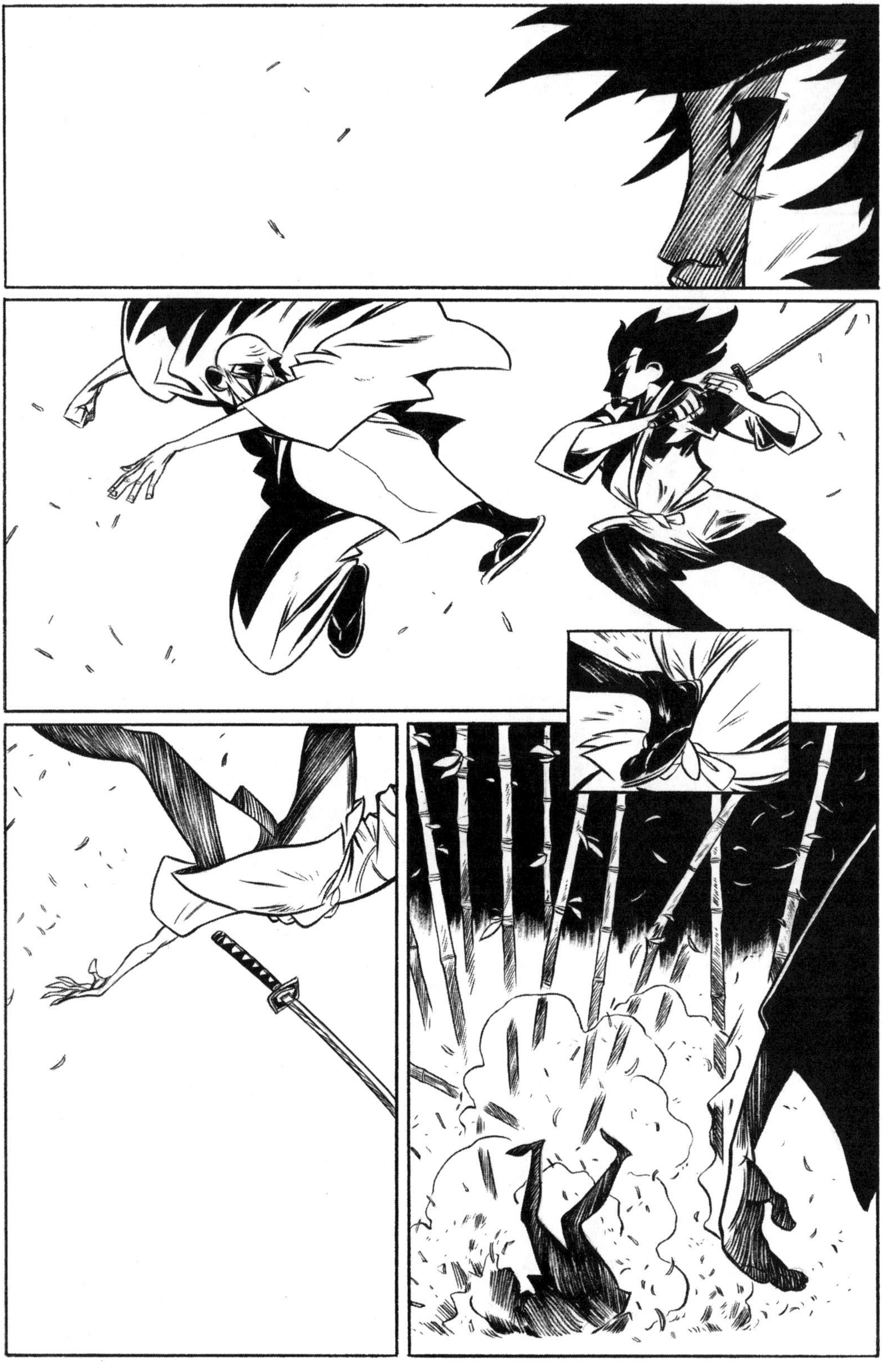

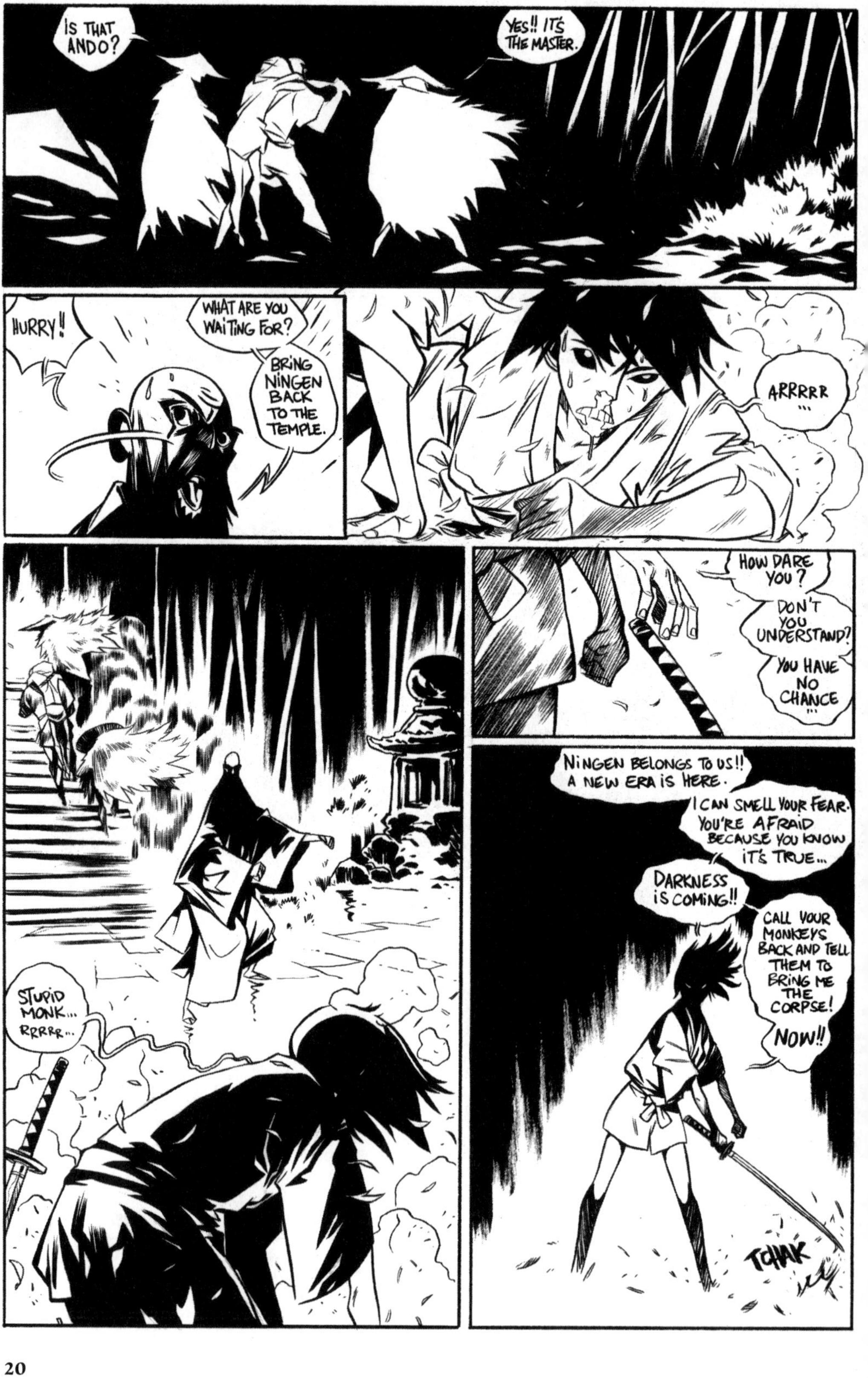
IS THAT ANDO?
YES!! IT'S THE MASTER.
HURRY!!
WHAT ARE YOU WAITING FOR?
BRING NINGEN BACK TO THE TEMPLE.
ARRRRR...
STUPID MONK... RRRRR...
HOW DARE YOU?
DON'T YOU UNDERSTAND?
YOU HAVE NO CHANCE...
NINGEN BELONGS TO US!! A NEW ERA IS HERE.
I CAN SMELL YOUR FEAR. YOU'RE AFRAID BECAUSE YOU KNOW IT'S TRUE...
DARKNESS IS COMING!!
CALL YOUR MONKEYS BACK AND TELL THEM TO BRING ME THE CORPSE!
NOW!!
TCHAK

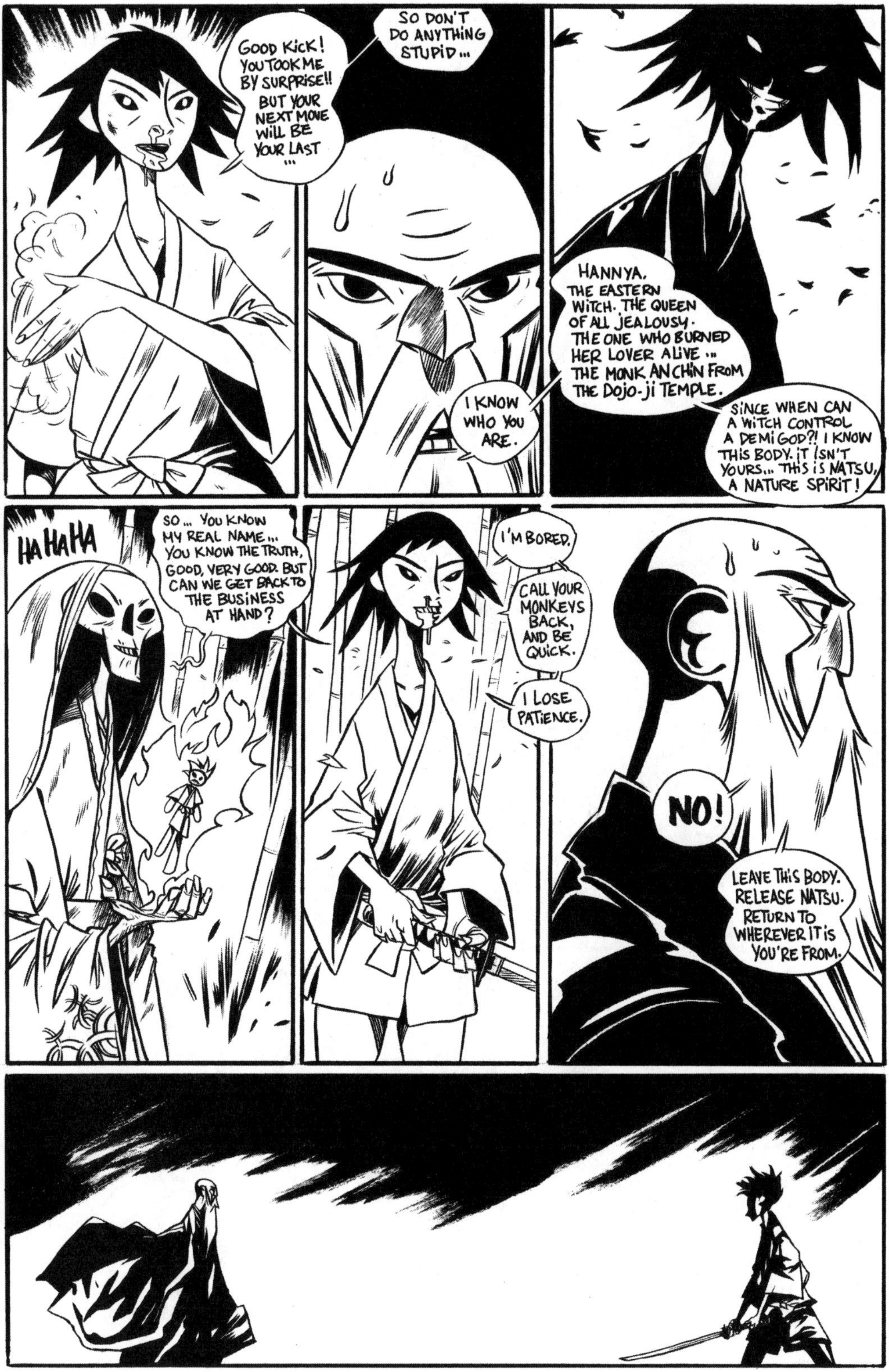
GOOD KICK! YOU TOOK ME BY SURPRISE!! BUT YOUR NEXT MOVE WILL BE YOUR LAST ...
SO DON'T DO ANYTHING STUPID...
I KNOW WHO YOU ARE.
HANNYA. THE EASTERN WITCH. THE QUEEN OF ALL JEALOUSY. THE ONE WHO BURNED HER LOVER ALIVE... THE MONK AN CHIN FROM THE DOJO-JI TEMPLE.
SINCE WHEN CAN A WITCH CONTROL A DEMI GOD?! I KNOW THIS BODY. IT ISN'T YOURS... THIS IS NATSU, A NATURE SPIRIT!
HA HA HA
SO... YOU KNOW MY REAL NAME... YOU KNOW THE TRUTH, GOOD, VERY GOOD. BUT CAN WE GET BACK TO THE BUSINESS AT HAND?
I'M BORED.
CALL YOUR MONKEYS BACK, AND BE QUICK.
I LOSE PATIENCE.
NO!
LEAVE THIS BODY. RELEASE NATSU. RETURN TO WHEREVER IT IS YOU'RE FROM.

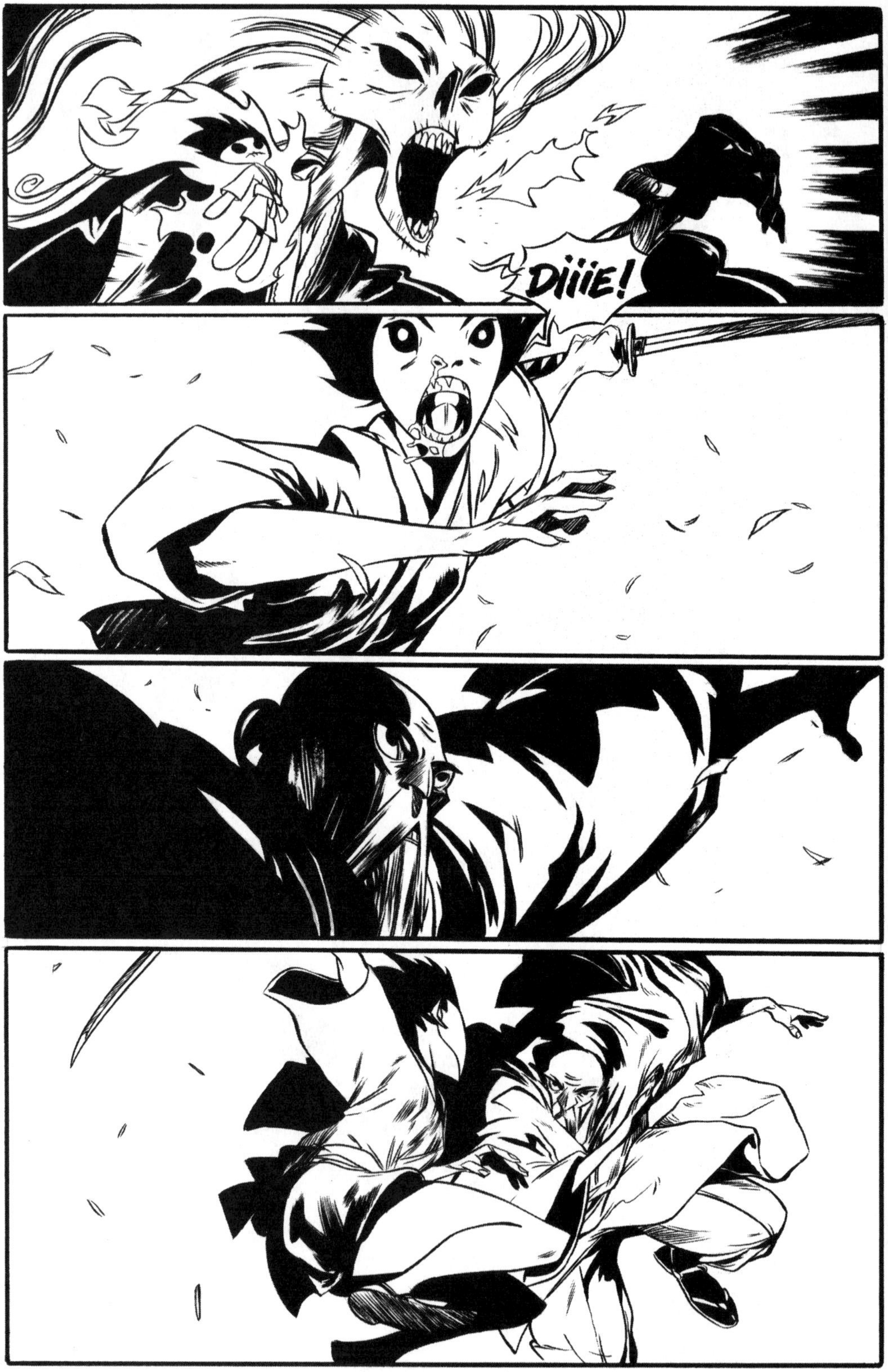
DIiiE!

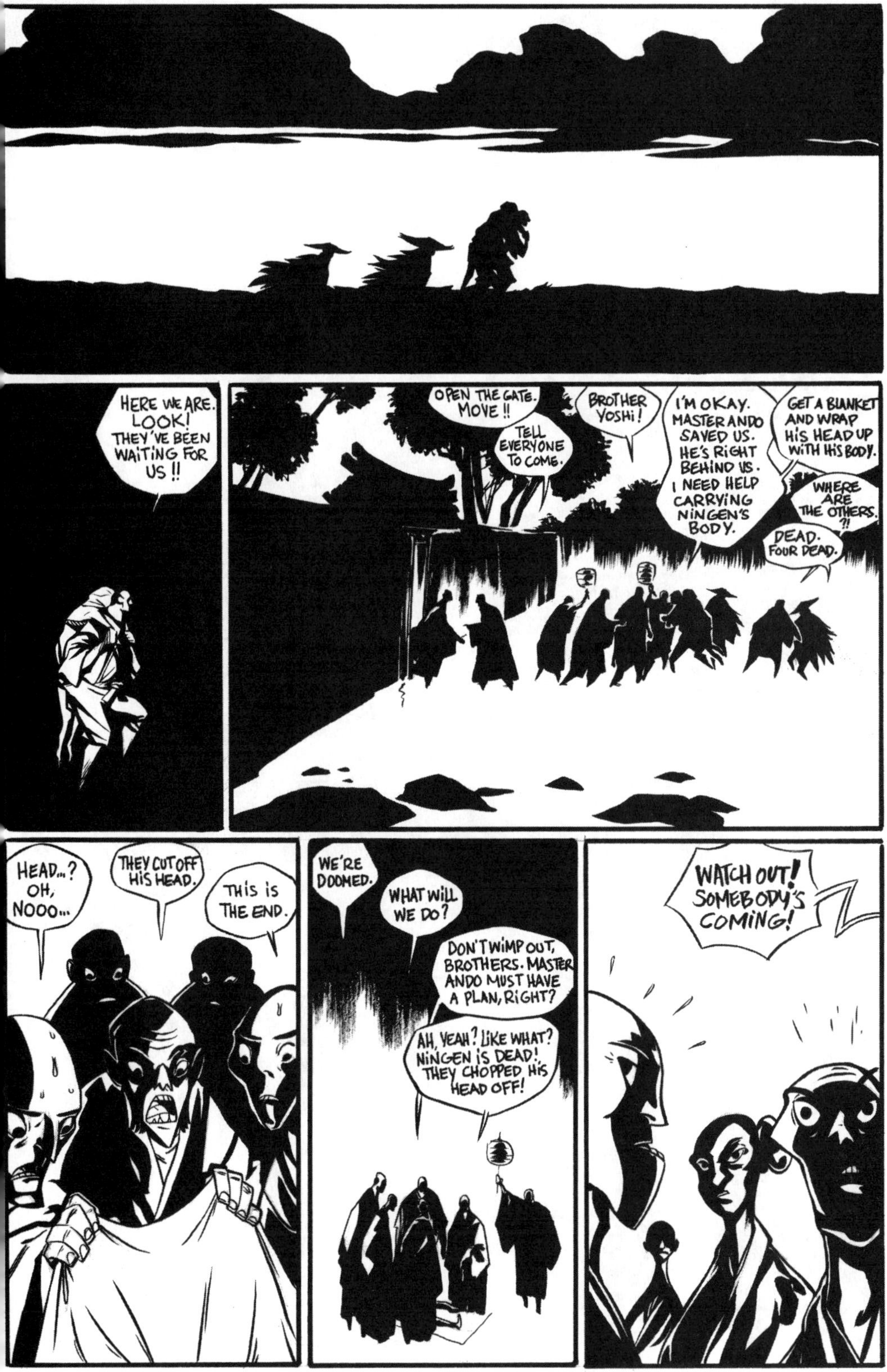
HERE WE ARE. LOOK! THEY'VE BEEN WAITING FOR US !!
OPEN THE GATE. MOVE !!
TELL EVERYONE TO COME.
BROTHER YOSHI!
I'M OKAY. MASTER ANDO SAVED US. HE'S RIGHT BEHIND US. I NEED HELP CARRYING NINGEN'S BODY.
GET A BLANKET AND WRAP HIS HEAD UP WITH HIS BODY.
WHERE ARE THE OTHERS. ?!
DEAD. FOUR DEAD.
HEAD...? OH, NOOO...
THEY CUT OFF HIS HEAD.
THIS IS THE END.
WE'RE DOOMED.
WHAT WILL WE DO?
DON'T WIMP OUT, BROTHERS. MASTER ANDO MUST HAVE A PLAN, RIGHT?
AH, YEAH? LIKE WHAT? NINGEN IS DEAD! THEY CHOPPED HIS HEAD OFF!
WATCH OUT! SOMEBODY'S COMING!

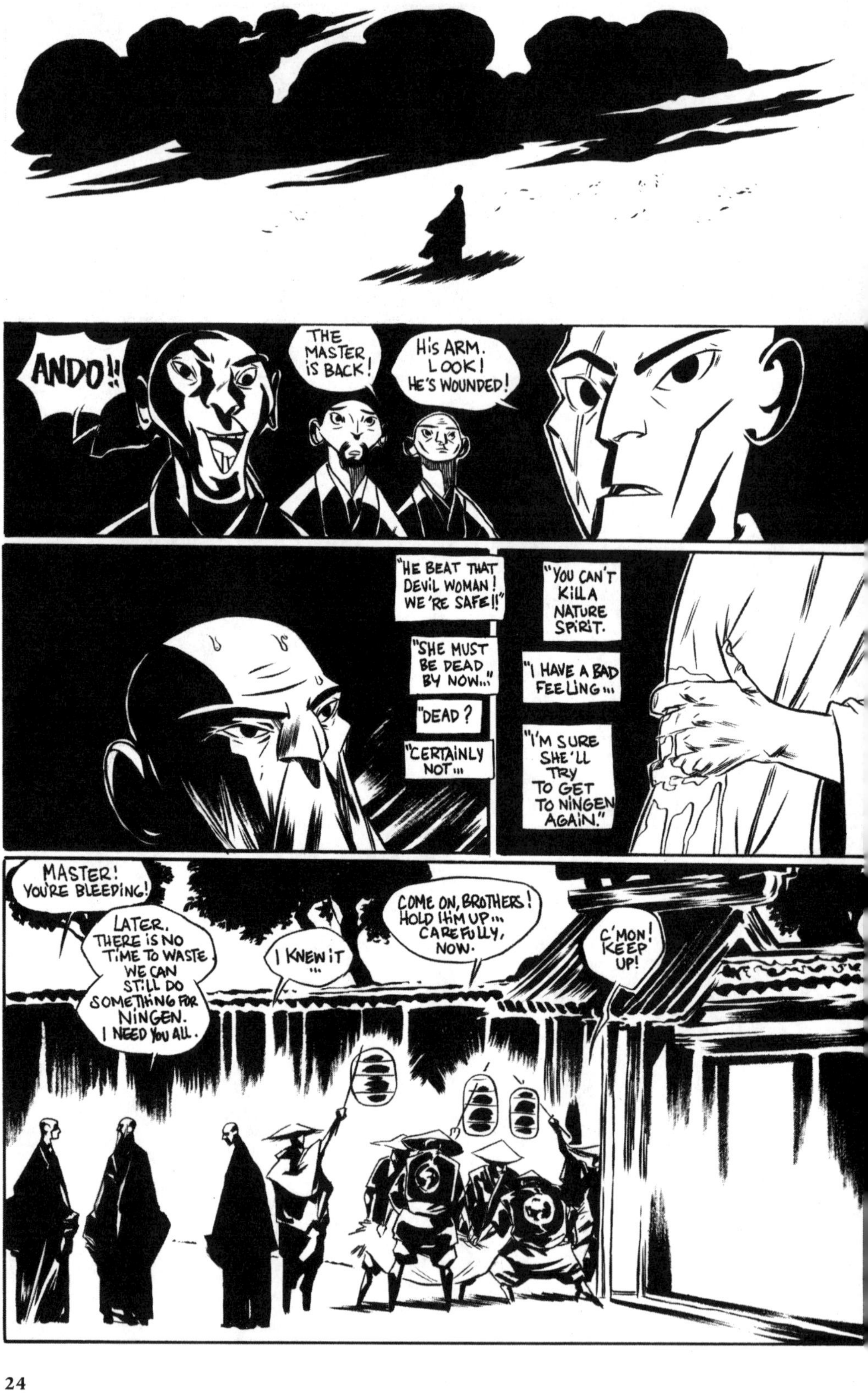
ANDO!!
THE MASTER IS BACK!
HiS ARM. LOOK! HE'S WOUNDED!
"HE BEAT THAT DEViL WOMAN! WE'RE SAFE!!"
"SHE MUST BE DEAD BY NOW..."
"DEAD?
"CERTAiNLY NOT...
"YOU CAN'T KiLL A NATURE SPiRiT.
"I HAVE A BAD FEELiNG...
"I'M SURE SHE'LL TRY TO GET TO NiNGEN AGAiN."
MASTER! YOU'RE BLEEDiNG!
LATER. THERE iS NO TiME TO WASTE. WE CAN STiLL DO SOMETHiNG FOR NiNGEN. I NEED YOU ALL.
I KNEW iT...
COME ON, BROTHERS! HOLD HiM UP... CAREFULLY, NOW.
C'MON! KEEP UP!

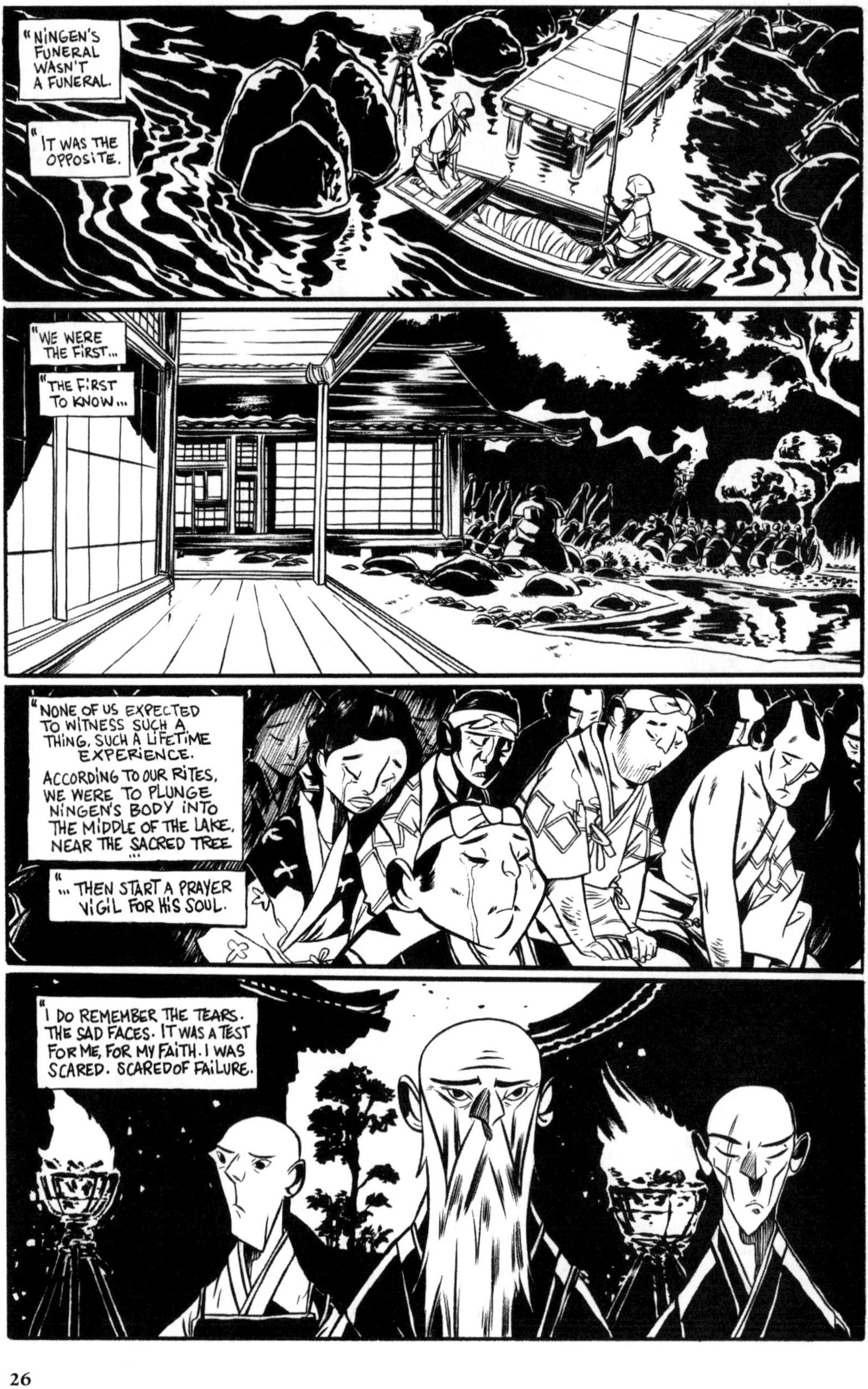
"NINGEN'S FUNERAL WASN'T A FUNERAL.
"IT WAS THE OPPOSITE.
"WE WERE THE FIRST...
"THE FIRST TO KNOW...
"NONE OF US EXPECTED TO WITNESS SUCH A THING, SUCH A LIFETIME EXPERIENCE. ACCORDING TO OUR RITES, WE WERE TO PLUNGE NINGEN'S BODY INTO THE MIDDLE OF THE LAKE, NEAR THE SACRED TREE ...
"... THEN START A PRAYER VIGIL FOR HIS SOUL.
"I DO REMEMBER THE TEARS. THE SAD FACES. IT WAS A TEST FOR ME, FOR MY FAITH. I WAS SCARED. SCAREDOF FAILURE.

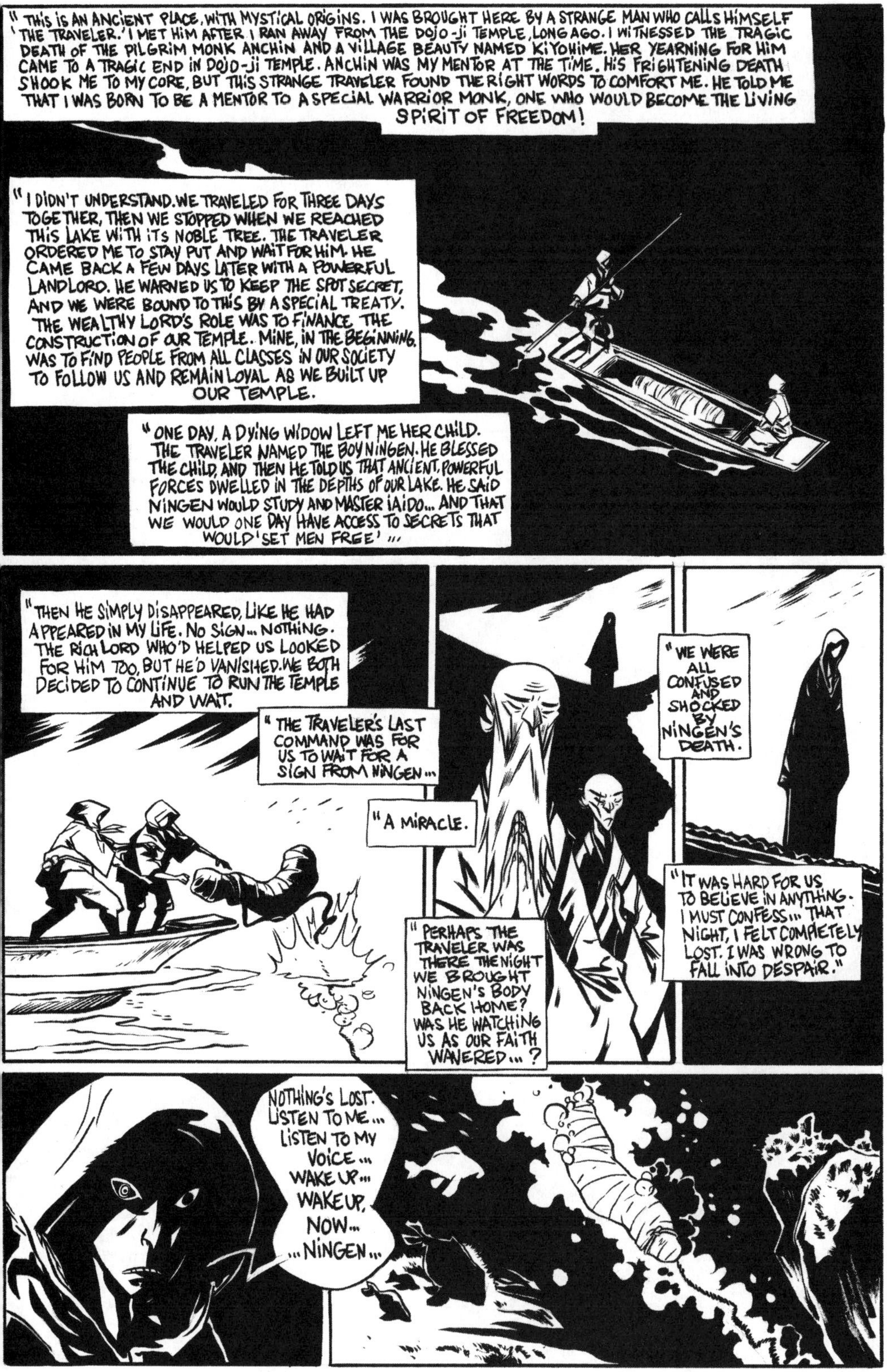
"This is an ancient place, with mystical origins. I was brought here by a strange man who calls himself 'The Traveler.' I met him after I ran away from the Dojo-ji Temple, long ago. I witnessed the tragic death of the pilgrim monk Anchin and a village beauty named Kiyohime. Her yearning for him came to a tragic end in Dojo-ji Temple. Anchin was my mentor at the time. His frightening death shook me to my core, but this strange traveler found the right words to comfort me. He told me that I was born to be a mentor to a special warrior monk, one who would become the living spirit of freedom!
"I didn't understand. We traveled for three days together, then we stopped when we reached this lake with its noble tree. The Traveler ordered me to stay put and wait for him. He came back a few days later with a powerful landlord. He warned us to keep the spot secret, and we were bound to this by a special treaty. The wealthy lord's role was to finance the construction of our temple. Mine, in the beginning, was to find people from all classes in our society to follow us and remain loyal as we built up our temple.
"One day, a dying widow left me her child. The Traveler named the boy Ningen. He blessed the child, and then he told us that ancient, powerful forces dwelled in the depths of our lake. He said Ningen would study and master iaido... and that we would one day have access to secrets that would 'set men free'...
"Then he simply disappeared, like he had appeared in my life. No sign... nothing. The rich lord who'd helped us looked for him too, but he'd vanished. We both decided to continue to run the temple and wait.
"The Traveler's last command was for us to wait for a sign from Ningen...
"A miracle.
"We were all confused and shocked by Ningen's death.
"Perhaps the Traveler was there the night we brought Ningen's body back home? Was he watching us as our faith wavered...?
"It was hard for us to believe in anything. I must confess... that night, I felt completely lost. I was wrong to fall into despair."
Nothing's lost. Listen to me... listen to my voice... wake up... wake up, now... ...Ningen...

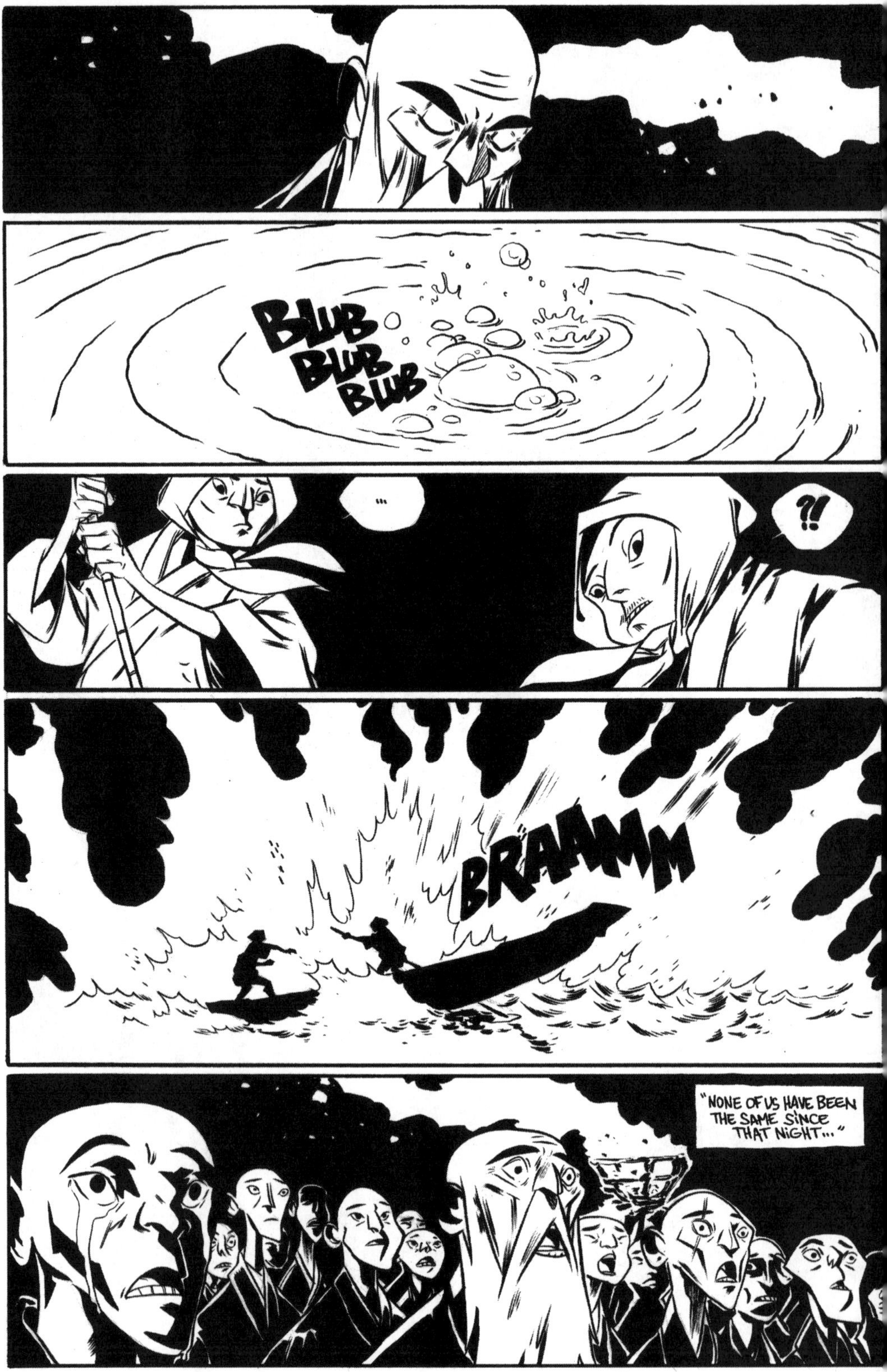
BLUB
BLUB BLUB
BLUB
...
?!
BRAAMM
"NONE OF US HAVE BEEN THE SAME SINCE THAT NIGHT..."

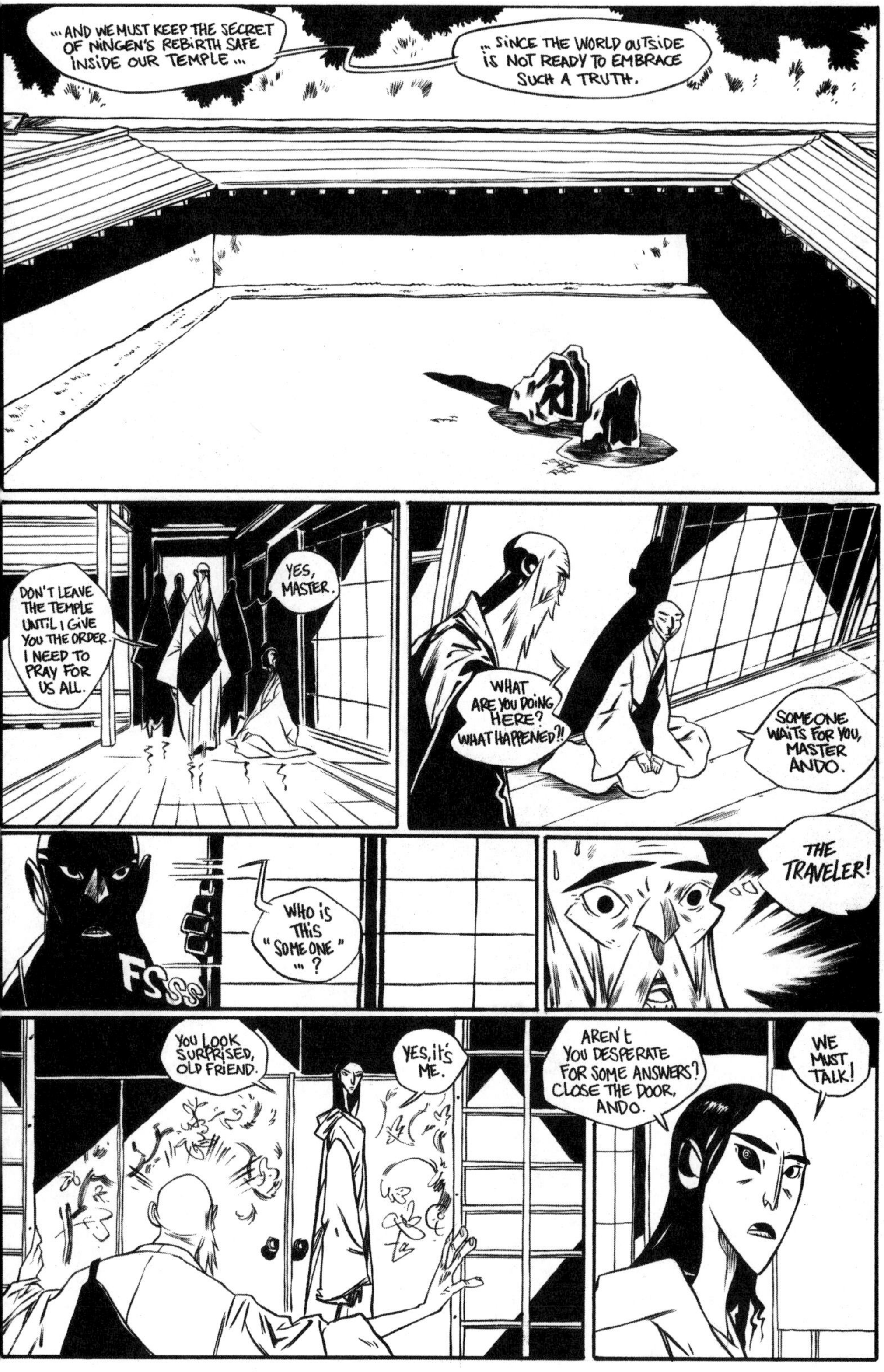
...AND WE MUST KEEP THE SECRET OF NINGEN'S REBIRTH SAFE INSIDE OUR TEMPLE...
...SINCE THE WORLD OUTSIDE IS NOT READY TO EMBRACE SUCH A TRUTH.
DON'T LEAVE THE TEMPLE UNTIL I GIVE YOU THE ORDER. I NEED TO PRAY FOR US ALL.
YES, MASTER.
WHAT ARE YOU DOING HERE? WHAT HAPPENED?!
SOMEONE WAITS FOR YOU, MASTER ANDO.
FSsss
WHO IS THIS "SOMEONE"...?
THE TRAVELER!
YOU LOOK SURPRISED, OLD FRIEND.
YES, IT'S ME.
AREN'T YOU DESPERATE FOR SOME ANSWERS? CLOSE THE DOOR, ANDO.
WE MUST TALK!

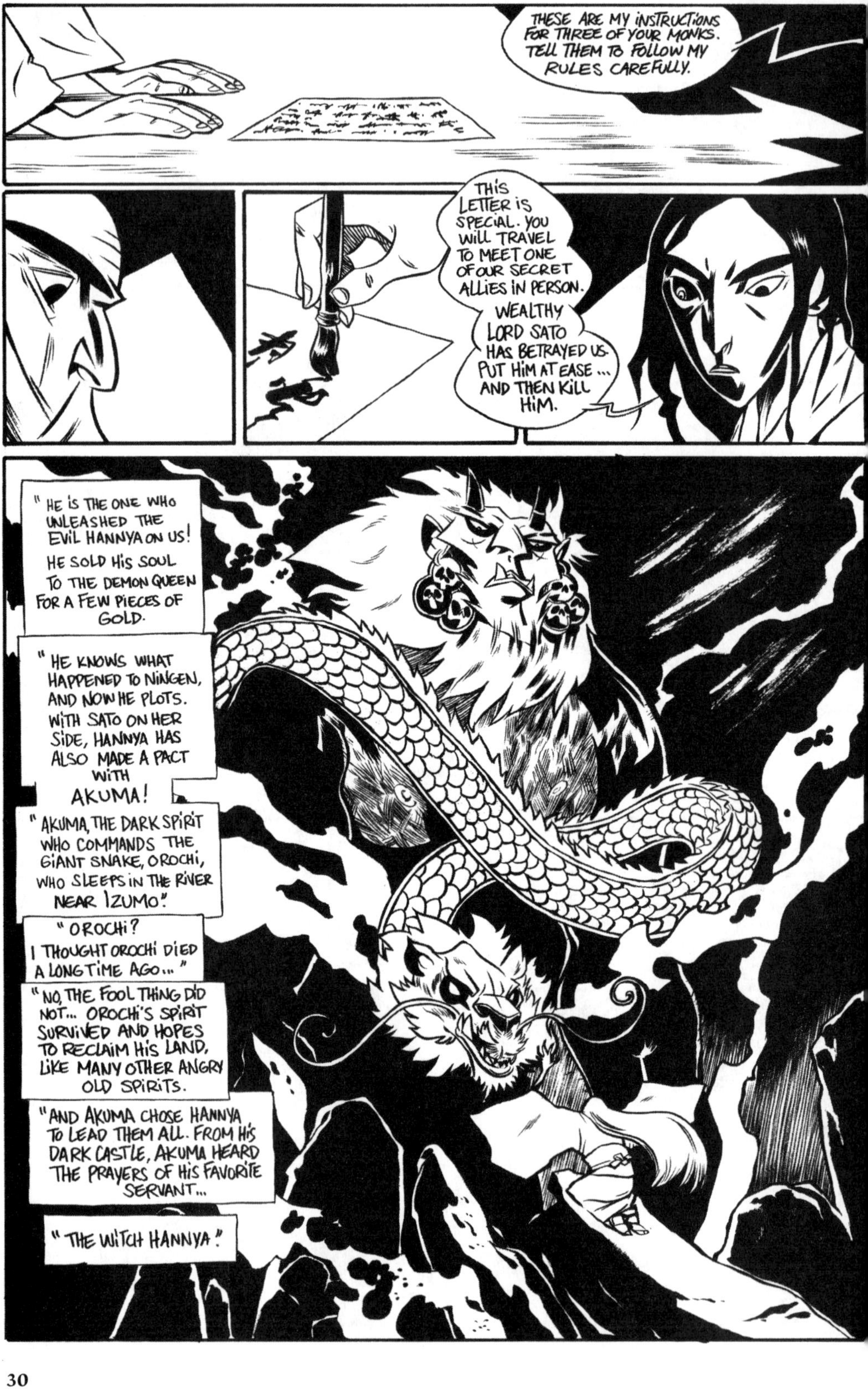
THESE ARE MY INSTRUCTIONS FOR THREE OF YOUR MONKS. TELL THEM TO FOLLOW MY RULES CAREFULLY.
THIS LETTER IS SPECIAL. YOU WILL TRAVEL TO MEET ONE OF OUR SECRET ALLIES IN PERSON.
WEALTHY LORD SATO HAS BETRAYED US. PUT HIM AT EASE ... AND THEN KILL HIM.
"HE IS THE ONE WHO UNLEASHED THE EVIL HANNYA ON US! HE SOLD HIS SOUL TO THE DEMON QUEEN FOR A FEW PIECES OF GOLD.
"HE KNOWS WHAT HAPPENED TO NINGEN, AND NOW HE PLOTS. WITH SATO ON HER SIDE, HANNYA HAS ALSO MADE A PACT WITH AKUMA!
"AKUMA, THE DARK SPIRIT WHO COMMANDS THE GIANT SNAKE, OROCHI, WHO SLEEPS IN THE RIVER NEAR IZUMO."
"OROCHI? I THOUGHT OROCHI DIED A LONG TIME AGO..."
"NO, THE FOOL THING DID NOT... OROCHI'S SPIRIT SURVIVED AND HOPES TO RECLAIM HIS LAND, LIKE MANY OTHER ANGRY OLD SPIRITS.
"AND AKUMA CHOSE HANNYA TO LEAD THEM ALL. FROM HIS DARK CASTLE, AKUMA HEARD THE PRAYERS OF HIS FAVORITE SERVANT...
"THE WITCH HANNYA."

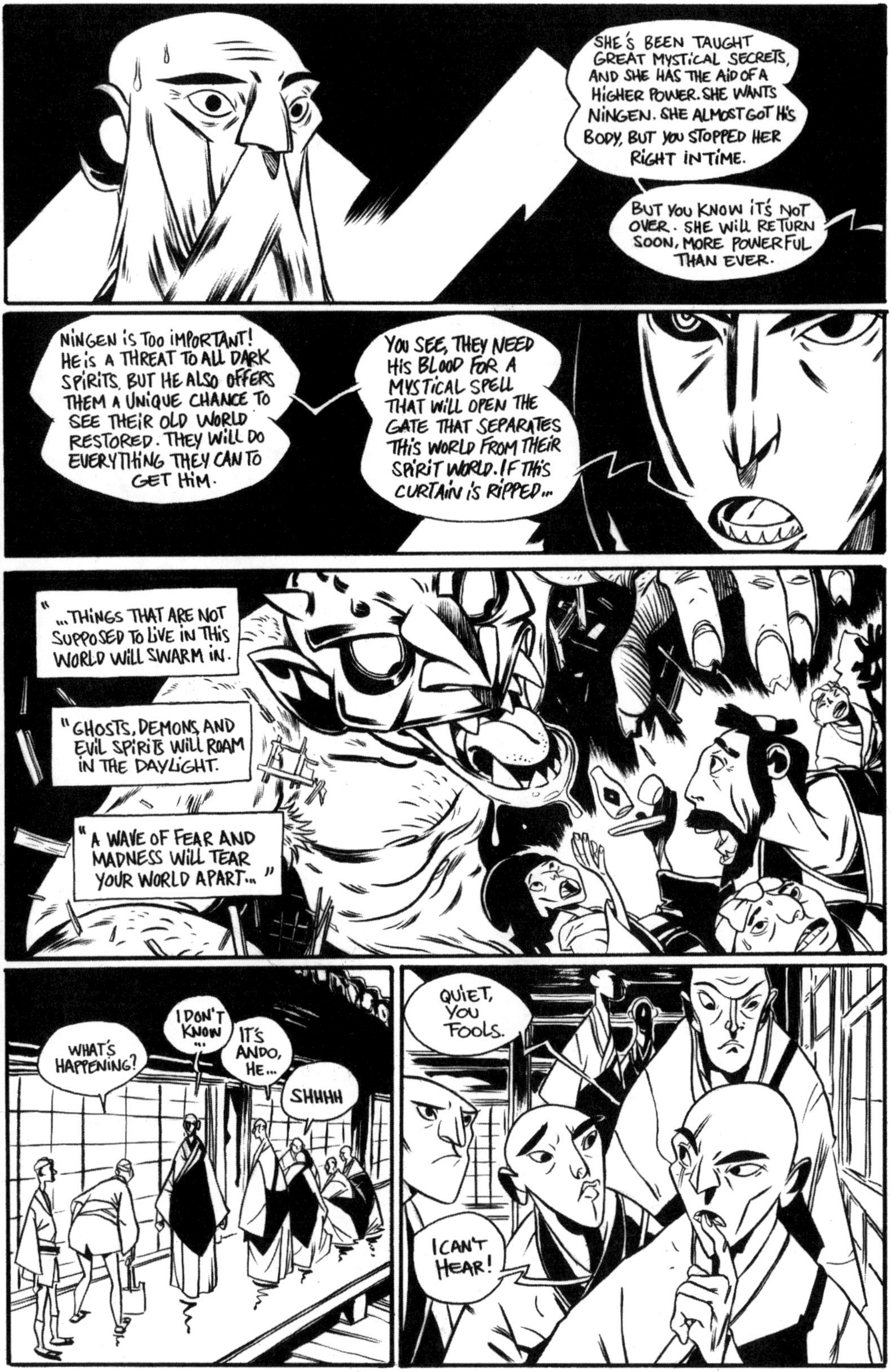

SHE'S BEEN TAUGHT GREAT MYSTICAL SECRETS, AND SHE HAS THE AID OF A HIGHER POWER. SHE WANTS NINGEN. SHE ALMOST GOT HIS BODY, BUT YOU STOPPED HER RIGHT IN TIME.
BUT YOU KNOW IT'S NOT OVER. SHE WILL RETURN SOON, MORE POWERFUL THAN EVER.
NINGEN IS TOO IMPORTANT! HE IS A THREAT TO ALL DARK SPIRITS, BUT HE ALSO OFFERS THEM A UNIQUE CHANCE TO SEE THEIR OLD WORLD RESTORED. THEY WILL DO EVERYTHING THEY CAN TO GET HIM.
YOU SEE, THEY NEED HIS BLOOD FOR A MYSTICAL SPELL THAT WILL OPEN THE GATE THAT SEPARATES THIS WORLD FROM THEIR SPIRIT WORLD. IF THIS CURTAIN IS RIPPED...
"...THINGS THAT ARE NOT SUPPOSED TO LIVE IN THIS WORLD WILL SWARM IN.
"GHOSTS, DEMONS AND EVIL SPIRITS WILL ROAM IN THE DAYLIGHT.
"A WAVE OF FEAR AND MADNESS WILL TEAR YOUR WORLD APART..."
WHAT'S HAPPENING?
I DON'T KNOW ...
IT'S ANDO, HE...
SHHHH
QUIET, YOU FOOLS.
I CAN'T HEAR!

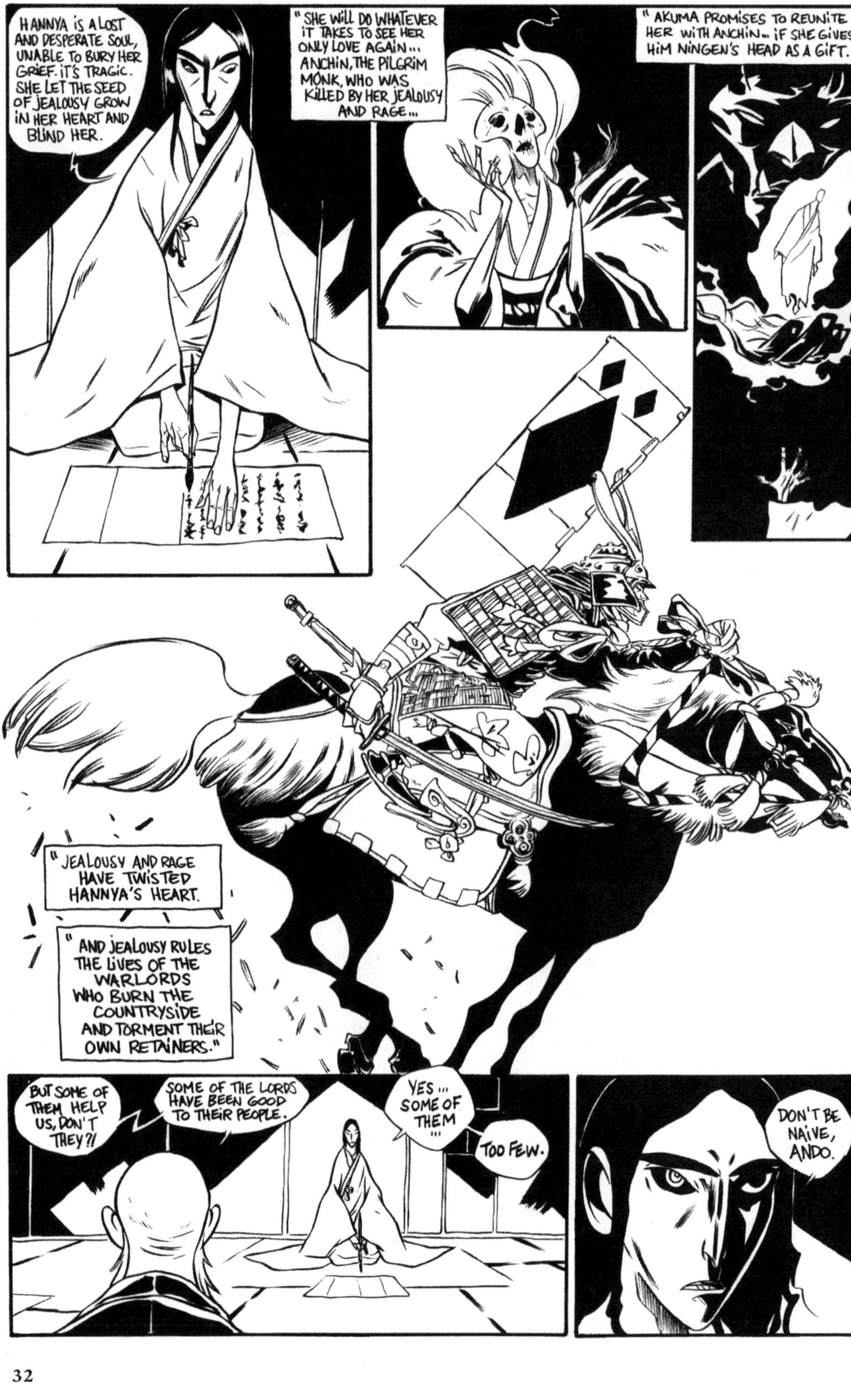
HANNYA IS A LOST AND DESPERATE SOUL, UNABLE TO BURY HER GRIEF. IT'S TRAGIC. SHE LET THE SEED OF JEALOUSY GROW IN HER HEART AND BLIND HER.
"SHE WILL DO WHATEVER IT TAKES TO SEE HER ONLY LOVE AGAIN... ANCHIN, THE PILGRIM MONK, WHO WAS KILLED BY HER JEALOUSY AND RAGE...
"AKUMA PROMISES TO REUNITE HER WITH ANCHIN... IF SHE GIVES HIM NINGEN'S HEAD AS A GIFT.
"JEALOUSY AND RAGE HAVE TWISTED HANNYA'S HEART.
"AND JEALOUSY RULES THE LIVES OF THE WARLORDS WHO BURN THE COUNTRYSIDE AND TORMENT THEIR OWN RETAINERS."
BUT SOME OF THEM HELP US, DON'T THEY?!
SOME OF THE LORDS HAVE BEEN GOOD TO THEIR PEOPLE.
YES... SOME OF THEM...
TOO FEW.
DON'T BE NAIVE, ANDO.

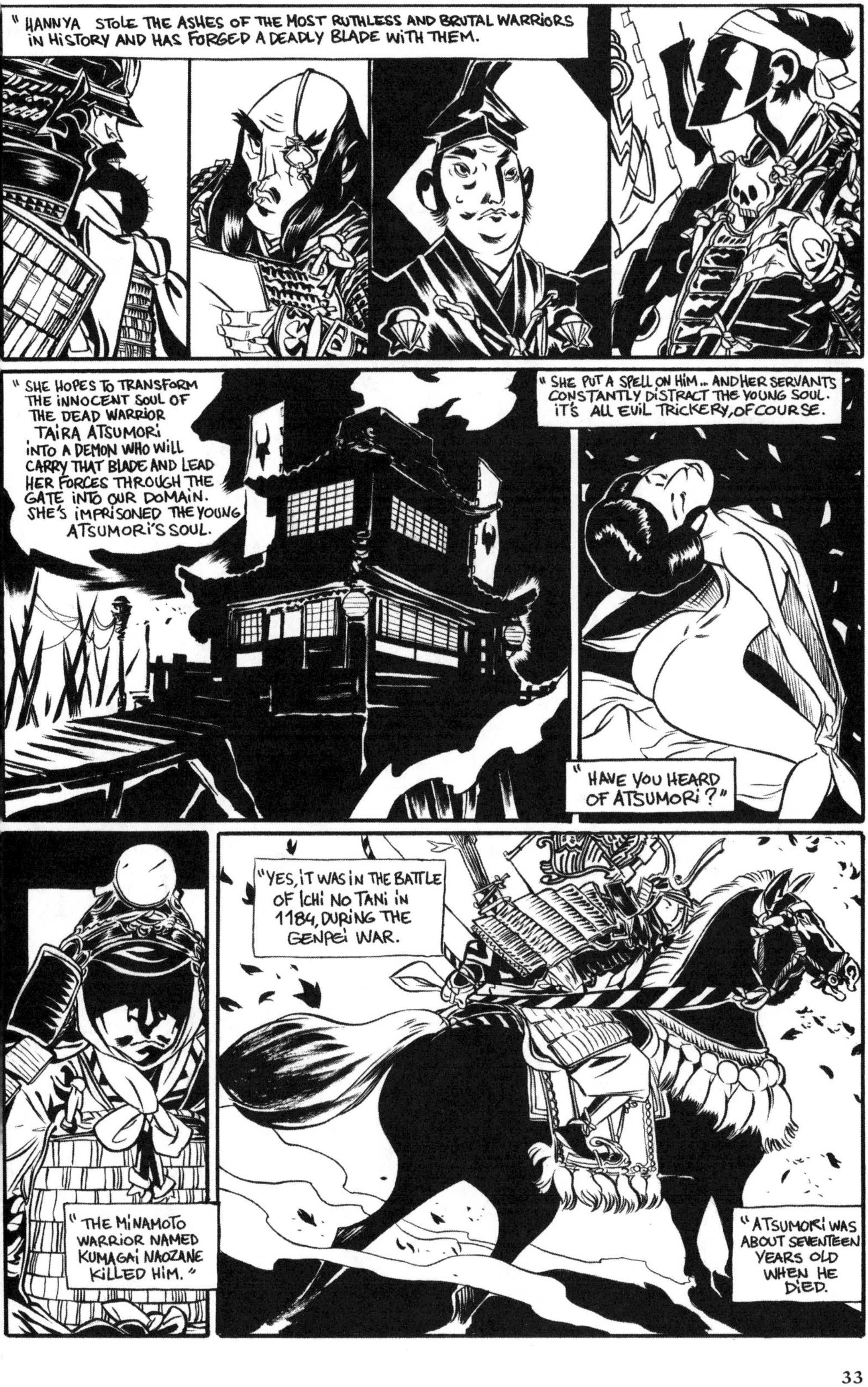
"HANNYA STOLE THE ASHES OF THE MOST RUTHLESS AND BRUTAL WARRIORS IN HISTORY AND HAS FORGED A DEADLY BLADE WITH THEM.
"SHE HOPES TO TRANSFORM THE INNOCENT SOUL OF THE DEAD WARRIOR TAIRA ATSUMORI INTO A DEMON WHO WILL CARRY THAT BLADE AND LEAD HER FORCES THROUGH THE GATE INTO OUR DOMAIN. SHE'S IMPRISONED THE YOUNG ATSUMORI'S SOUL.
"SHE PUT A SPELL ON HIM... AND HER SERVANTS CONSTANTLY DISTRACT THE YOUNG SOUL. IT'S ALL EVIL TRICKERY, OF COURSE.
"HAVE YOU HEARD OF ATSUMORI?"
"THE MINAMOTO WARRIOR NAMED KUMAGAI NAOZANE KILLED HIM."
"YES, IT WAS IN THE BATTLE OF ICHI NO TANI IN 1184, DURING THE GENPEI WAR.
"ATSUMORI WAS ABOUT SEVENTEEN YEARS OLD WHEN HE DIED.

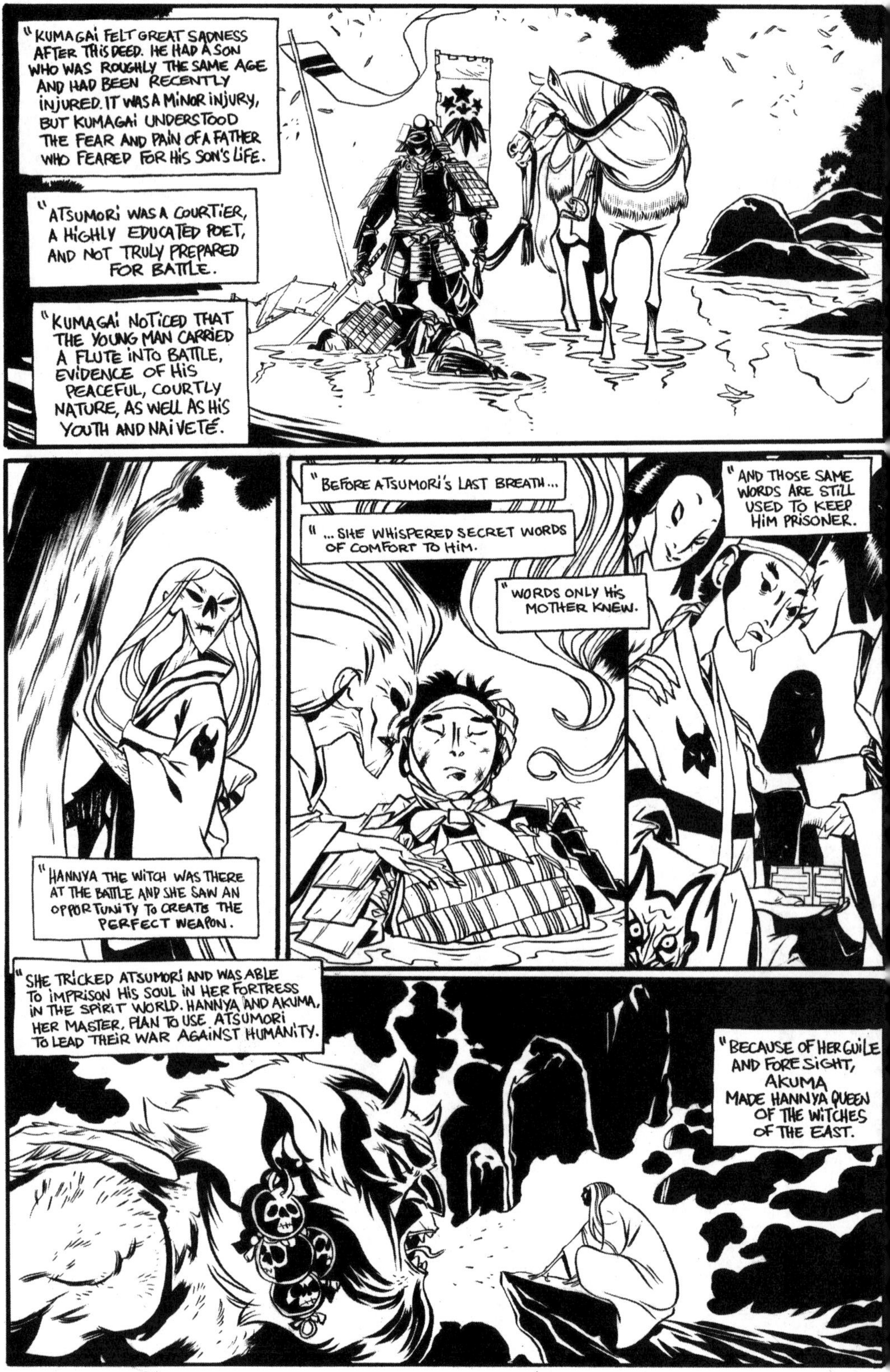
"KUMAGAI FELT GREAT SADNESS AFTER THIS DEED. HE HAD A SON WHO WAS ROUGHLY THE SAME AGE AND HAD BEEN RECENTLY INJURED. IT WAS A MINOR INJURY, BUT KUMAGAI UNDERSTOOD THE FEAR AND PAIN OF A FATHER WHO FEARED FOR HIS SON'S LIFE.
"ATSUMORI WAS A COURTIER, A HIGHLY EDUCATED POET, AND NOT TRULY PREPARED FOR BATTLE.
"KUMAGAI NOTICED THAT THE YOUNG MAN CARRIED A FLUTE INTO BATTLE, EVIDENCE OF HIS PEACEFUL, COURTLY NATURE, AS WELL AS HIS YOUTH AND NAIVETÉ.
"HANNYA THE WITCH WAS THERE AT THE BATTLE AND SHE SAW AN OPPORTUNITY TO CREATE THE PERFECT WEAPON.
"BEFORE ATSUMORI'S LAST BREATH...
"...SHE WHISPERED SECRET WORDS OF COMFORT TO HIM.
"WORDS ONLY HIS MOTHER KNEW.
"AND THOSE SAME WORDS ARE STILL USED TO KEEP HIM PRISONER.
"SHE TRICKED ATSUMORI AND WAS ABLE TO IMPRISON HIS SOUL IN HER FORTRESS IN THE SPIRIT WORLD. HANNYA AND AKUMA, HER MASTER, PLAN TO USE ATSUMORI TO LEAD THEIR WAR AGAINST HUMANITY.
"BECAUSE OF HER GUILE AND FORESIGHT, AKUMA MADE HANNYA QUEEN OF THE WITCHES OF THE EAST.

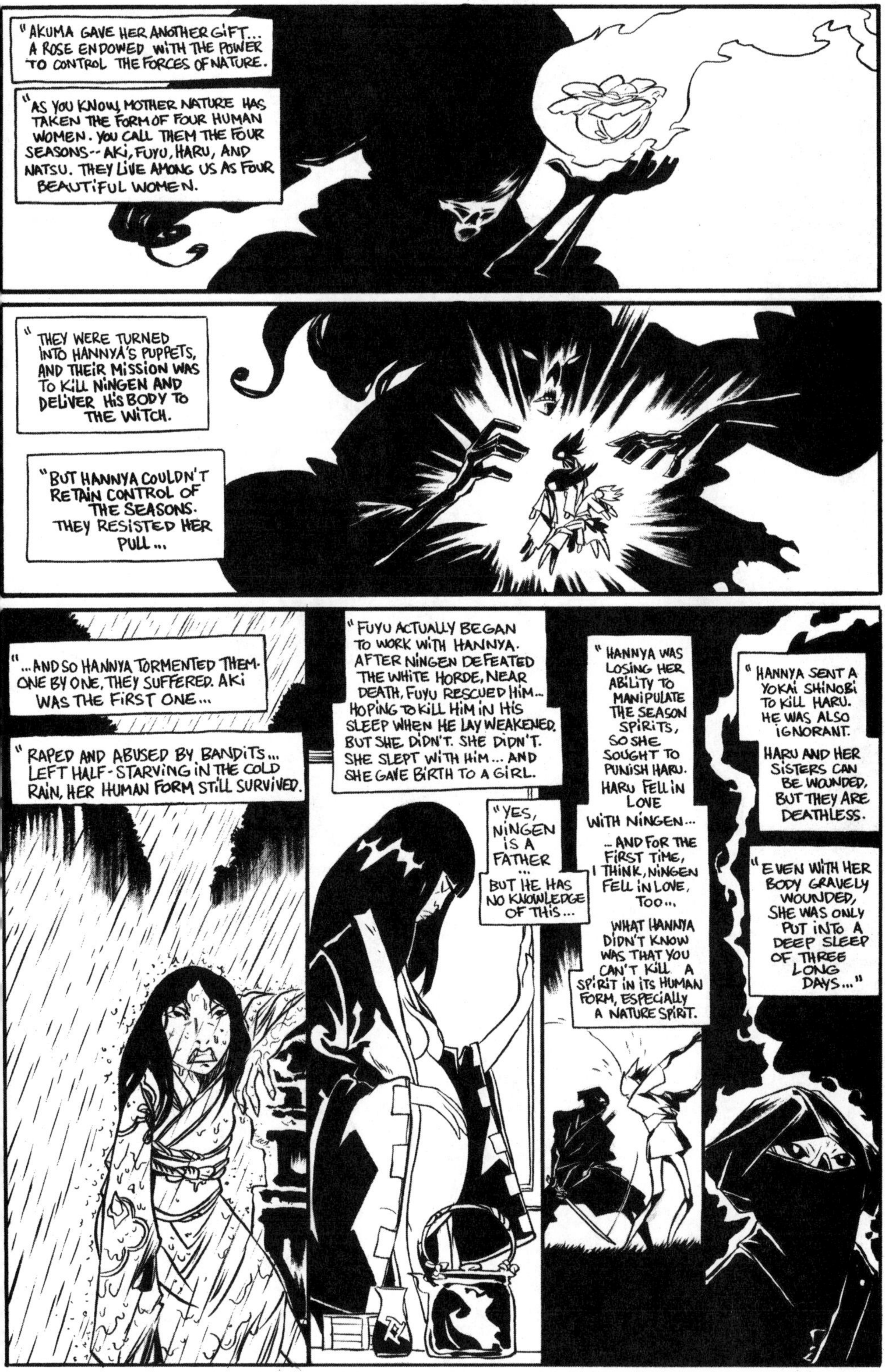
"AKUMA GAVE HER ANOTHER GIFT... A ROSE ENDOWED WITH THE POWER TO CONTROL THE FORCES OF NATURE.
"AS YOU KNOW, MOTHER NATURE HAS TAKEN THE FORM OF FOUR HUMAN WOMEN. YOU CALL THEM THE FOUR SEASONS-- AKI, FUYU, HARU, AND NATSU. THEY LIVE AMONG US AS FOUR BEAUTIFUL WOMEN.
"THEY WERE TURNED INTO HANNYA'S PUPPETS, AND THEIR MISSION WAS TO KILL NINGEN AND DELIVER HIS BODY TO THE WITCH.
"BUT HANNYA COULDN'T RETAIN CONTROL OF THE SEASONS. THEY RESISTED HER PULL...
"...AND SO HANNYA TORMENTED THEM. ONE BY ONE, THEY SUFFERED. AKI WAS THE FIRST ONE...
"RAPED AND ABUSED BY BANDITS... LEFT HALF-STARVING IN THE COLD RAIN, HER HUMAN FORM STILL SURVIVED.
"FUYU ACTUALLY BEGAN TO WORK WITH HANNYA. AFTER NINGEN DEFEATED THE WHITE HORDE, NEAR DEATH, FUYU RESCUED HIM... HOPING TO KILL HIM IN HIS SLEEP WHEN HE LAY WEAKENED. BUT SHE DIDN'T. SHE DIDN'T. SHE SLEPT WITH HIM... AND SHE GAVE BIRTH TO A GIRL.
"YES, NINGEN IS A FATHER ... BUT HE HAS NO KNOWLEDGE OF THIS...
"HANNYA WAS LOSING HER ABILITY TO MANIPULATE THE SEASON SPIRITS, SO SHE SOUGHT TO PUNISH HARU. HARU FELL IN LOVE WITH NINGEN...
...AND FOR THE FIRST TIME, I THINK, NINGEN FELL IN LOVE, TOO...
WHAT HANNYA DIDN'T KNOW WAS THAT YOU CAN'T KILL A SPIRIT IN ITS HUMAN FORM, ESPECIALLY A NATURE SPIRIT.
"HANNYA SENT A YOKAI SHINOBI TO KILL HARU. HE WAS ALSO IGNORANT.
HARU AND HER SISTERS CAN BE WOUNDED, BUT THEY ARE DEATHLESS.
"EVEN WITH HER BODY GRAVELY WOUNDED, SHE WAS ONLY PUT INTO A DEEP SLEEP OF THREE LONG DAYS..."

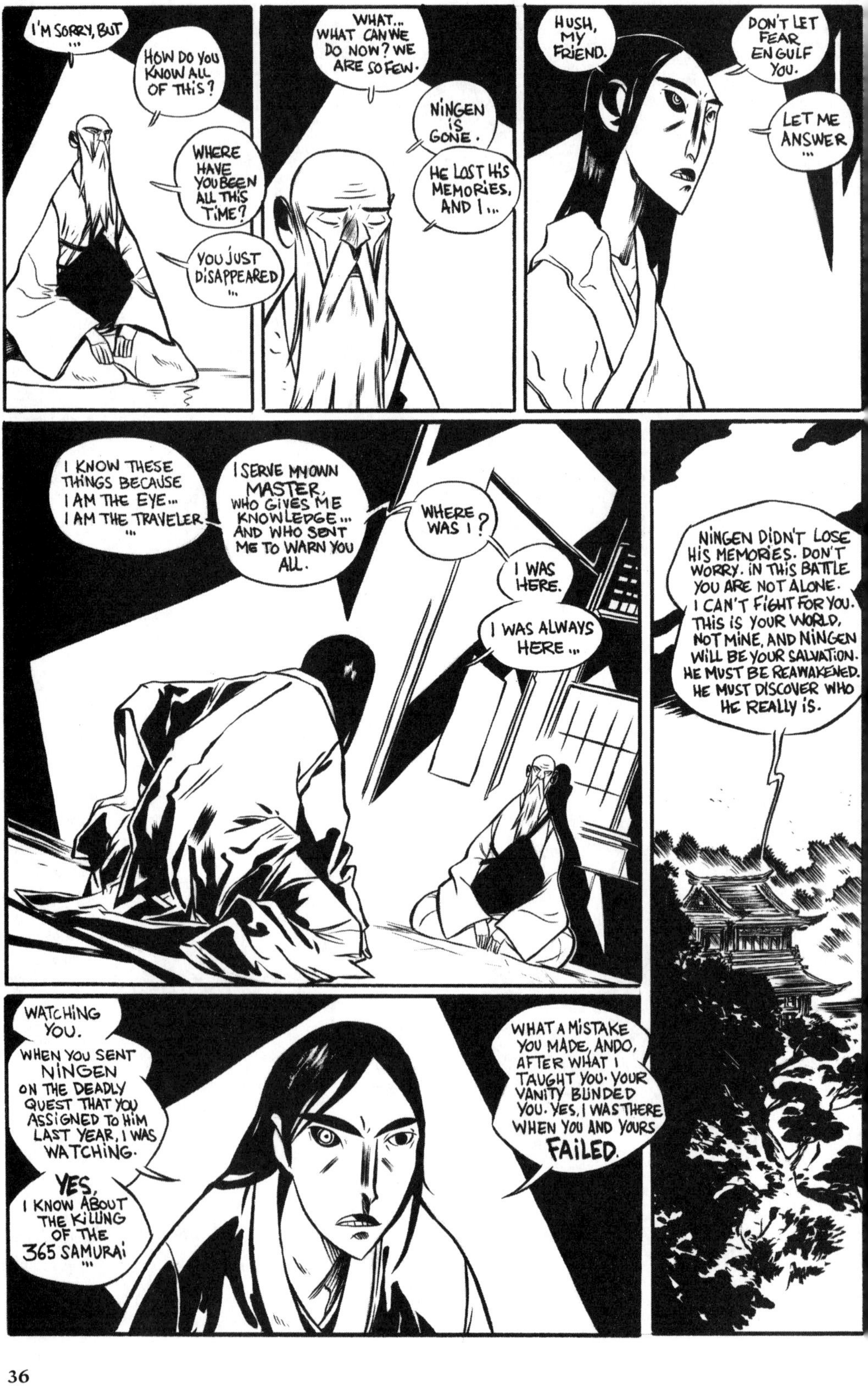
I'M SORRY, BUT ...
HOW DO YOU KNOW ALL OF THIS?
WHERE HAVE YOU BEEN ALL THIS TIME?
YOU JUST DISAPPEARED ...
WHAT... WHAT CAN WE DO NOW? WE ARE SO FEW.
NINGEN IS GONE.
HE LOST HIS MEMORIES, AND I...
HUSH, MY FRIEND.
DON'T LET FEAR ENGULF YOU.
LET ME ANSWER ...
I KNOW THESE THINGS BECAUSE I AM THE EYE... I AM THE TRAVELER ...
I SERVE MY OWN MASTER, WHO GIVES ME KNOWLEDGE... AND WHO SENT ME TO WARN YOU ALL.
WHERE WAS I?
I WAS HERE.
I WAS ALWAYS HERE...
NINGEN DIDN'T LOSE HIS MEMORIES. DON'T WORRY. IN THIS BATTLE YOU ARE NOT ALONE. I CAN'T FIGHT FOR YOU. THIS IS YOUR WORLD, NOT MINE, AND NINGEN WILL BE YOUR SALVATION. HE MUST BE REAWAKENED. HE MUST DISCOVER WHO HE REALLY IS.
WATCHING YOU.
WHEN YOU SENT NINGEN ON THE DEADLY QUEST THAT YOU ASSIGNED TO HIM LAST YEAR, I WAS WATCHING.
YES, I KNOW ABOUT THE KILLING OF THE 365 SAMURAI ...
WHAT A MISTAKE YOU MADE, ANDO, AFTER WHAT I TAUGHT YOU. YOUR VANITY BLINDED YOU. YES, I WAS THERE WHEN YOU AND YOURS FAILED.

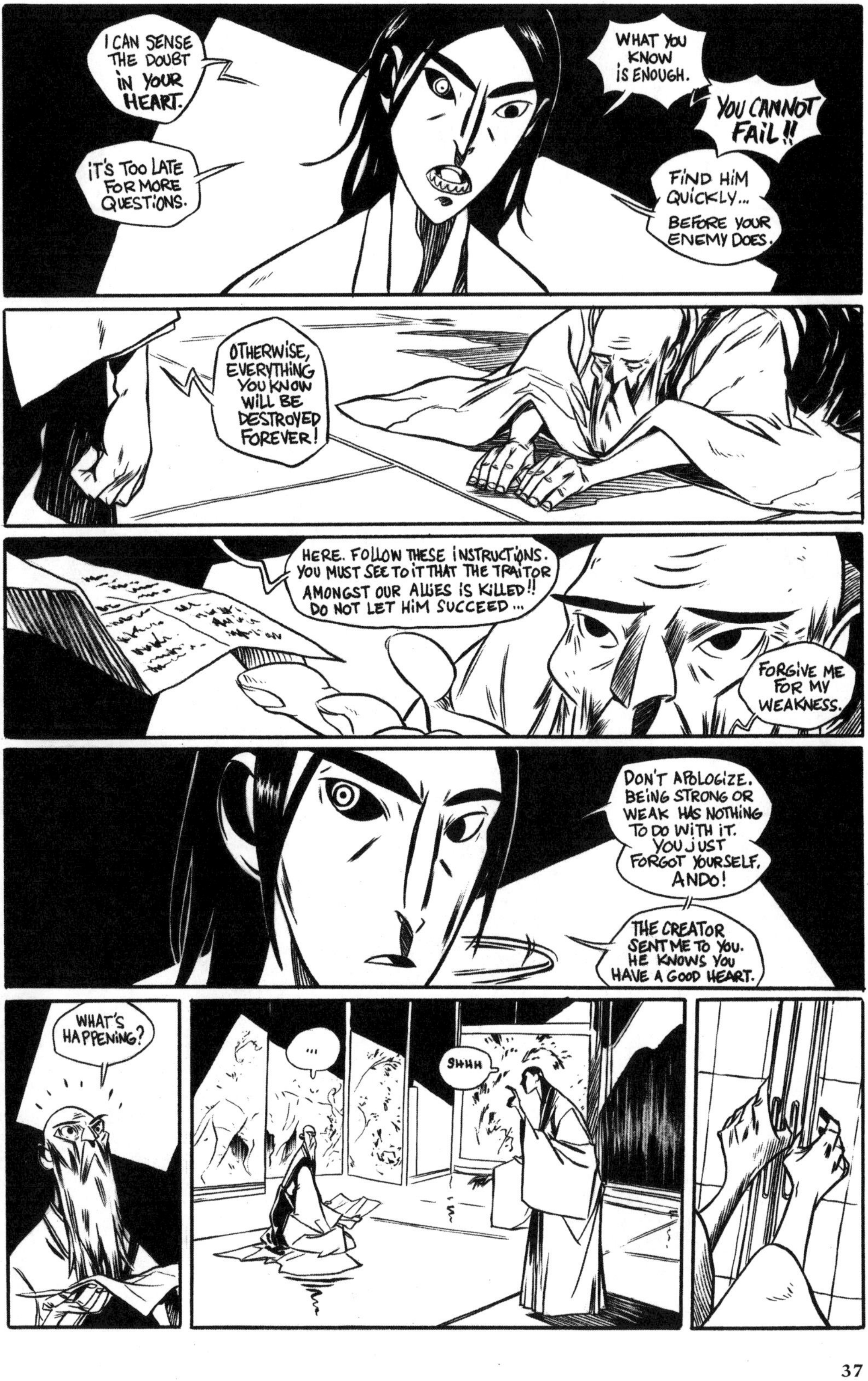
I CAN SENSE THE DOUBT IN YOUR HEART.
IT'S TOO LATE FOR MORE QUESTIONS.
WHAT YOU KNOW IS ENOUGH.
YOU CANNOT FAIL!!
FIND HIM QUICKLY... BEFORE YOUR ENEMY DOES.
OTHERWISE, EVERYTHING YOU KNOW WILL BE DESTROYED FOREVER!
HERE. FOLLOW THESE INSTRUCTIONS. YOU MUST SEE TO IT THAT THE TRAITOR AMONGST OUR ALLIES IS KILLED!! DO NOT LET HIM SUCCEED...
FORGIVE ME FOR MY WEAKNESS.
DON'T APOLOGIZE. BEING STRONG OR WEAK HAS NOTHING TO DO WITH IT. YOU JUST FORGOT YOURSELF, ANDO!
THE CREATOR SENT ME TO YOU. HE KNOWS YOU HAVE A GOOD HEART.
WHAT'S HAPPENING?
...
SHHH

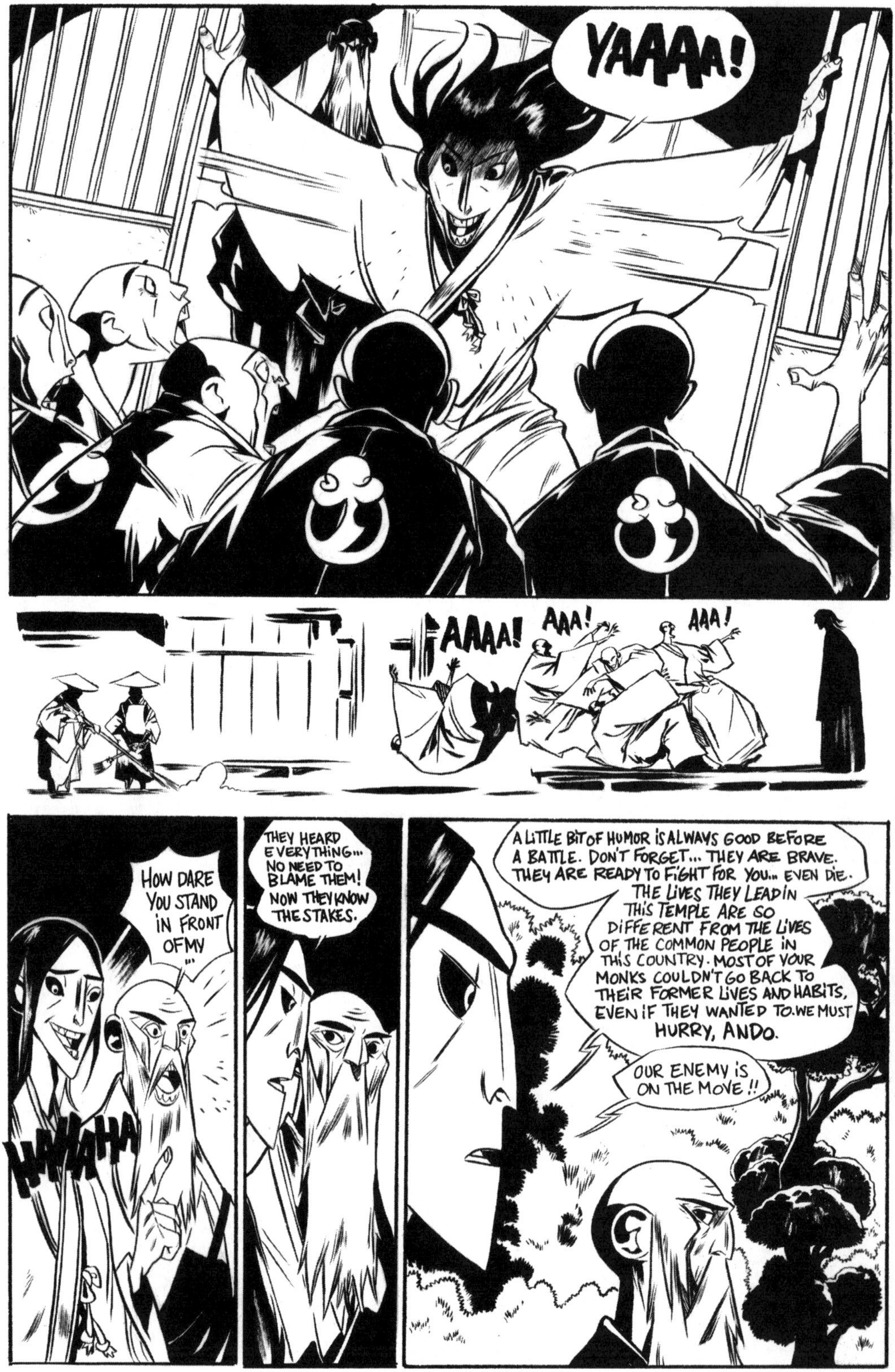
YAAAA!
AAAA!
AAA!
AAA!
HOW DARE YOU STAND IN FRONT OF MY ...
HAHAHA
THEY HEARD EVERYTHING... NO NEED TO BLAME THEM! NOW THEY KNOW THE STAKES.
A LITTLE BIT OF HUMOR IS ALWAYS GOOD BEFORE A BATTLE. DON'T FORGET... THEY ARE BRAVE. THEY ARE READY TO FIGHT FOR YOU... EVEN DIE. THE LIVES THEY LEAD IN THIS TEMPLE ARE SO DIFFERENT FROM THE LIVES OF THE COMMON PEOPLE IN THIS COUNTRY. MOST OF YOUR MONKS COULDN'T GO BACK TO THEIR FORMER LIVES AND HABITS, EVEN IF THEY WANTED TO. WE MUST HURRY, ANDO.
OUR ENEMY IS ON THE MOVE!!

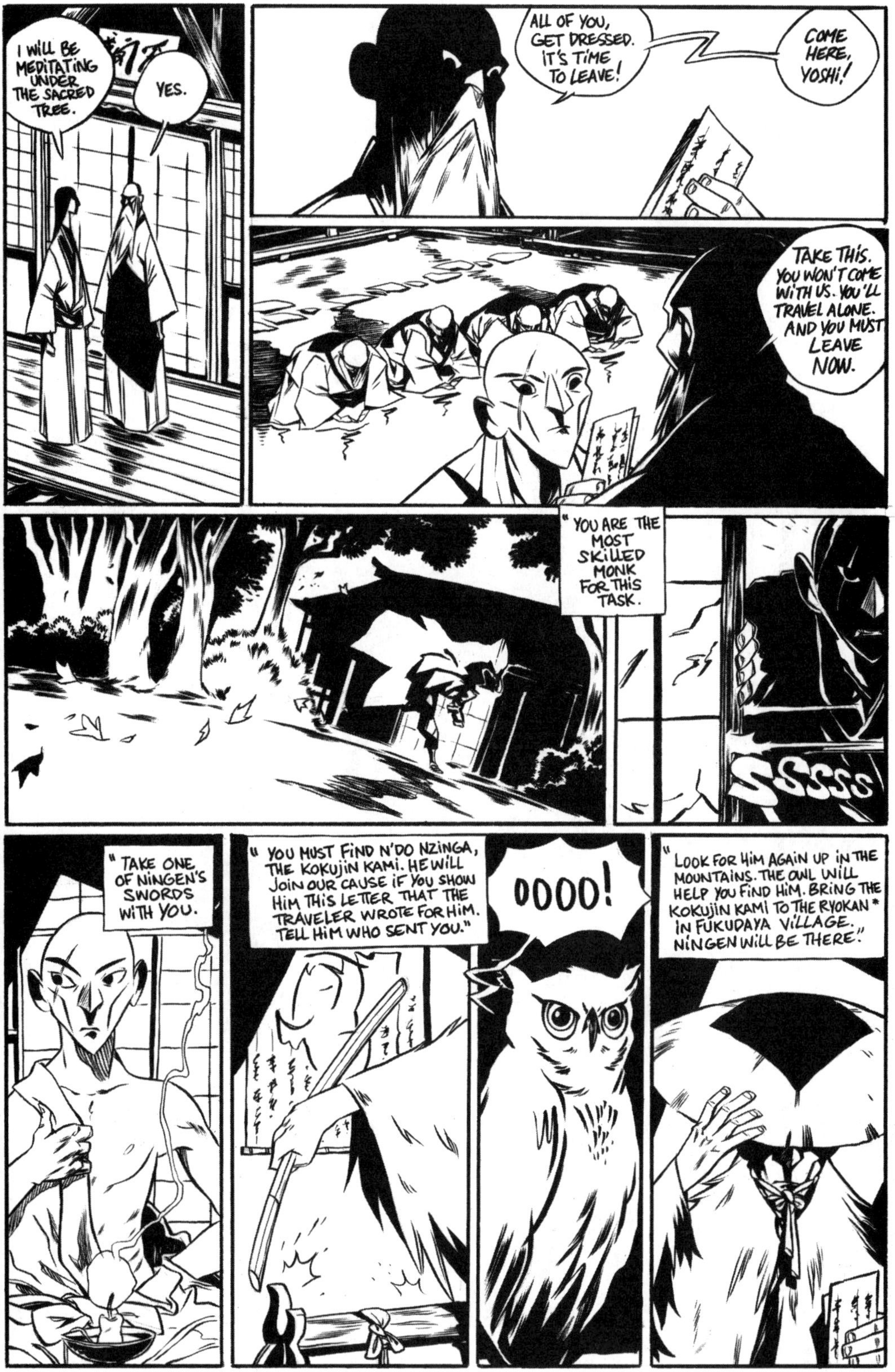
I WILL BE MEDITATING UNDER THE SACRED TREE.
YES.
ALL OF YOU, GET DRESSED. IT'S TIME TO LEAVE!
COME HERE, YOSHI!
TAKE THIS. YOU WON'T COME WITH US. YOU'LL TRAVEL ALONE. AND YOU MUST LEAVE NOW.
"YOU ARE THE MOST SKILLED MONK FOR THIS TASK.
SSSSS
"TAKE ONE OF NINGEN'S SWORDS WITH YOU.
"YOU MUST FIND N'DO NZINGA, THE KOKUJIN KAMI. HE WILL JOIN OUR CAUSE IF YOU SHOW HIM THIS LETTER THAT THE TRAVELER WROTE FOR HIM. TELL HIM WHO SENT YOU."
OOOO!
"LOOK FOR HIM AGAIN UP IN THE MOUNTAINS. THE OWL WILL HELP YOU FIND HIM. BRING THE KOKUJIN KAMI TO THE RYOKAN* IN FUKUDAYA VILLAGE. NINGEN WILL BE THERE."

*RYOKAN: A TRADITIONAL JAPANESE HOTEL

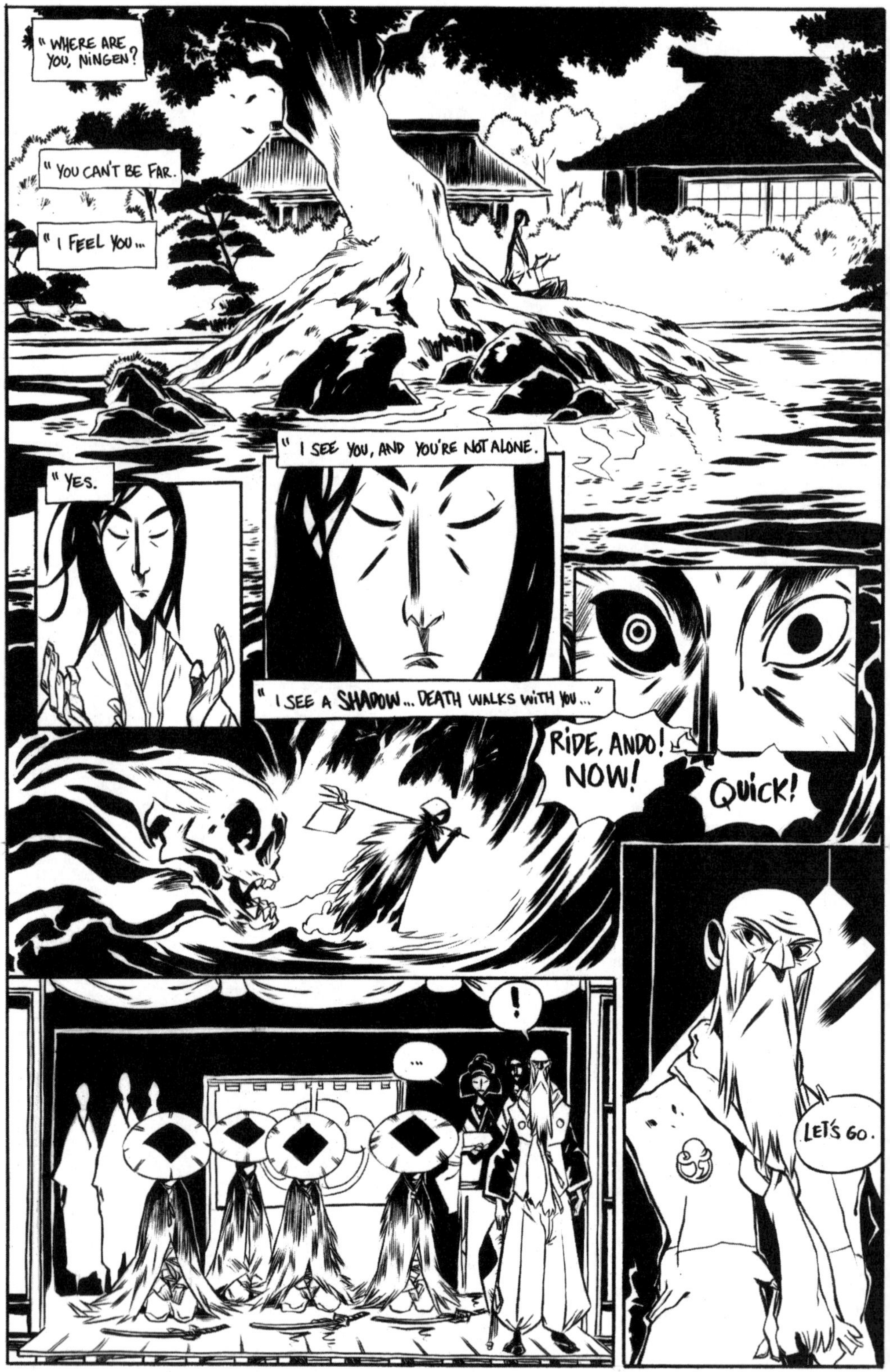
"WHERE ARE YOU, NINGEN?
"YOU CAN'T BE FAR.
"I FEEL YOU...
"YES.
"I SEE YOU, AND YOU'RE NOT ALONE.
"I SEE A SHADOW... DEATH WALKS WITH YOU..."
RIDE, ANDO! NOW!
QUICK!
!
...
LET'S GO.

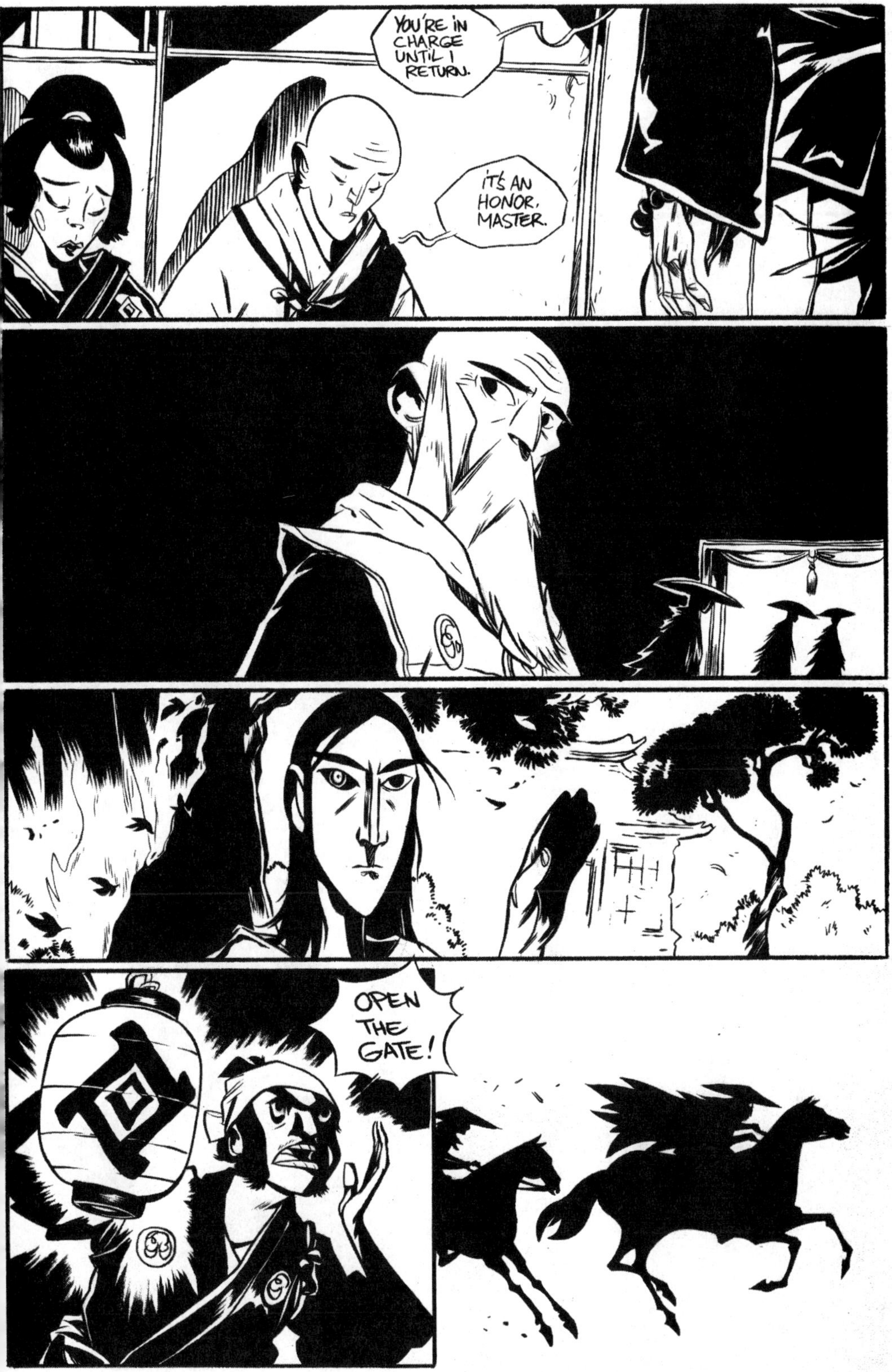
YOU'RE IN CHARGE UNTIL I RETURN.
IT'S AN HONOR, MASTER.
OPEN THE GATE!

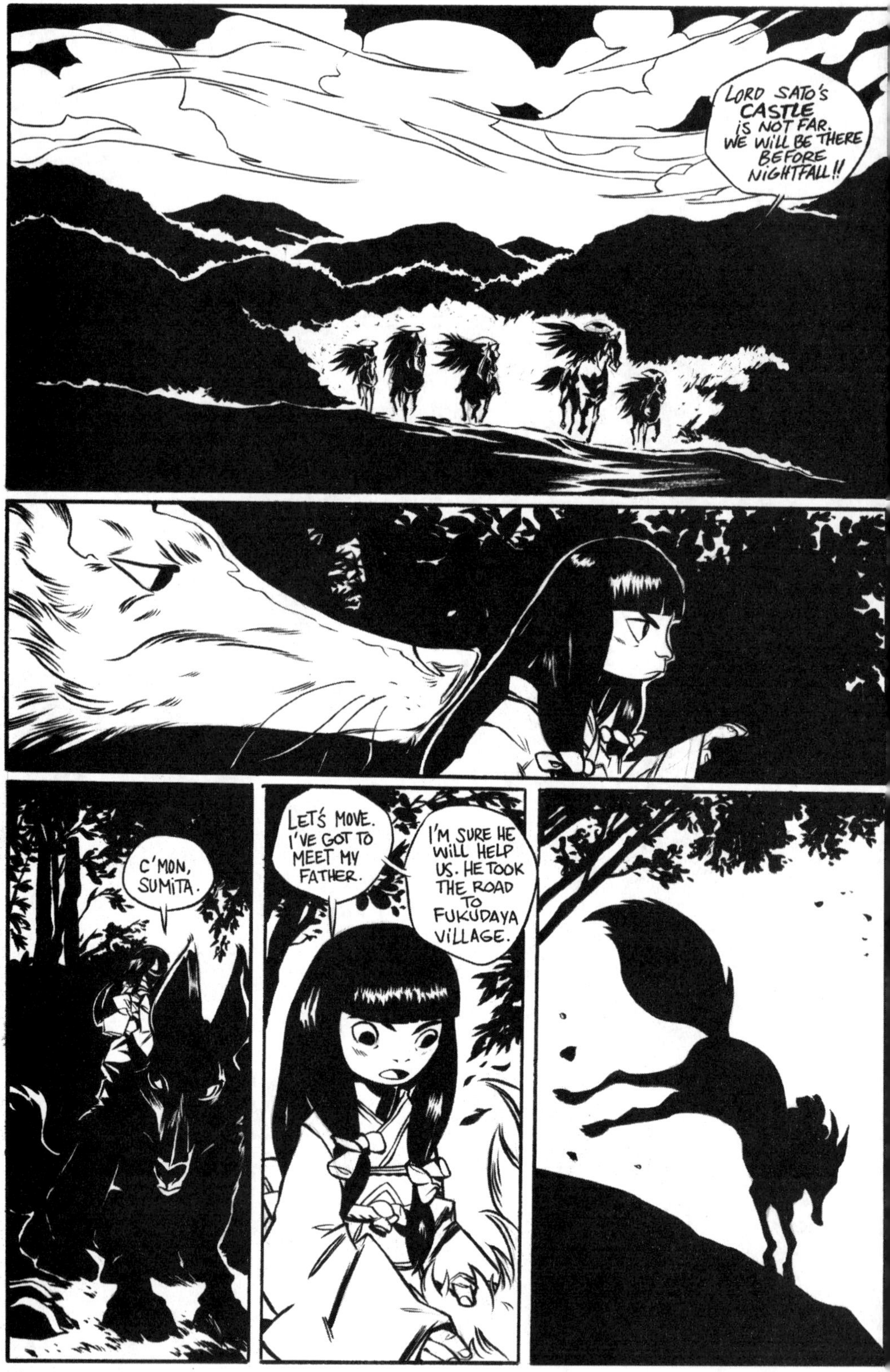
LORD SATO'S CASTLE IS NOT FAR. WE WILL BE THERE BEFORE NIGHTFALL!!
C'MON, SUMITA.
LET'S MOVE. I'VE GOT TO MEET MY FATHER.
I'M SURE HE WILL HELP US. HE TOOK THE ROAD TO FUKUDAYA VILLAGE.

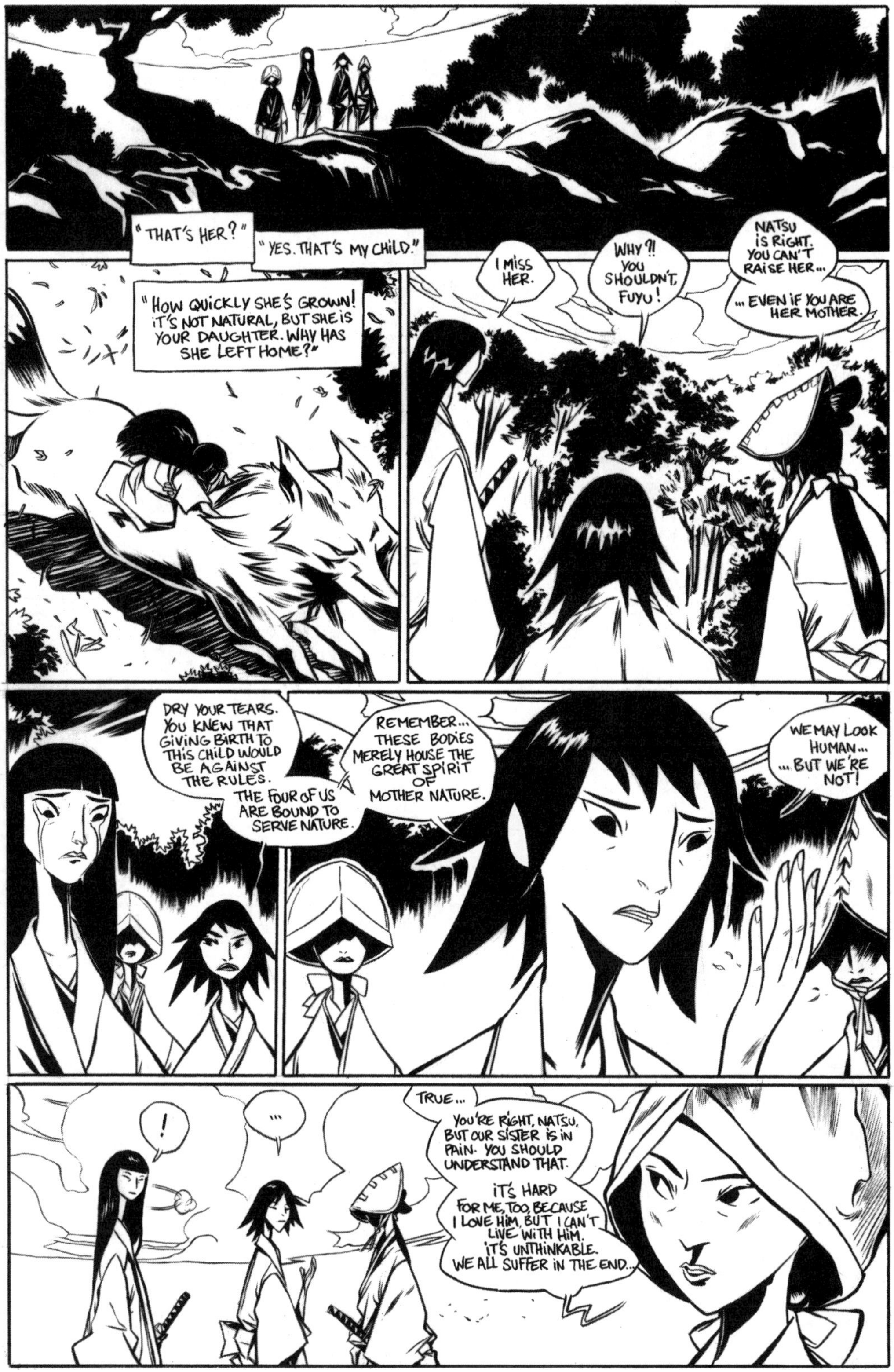
"THAT'S HER?"
"YES. THAT'S MY CHILD."
"HOW QUICKLY SHE'S GROWN! IT'S NOT NATURAL, BUT SHE IS YOUR DAUGHTER. WHY HAS SHE LEFT HOME?"
I MISS HER.
WHY?! YOU SHOULDN'T, FUYU!
NATSU IS RIGHT. YOU CAN'T RAISE HER...
... EVEN IF YOU ARE HER MOTHER.
DRY YOUR TEARS. YOU KNEW THAT GIVING BIRTH TO THIS CHILD WOULD BE AGAINST THE RULES.
THE FOUR OF US ARE BOUND TO SERVE NATURE.
REMEMBER... THESE BODIES MERELY HOUSE THE GREAT SPIRIT OF MOTHER NATURE.
WE MAY LOOK HUMAN...
... BUT WE'RE NOT!
!
...
TRUE...
YOU'RE RIGHT, NATSU, BUT OUR SISTER IS IN PAIN. YOU SHOULD UNDERSTAND THAT.
IT'S HARD FOR ME, TOO, BECAUSE I LOVE HIM, BUT I CAN'T LIVE WITH HIM. IT'S UNTHINKABLE. WE ALL SUFFER IN THE END...

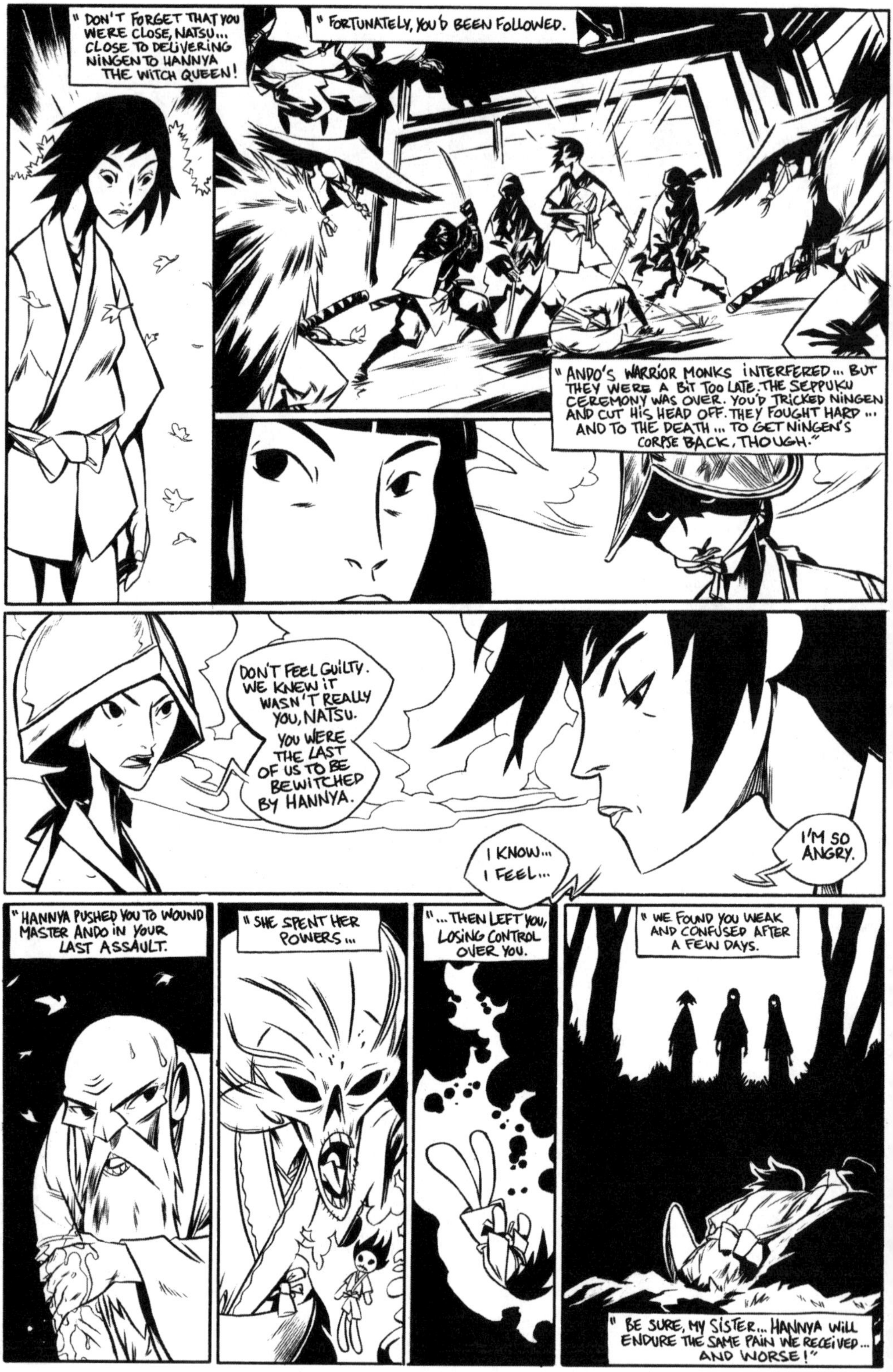
"DON'T FORGET THAT YOU WERE CLOSE, NATSU... CLOSE TO DELIVERING NINGEN TO HANNYA THE WITCH QUEEN!
"FORTUNATELY, YOU'D BEEN FOLLOWED.
"ANDO'S WARRIOR MONKS INTERFERED... BUT THEY WERE A BIT TOO LATE. THE SEPPUKU CEREMONY WAS OVER. YOU'D TRICKED NINGEN AND CUT HIS HEAD OFF. THEY FOUGHT HARD... AND TO THE DEATH... TO GET NINGEN'S CORPSE BACK, THOUGH."
DON'T FEEL GUILTY. WE KNEW IT WASN'T REALLY YOU, NATSU. YOU WERE THE LAST OF US TO BE BEWITCHED BY HANNYA.
I KNOW... I FEEL...
I'M SO ANGRY.
"HANNYA PUSHED YOU TO WOUND MASTER ANDO IN YOUR LAST ASSAULT.
"SHE SPENT HER POWERS...
"...THEN LEFT YOU, LOSING CONTROL OVER YOU.
"WE FOUND YOU WEAK AND CONFUSED AFTER A FEW DAYS.
"BE SURE, MY SISTER... HANNYA WILL ENDURE THE SAME PAIN WE RECEIVED... AND WORSE!"

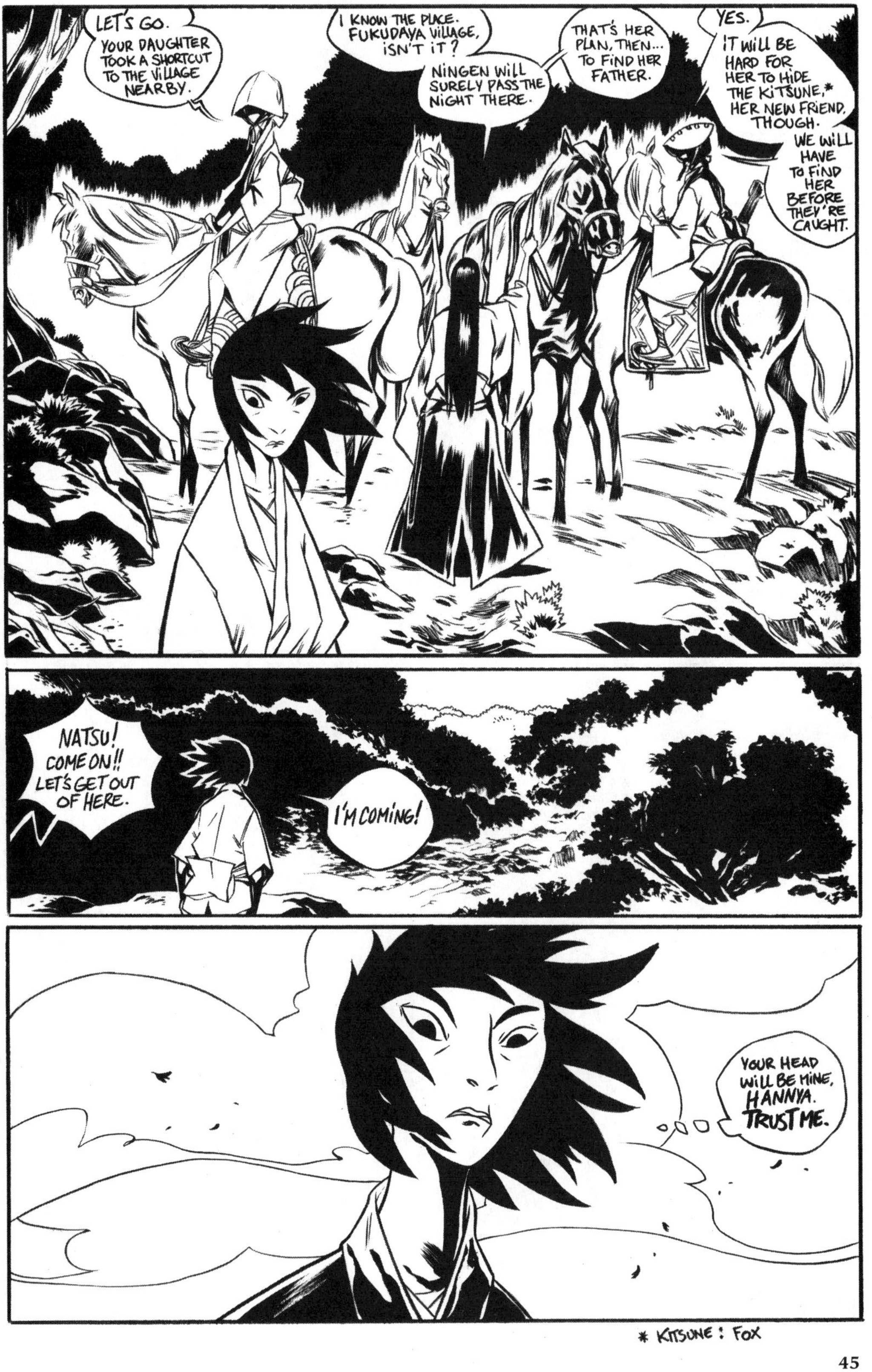
LET'S GO.
YOUR DAUGHTER TOOK A SHORTCUT TO THE VILLAGE NEARBY.
I KNOW THE PLACE. FUKUDAYA VILLAGE, ISN'T IT?
NINGEN WILL SURELY PASS THE NIGHT THERE.
THAT'S HER PLAN, THEN... TO FIND HER FATHER.
YES.
IT WILL BE HARD FOR HER TO HIDE THE KITSUNE,* HER NEW FRIEND, THOUGH.
WE WILL HAVE TO FIND HER BEFORE THEY'RE CAUGHT.
NATSU! COME ON!! LET'S GET OUT OF HERE.
I'M COMING!
YOUR HEAD WILL BE MINE, HANNYA. TRUST ME.

* KITSUNE: FOX

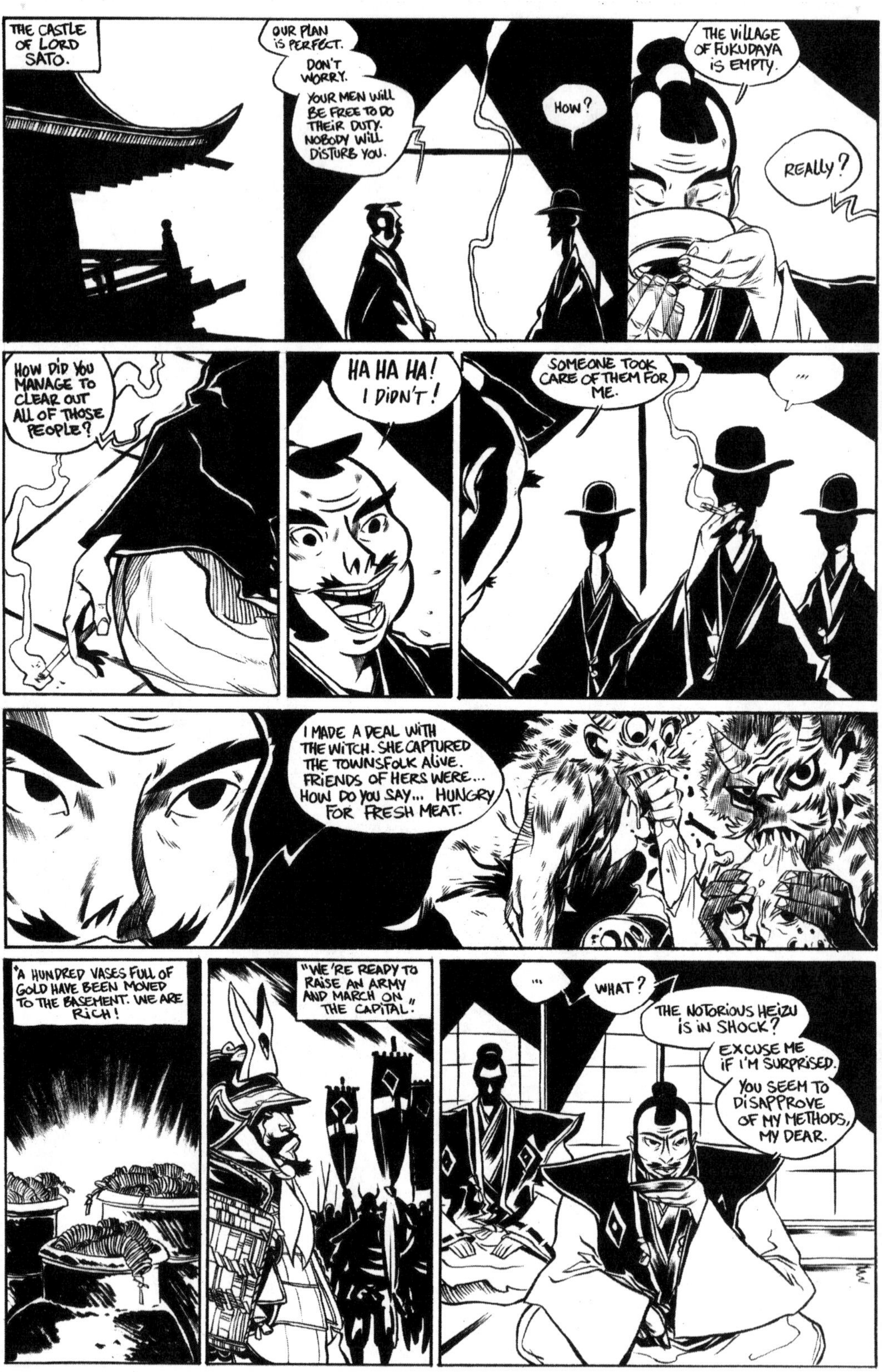
THE CASTLE OF LORD SATO.
OUR PLAN IS PERFECT.
DON'T WORRY.
YOUR MEN WILL BE FREE TO DO THEIR DUTY. NOBODY WILL DISTURB YOU.
HOW?
THE VILLAGE OF FUKUDAYA IS EMPTY.
REALLY?
HOW DID YOU MANAGE TO CLEAR OUT ALL OF THOSE PEOPLE?
HA HA HA! I DIDN'T!
SOMEONE TOOK CARE OF THEM FOR ME.
...
I MADE A DEAL WITH THE WITCH. SHE CAPTURED THE TOWNSFOLK ALIVE. FRIENDS OF HERS WERE... HOW DO YOU SAY... HUNGRY FOR FRESH MEAT.
"A HUNDRED VASES FULL OF GOLD HAVE BEEN MOVED TO THE BASEMENT. WE ARE RICH!
"WE'RE READY TO RAISE AN ARMY AND MARCH ON THE CAPITAL."
...
WHAT?
THE NOTORIOUS HEIZU IS IN SHOCK?
EXCUSE ME IF I'M SURPRISED.
YOU SEEM TO DISAPPROVE OF MY METHODS, MY DEAR.

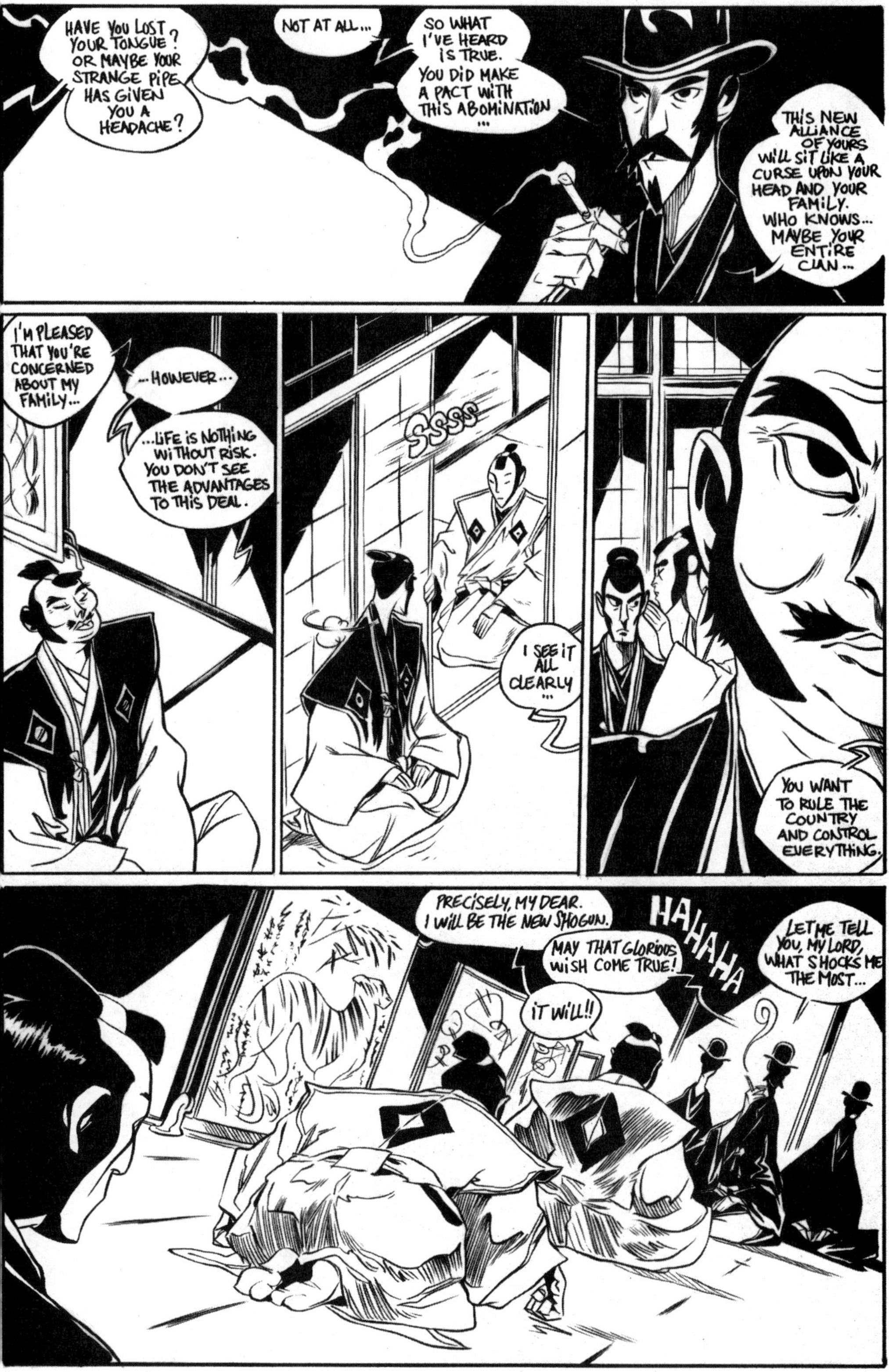
HAVE YOU LOST YOUR TONGUE? OR MAYBE YOUR STRANGE PIPE HAS GIVEN YOU A HEADACHE?
NOT AT ALL...
SO WHAT I'VE HEARD IS TRUE.
YOU DID MAKE A PACT WITH THIS ABOMINATION...
THIS NEW ALLIANCE OF YOURS WILL SIT LIKE A CURSE UPON YOUR HEAD AND YOUR FAMILY. WHO KNOWS... MAYBE YOUR ENTIRE CLAN...
I'M PLEASED THAT YOU'RE CONCERNED ABOUT MY FAMILY...
...HOWEVER...
...LIFE IS NOTHING WITHOUT RISK. YOU DON'T SEE THE ADVANTAGES TO THIS DEAL.
SSSS
I SEE IT ALL CLEARLY...
YOU WANT TO RULE THE COUNTRY AND CONTROL EVERYTHING.
PRECISELY, MY DEAR. I WILL BE THE NEW SHOGUN.
MAY THAT GLORIOUS WISH COME TRUE!
IT WILL!!
HAHAHA
LET ME TELL YOU, MY LORD, WHAT SHOCKS ME THE MOST...

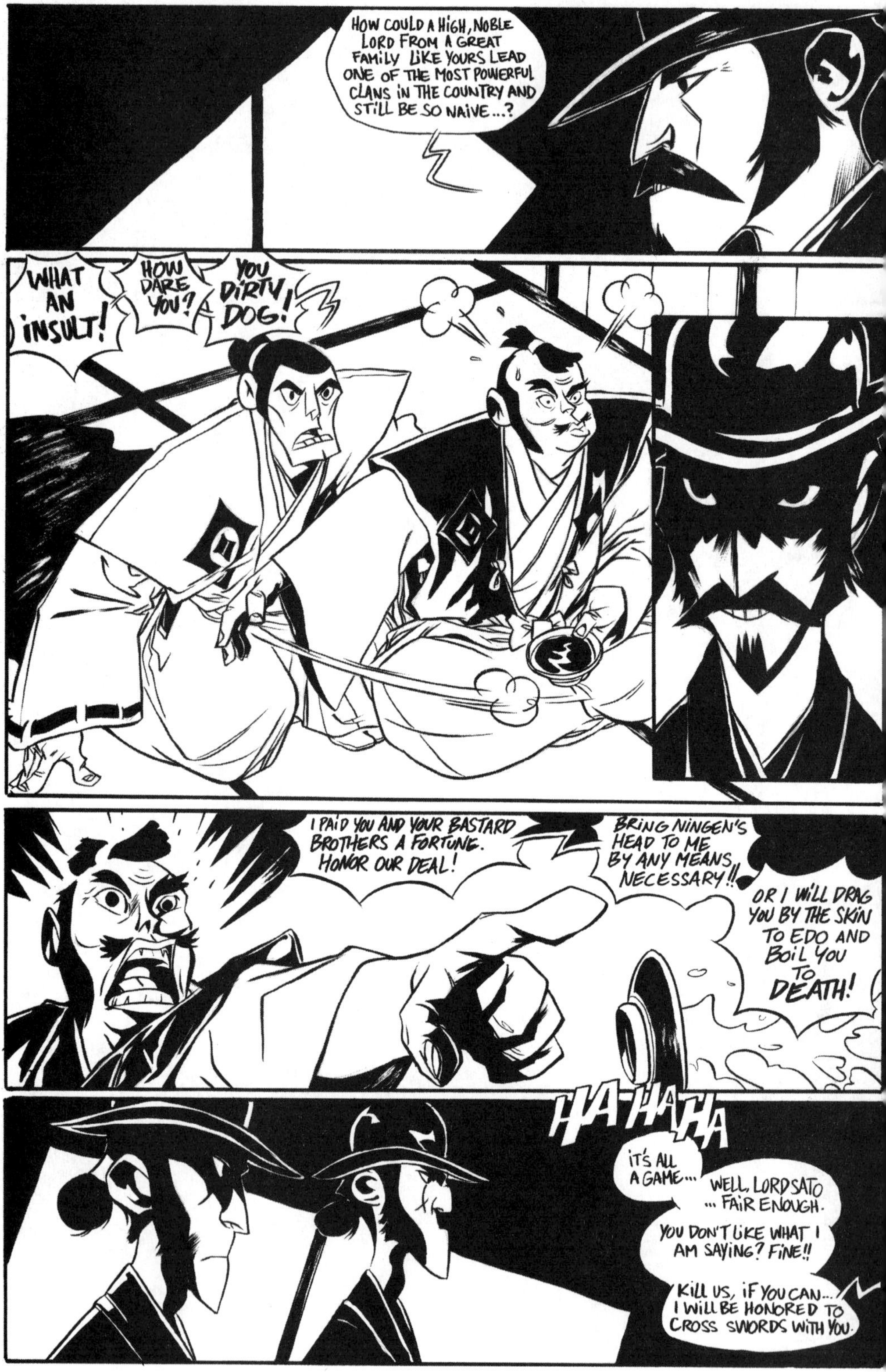
HOW COULD A HIGH, NOBLE LORD FROM A GREAT FAMILY LIKE YOURS LEAD ONE OF THE MOST POWERFUL CLANS IN THE COUNTRY AND STILL BE SO NAIVE...?
WHAT AN INSULT!
HOW DARE YOU?!
YOU DIRTY DOG!
I PAID YOU AND YOUR BASTARD BROTHERS A FORTUNE. HONOR OUR DEAL!
BRING NINGEN'S HEAD TO ME BY ANY MEANS NECESSARY!!
OR I WILL DRAG YOU BY THE SKIN TO EDO AND BOIL YOU TO DEATH!
HA HA HA HA
IT'S ALL A GAME...
WELL, LORD SATO ... FAIR ENOUGH.
YOU DON'T LIKE WHAT I AM SAYING? FINE!!
KILL US, IF YOU CAN... I WILL BE HONORED TO CROSS SWORDS WITH YOU.

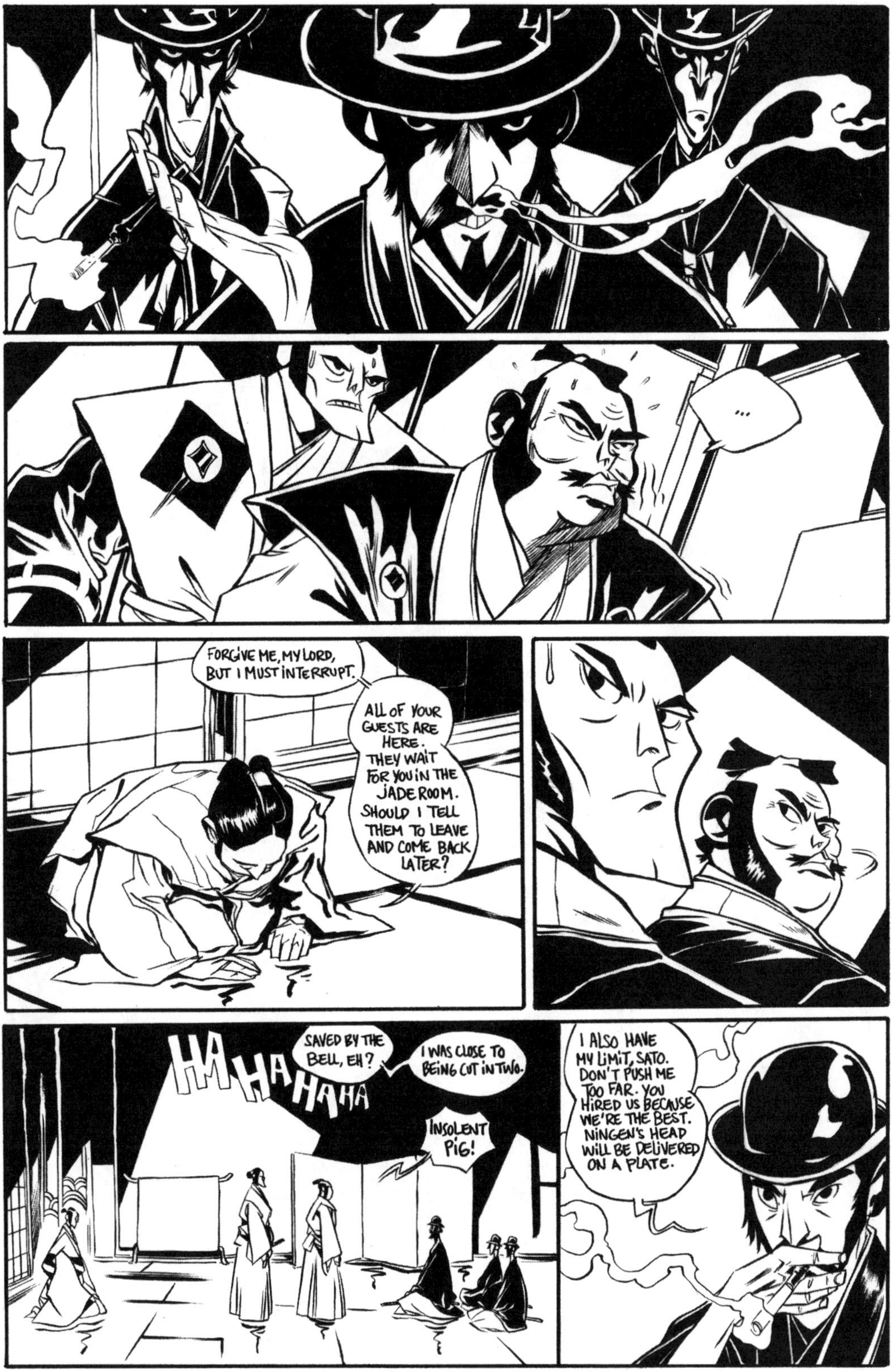
...
FORGIVE ME, MY LORD, BUT I MUST INTERRUPT.
ALL OF YOUR GUESTS ARE HERE. THEY WAIT FOR YOU IN THE JADE ROOM. SHOULD I TELL THEM TO LEAVE AND COME BACK LATER?
HAHAHAHAHA
SAVED BY THE BELL, EH?
I WAS CLOSE TO BEING CUT IN TWO.
INSOLENT PIG!
I ALSO HAVE MY LIMIT, SATO. DON'T PUSH ME TOO FAR. YOU HIRED US BECAUSE WE'RE THE BEST. NINGEN'S HEAD WILL BE DELIVERED ON A PLATE.

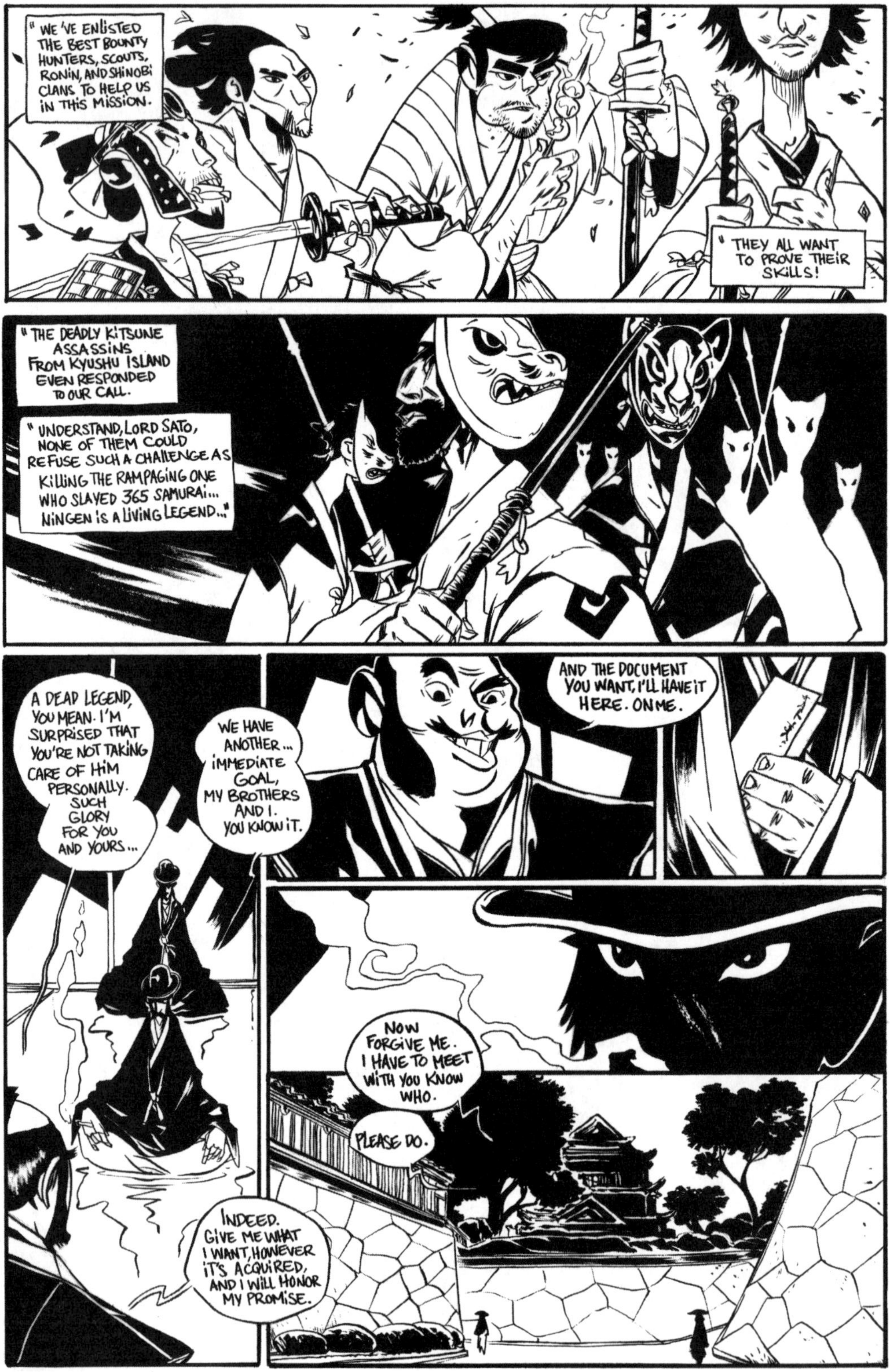
"WE'VE ENLISTED THE BEST BOUNTY HUNTERS, SCOUTS, RONIN, AND SHINOBI CLANS TO HELP US IN THIS MISSION.
"THEY ALL WANT TO PROVE THEIR SKILLS!
"THE DEADLY KITSUNE ASSASSINS FROM KYUSHU ISLAND EVEN RESPONDED TO OUR CALL.
"UNDERSTAND, LORD SATO, NONE OF THEM COULD REFUSE SUCH A CHALLENGE AS KILLING THE RAMPAGING ONE WHO SLAYED 365 SAMURAI... NINGEN IS A LIVING LEGEND..."
A DEAD LEGEND, YOU MEAN. I'M SURPRISED THAT YOU'RE NOT TAKING CARE OF HIM PERSONALLY. SUCH GLORY FOR YOU AND YOURS...
WE HAVE ANOTHER... IMMEDIATE GOAL, MY BROTHERS AND I. YOU KNOW IT.
AND THE DOCUMENT YOU WANT, I'LL HAVE IT HERE. ON ME.
INDEED. GIVE ME WHAT I WANT, HOWEVER IT'S ACQUIRED, AND I WILL HONOR MY PROMISE.
NOW FORGIVE ME. I HAVE TO MEET WITH YOU KNOW WHO.
PLEASE DO.

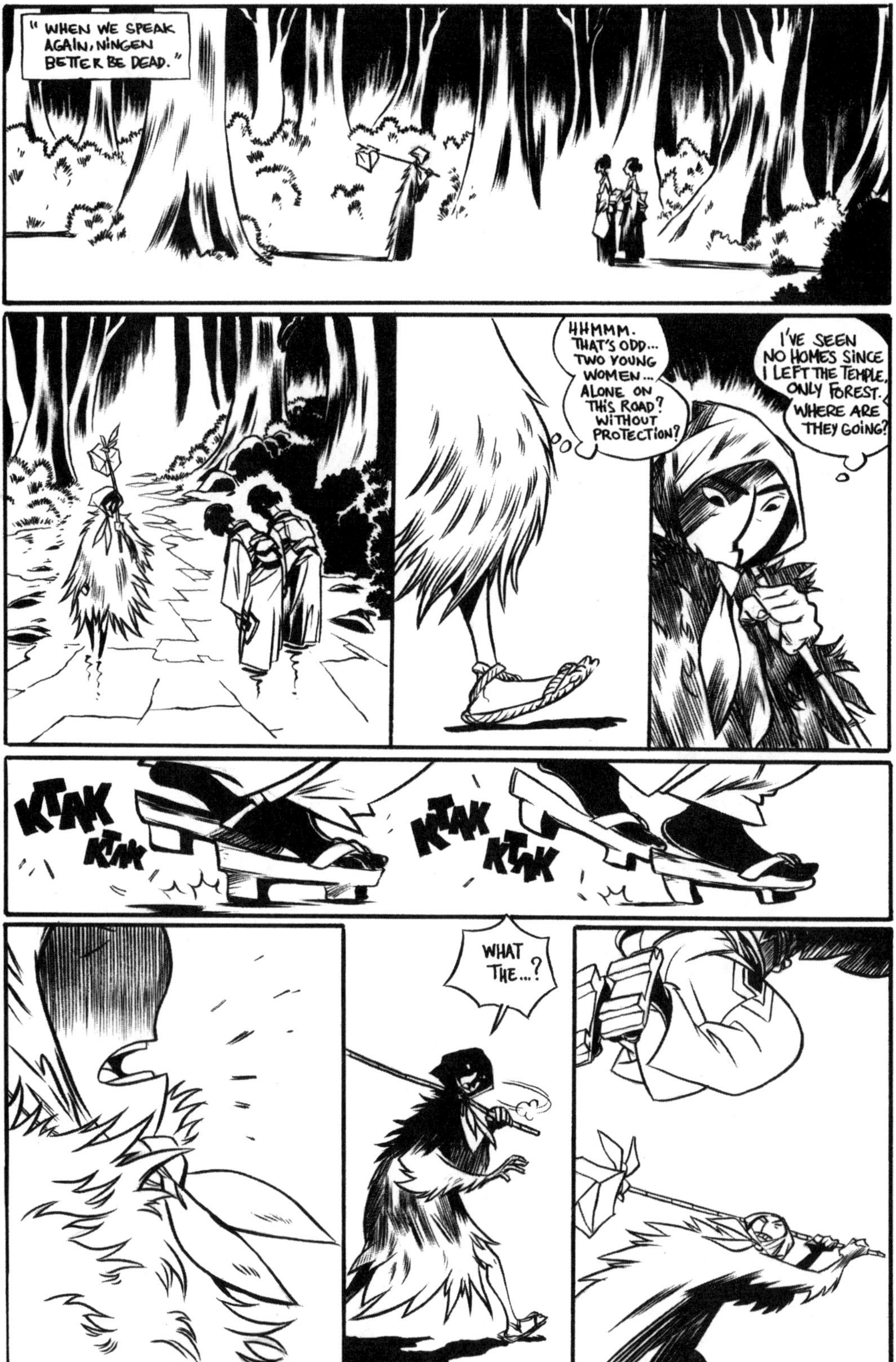

"WHEN WE SPEAK AGAIN, NINGEN BETTER BE DEAD."
HHMMM. THAT'S ODD... TWO YOUNG WOMEN... ALONE ON THIS ROAD? WITHOUT PROTECTION?
I'VE SEEN NO HOMES SINCE I LEFT THE TEMPLE, ONLY FOREST. WHERE ARE THEY GOING?
KTAK KTAK
KTAK KTAK
WHAT THE...?

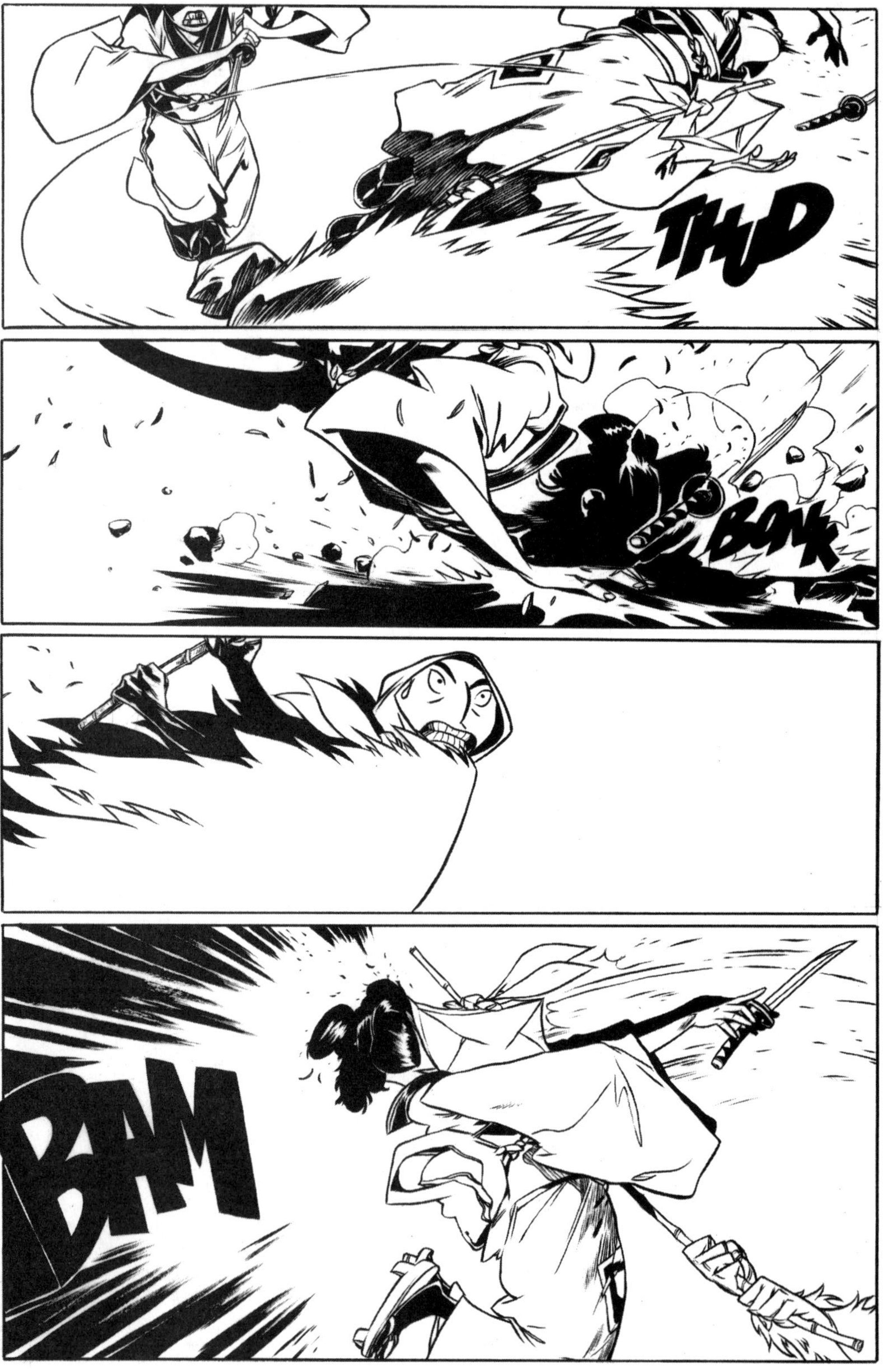
THUD
BONK
BAM

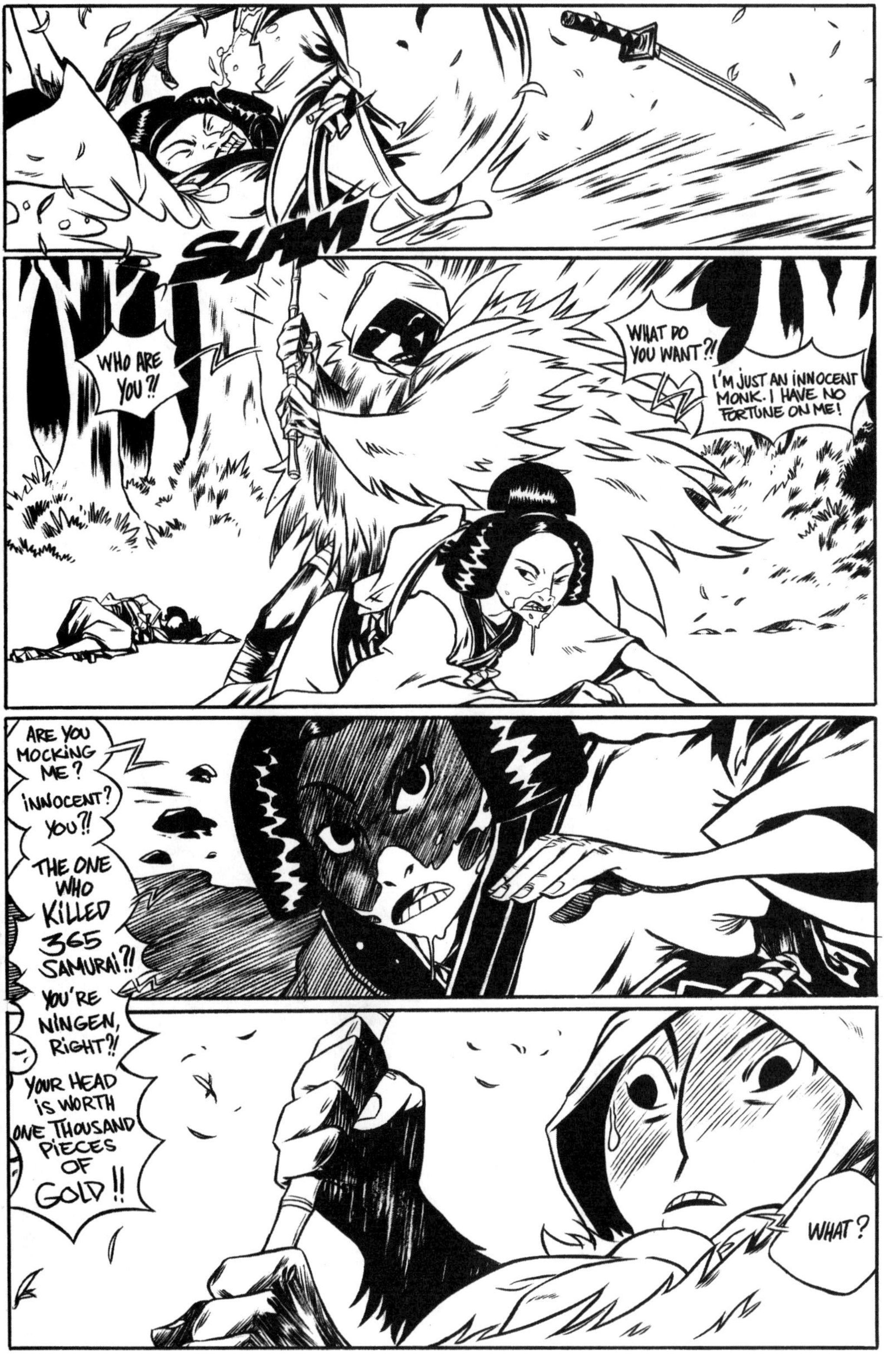
SLAM
WHO ARE YOU?!
WHAT DO YOU WANT?!
I'M JUST AN INNOCENT MONK. I HAVE NO FORTUNE ON ME!
ARE YOU MOCKING ME?
INNOCENT? YOU?!
THE ONE WHO KILLED 365 SAMURAI?!
YOU'RE NINGEN, RIGHT?!
YOUR HEAD IS WORTH ONE THOUSAND PIECES OF GOLD!!
WHAT?

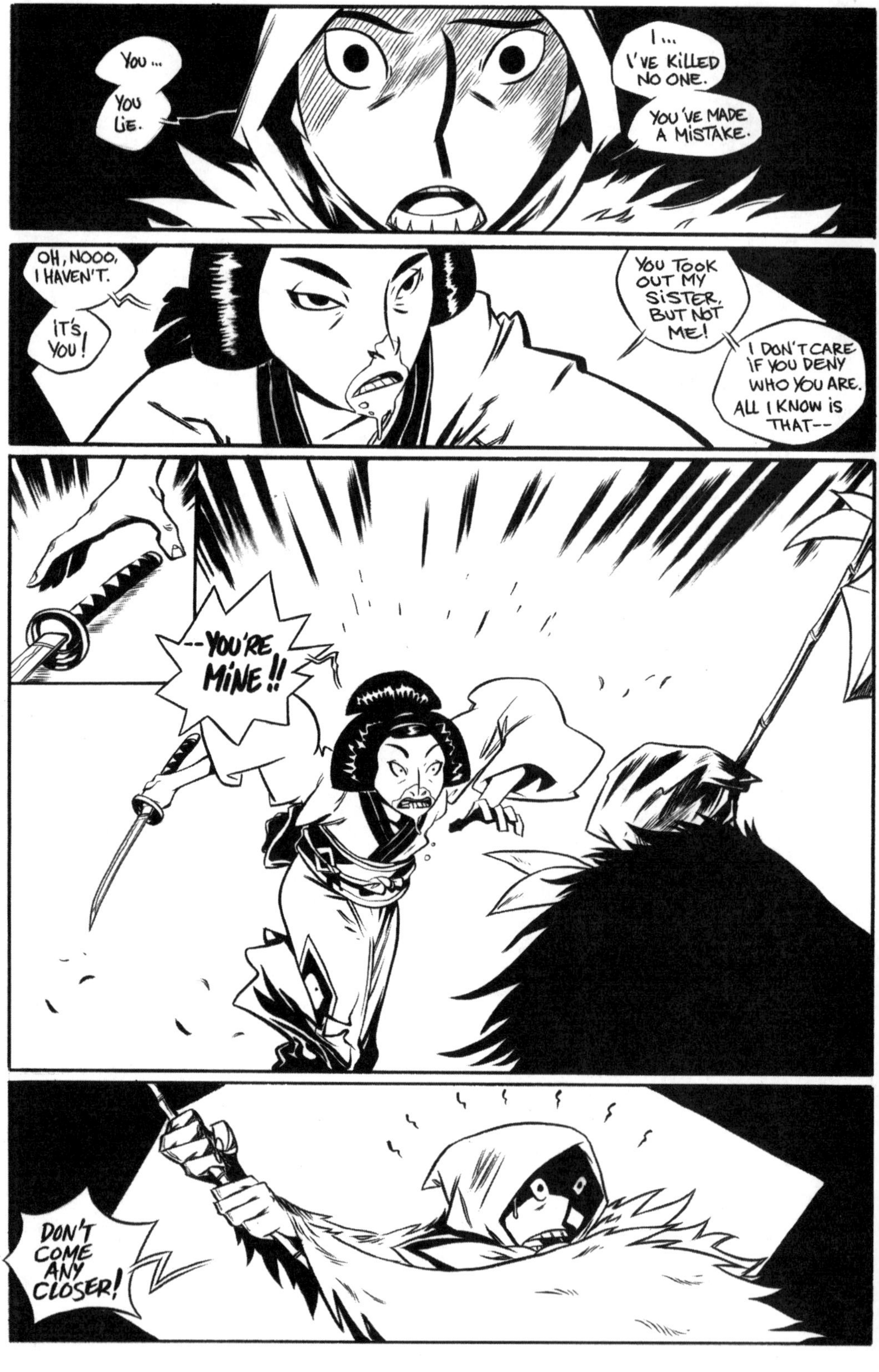
YOU...
YOU LIE.
I...
I'VE KILLED NO ONE.
YOU'VE MADE A MISTAKE.
OH, NOOO, I HAVEN'T.
IT'S YOU!
YOU TOOK OUT MY SISTER, BUT NOT ME!
I DON'T CARE IF YOU DENY WHO YOU ARE.
ALL I KNOW IS THAT--
--YOU'RE MINE!!
DON'T COME ANY CLOSER!

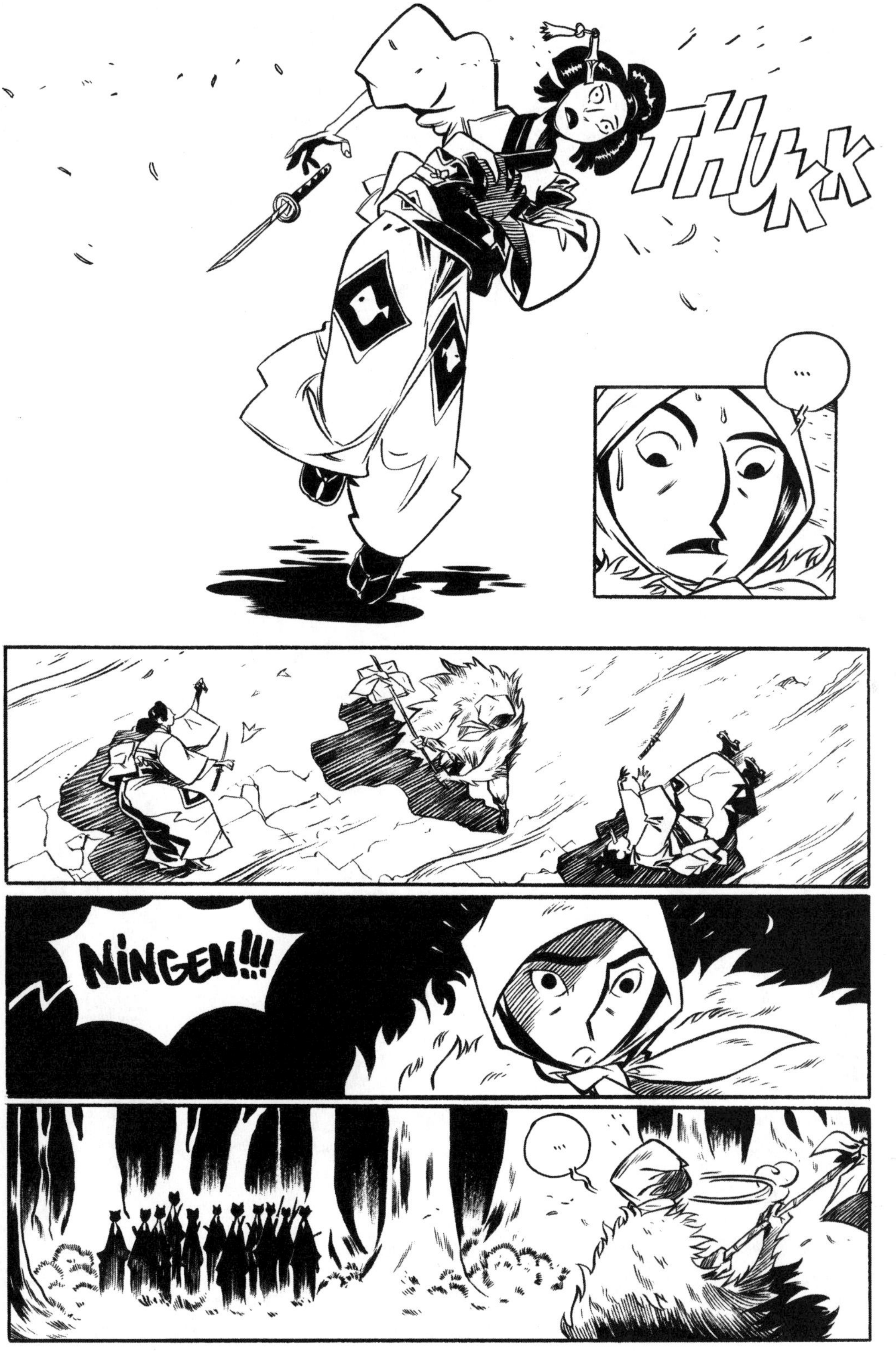
THUKK
...
NINGEN!!!
...

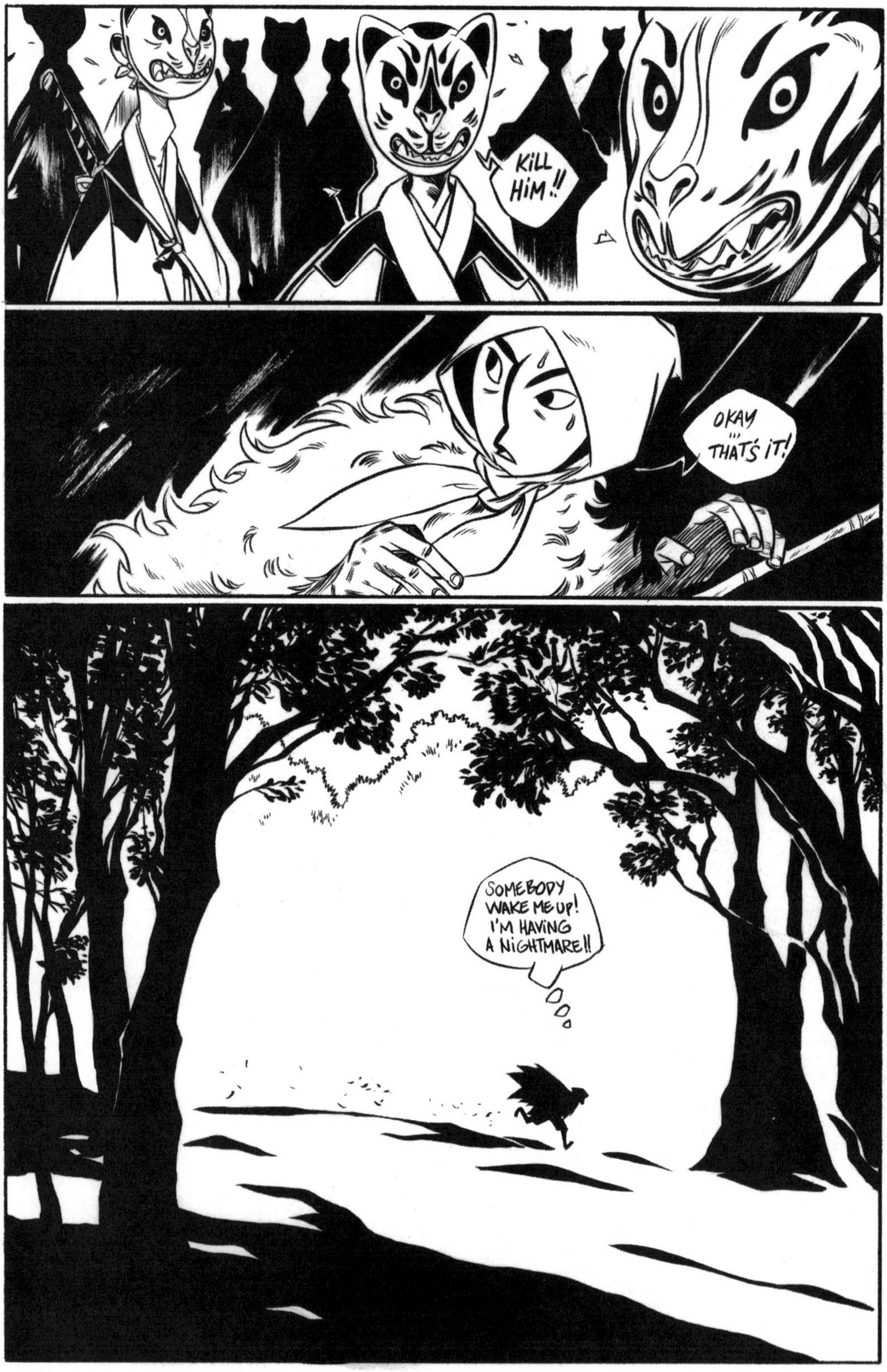
KILL HIM!!
OKAY ... THAT'S IT!
SOMEBODY WAKE ME UP! I'M HAVING A NIGHTMARE!!

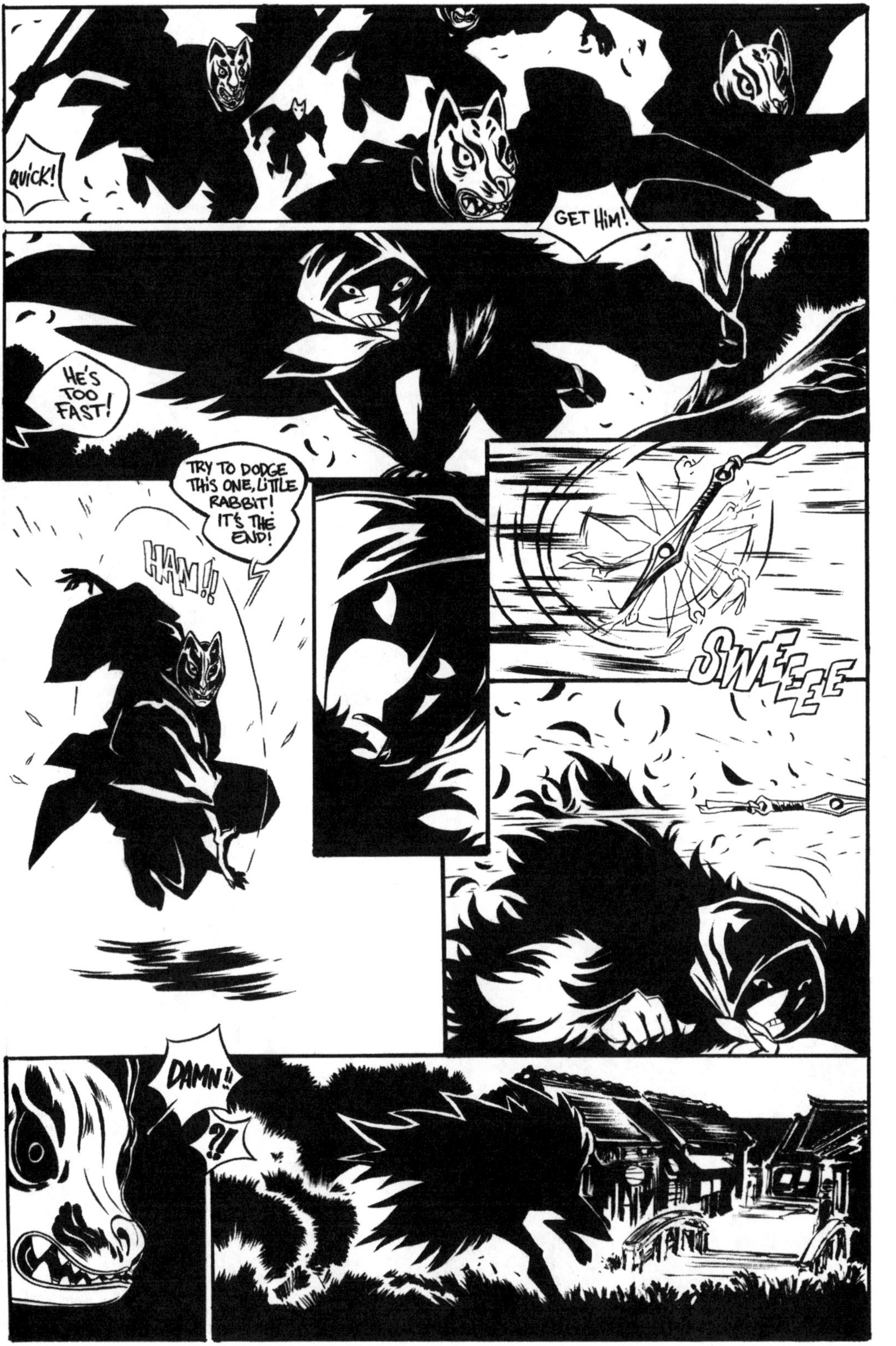
QUICK!
GET HIM!
HE'S TOO FAST!
TRY TO DODGE THIS ONE, LITTLE RABBIT! IT'S THE END!
HAN!!
SWEEEE
DAMN!!
?!

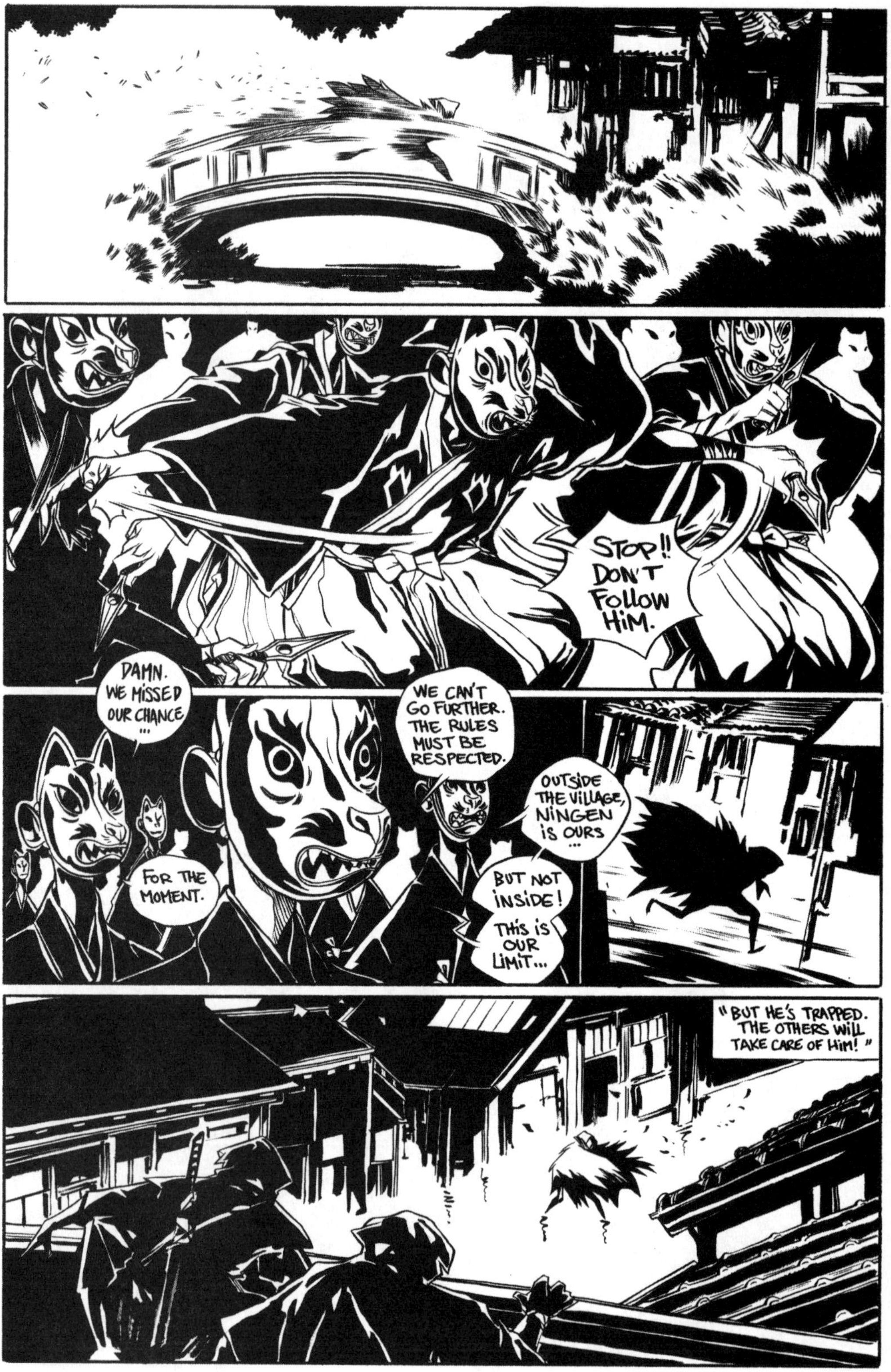
STOP!! DON'T FOLLOW HIM.
DAMN. WE MISSED OUR CHANCE...
FOR THE MOMENT.
WE CAN'T GO FURTHER. THE RULES MUST BE RESPECTED.
OUTSIDE THE VILLAGE, NINGEN IS OURS...
BUT NOT INSIDE!
THIS IS OUR LIMIT...
"BUT HE'S TRAPPED. THE OTHERS WILL TAKE CARE OF HIM!"

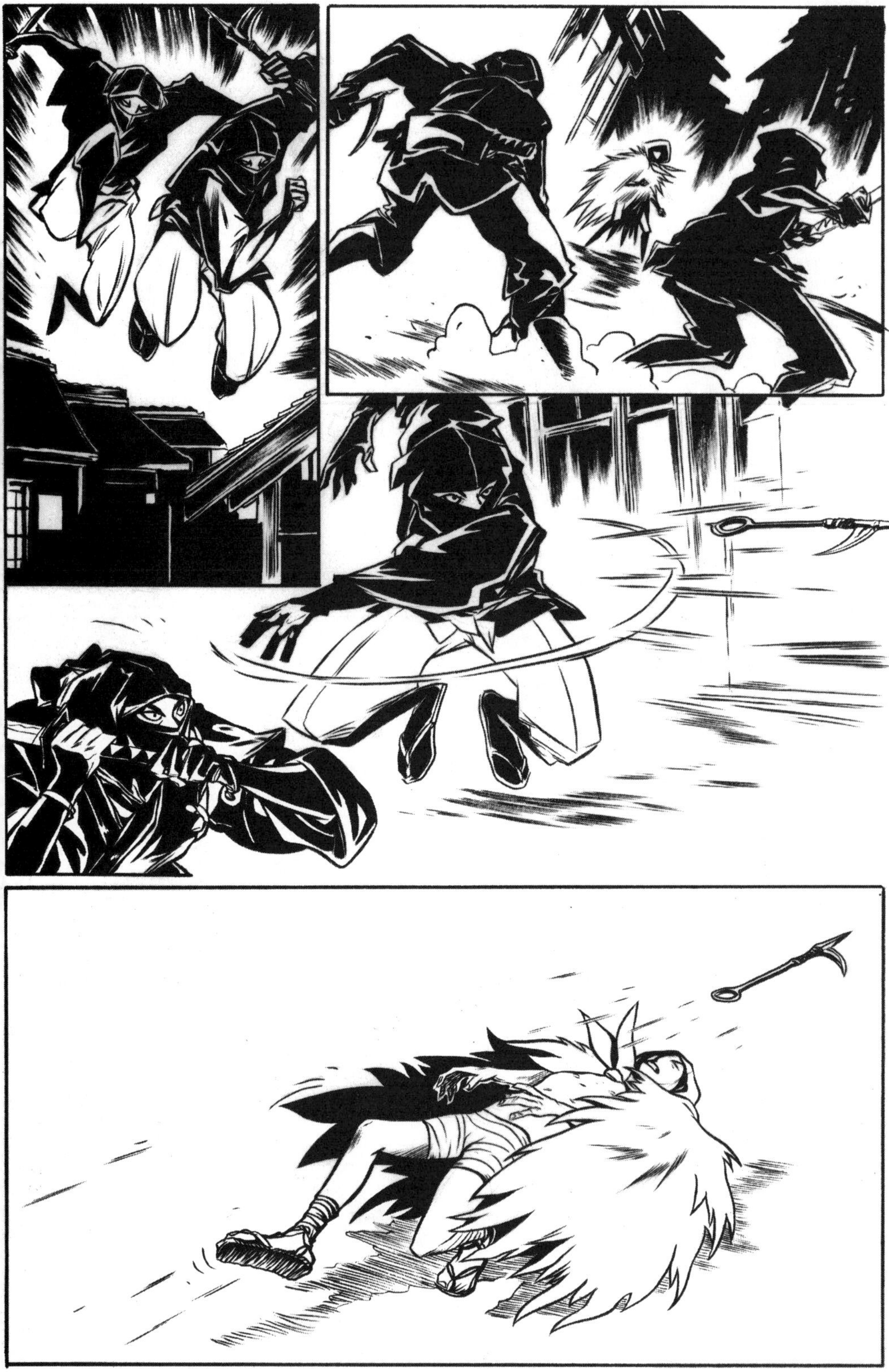

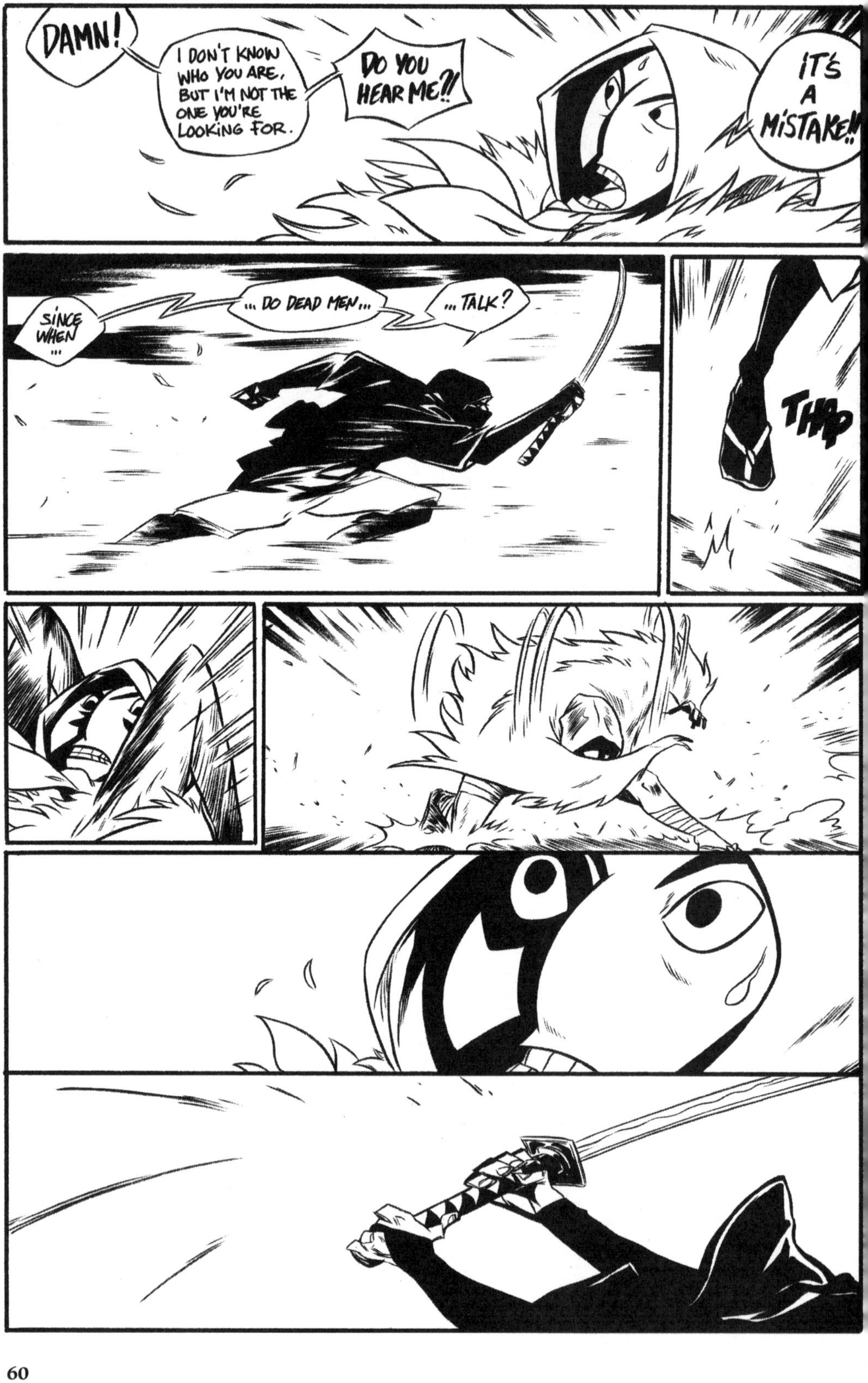
DAMN!
I DON'T KNOW WHO YOU ARE, BUT I'M NOT THE ONE YOU'RE LOOKING FOR.
DO YOU HEAR ME?!
IT'S A MISTAKE!!
SINCE WHEN ...
... DO DEAD MEN...
... TALK?
THAP

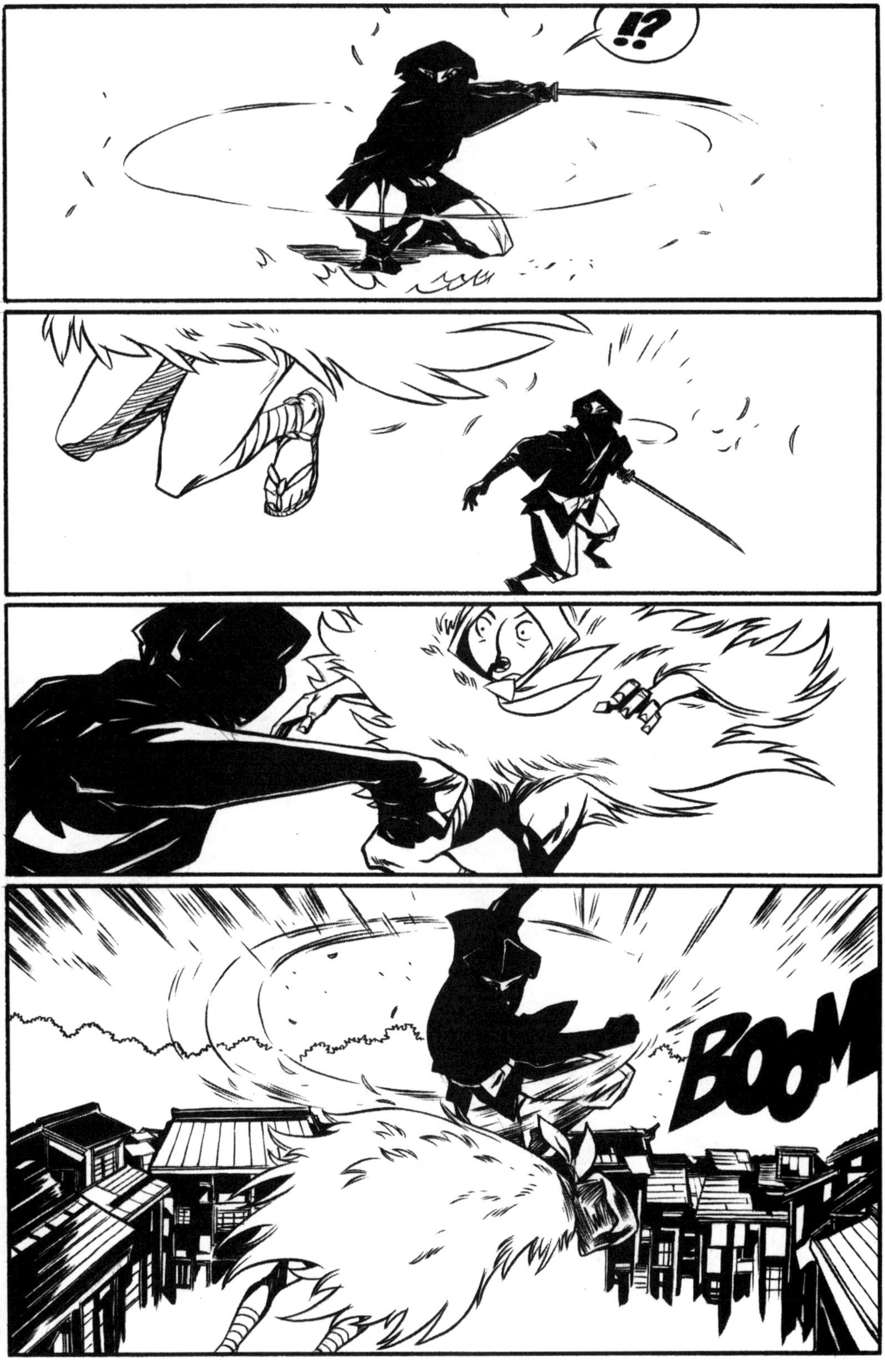
!?
BOOM

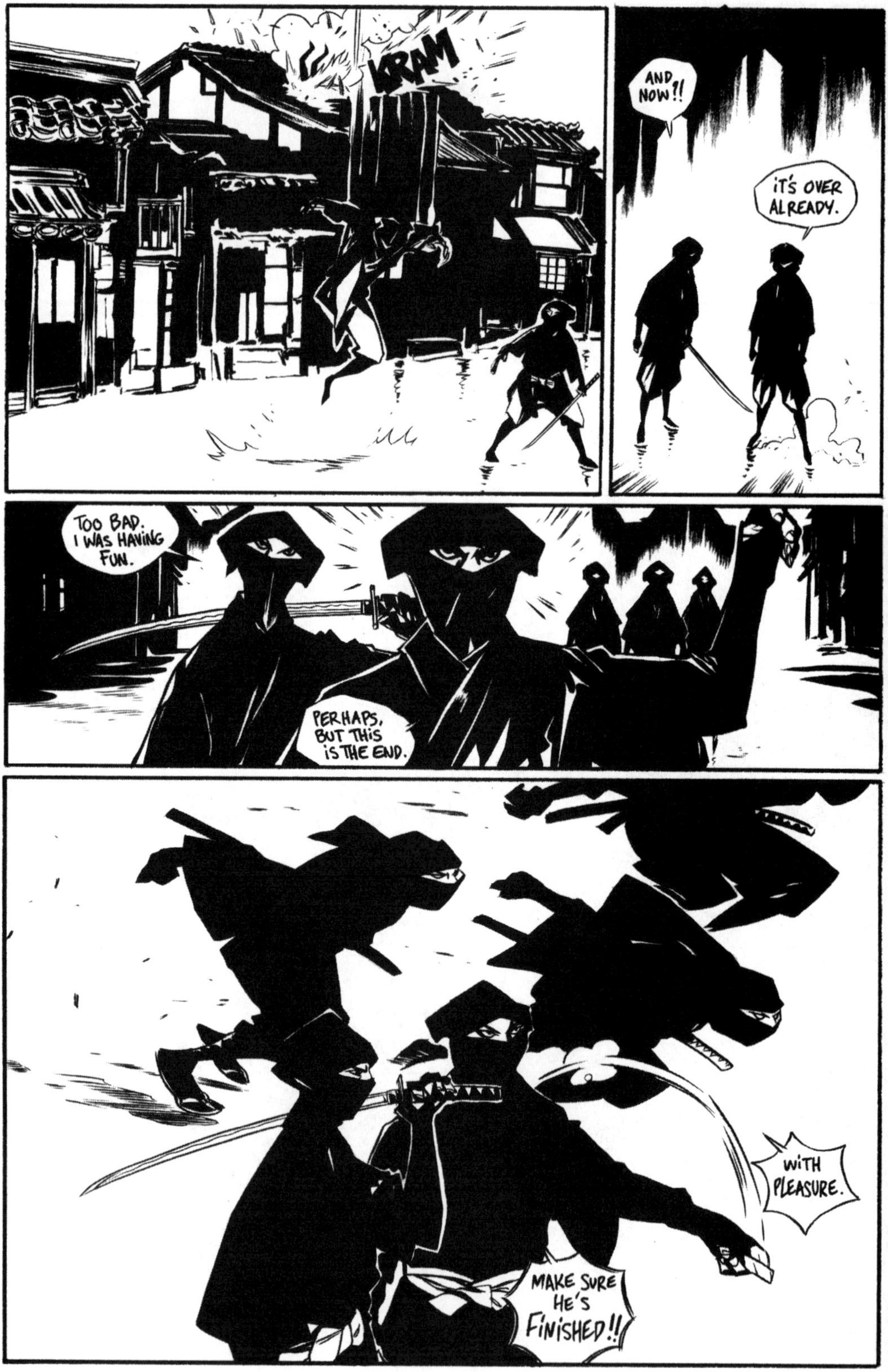
KRAM
AND NOW?!
IT'S OVER ALREADY.
TOO BAD. I WAS HAVING FUN.
PERHAPS, BUT THIS IS THE END.
WITH PLEASURE.
MAKE SURE HE'S FINISHED!!

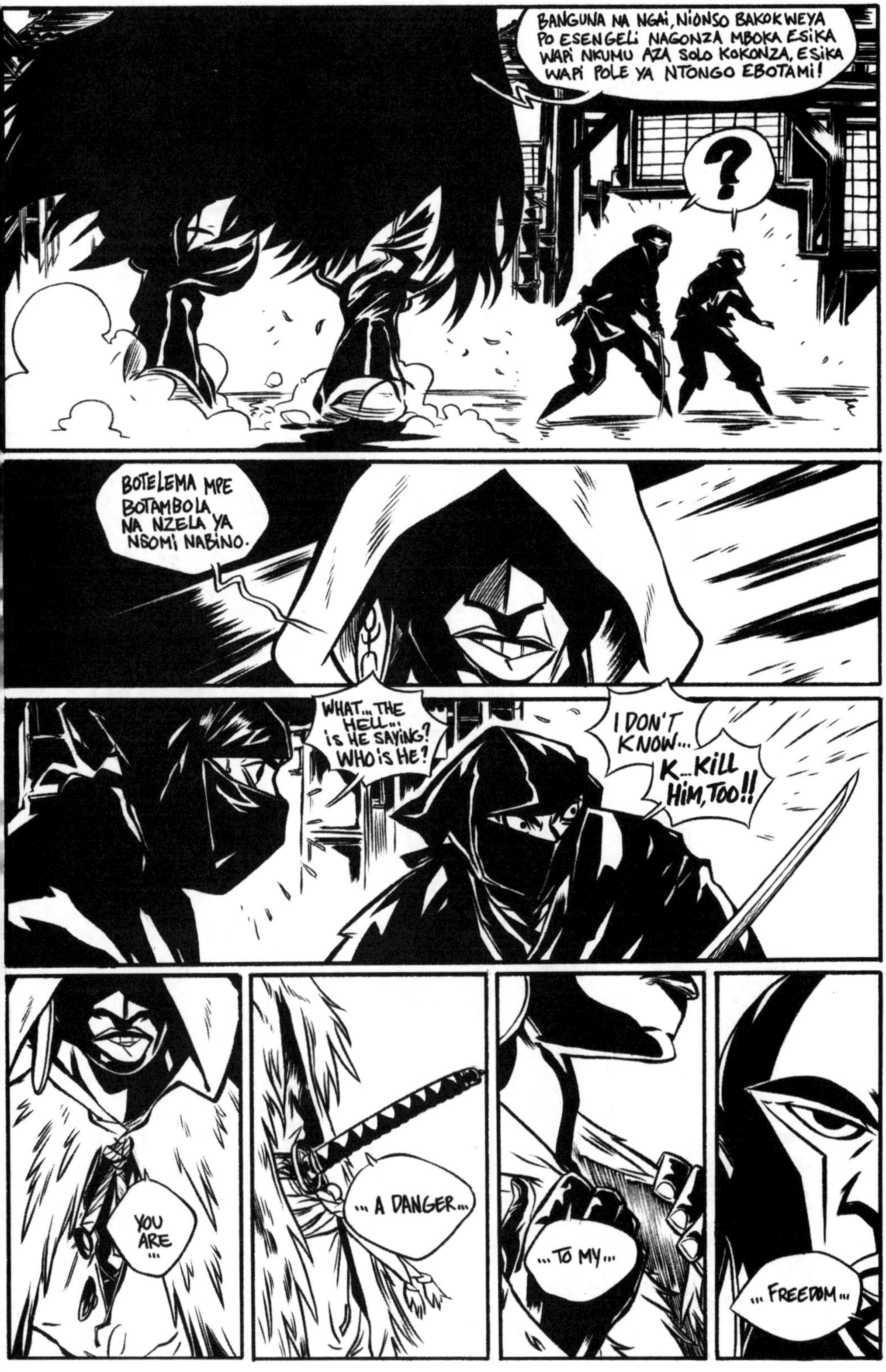
BANGUNA NA NGAi, NiONSO BAKOKWEYA PO ESENGELi NAGONZA MBOKA ESiKA WAPi NKUMU AZA SOLO KOKONZA, ESiKA WAPi POLE YA NTONGO EBOTAMi!
?
BOTELEMA MPE BOTAMBOLA NA NZELA YA NSOMi NABiNO.
WHAT... THE HELL... iS HE SAYiNG? WHO iS HE?
I DON'T KNOW... K... KiLL HiM, TOO!!
YOU ARE ...
... A DANGER...
... TO MY...
... FREEDOM...

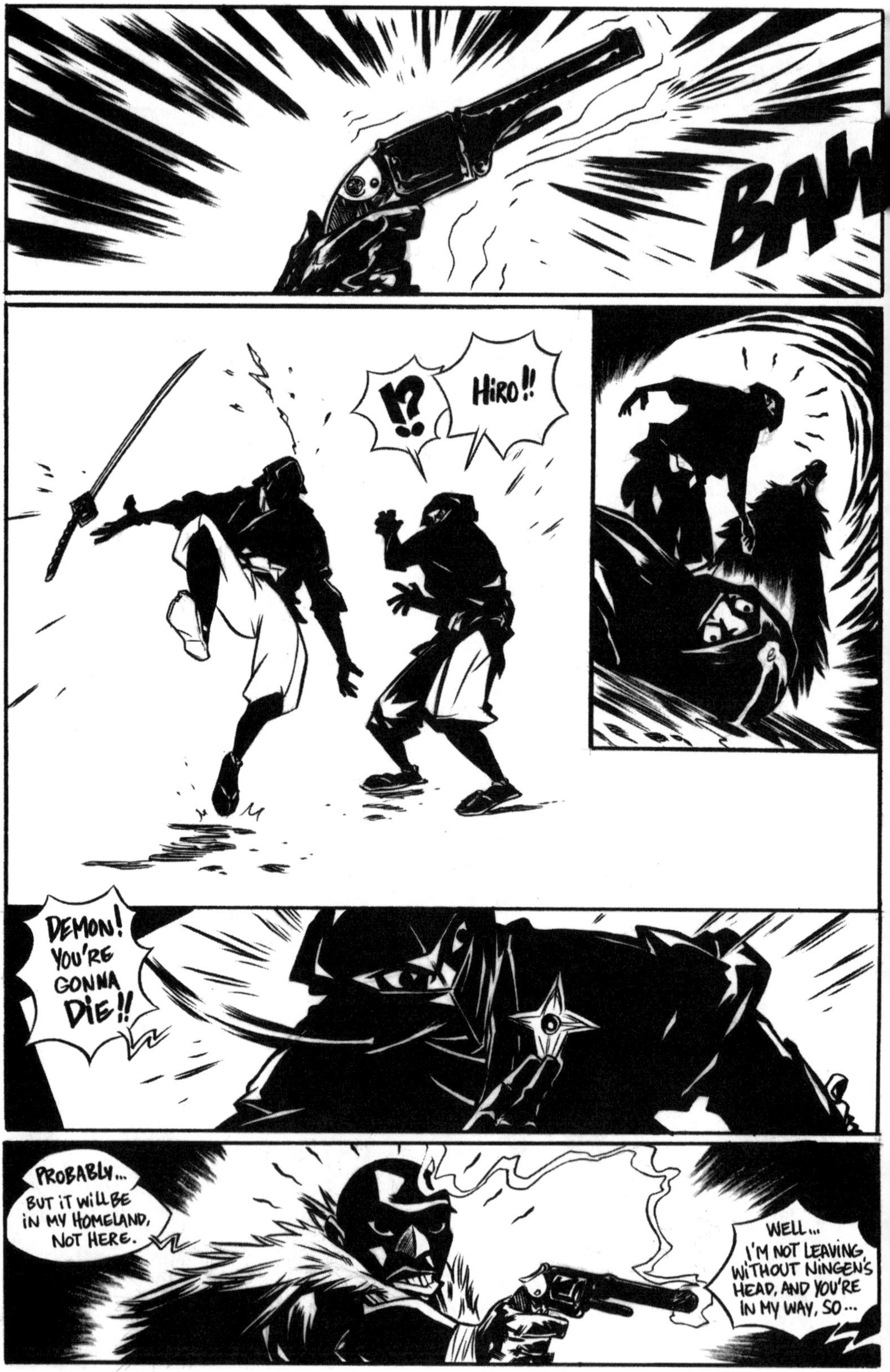
BAM
!?
HIRO!!
DEMON! YOU'RE GONNA DIE!!
PROBABLY...
BUT IT WILL BE IN MY HOMELAND, NOT HERE.
WELL... I'M NOT LEAVING WITHOUT NINGEN'S HEAD, AND YOU'RE IN MY WAY, SO...

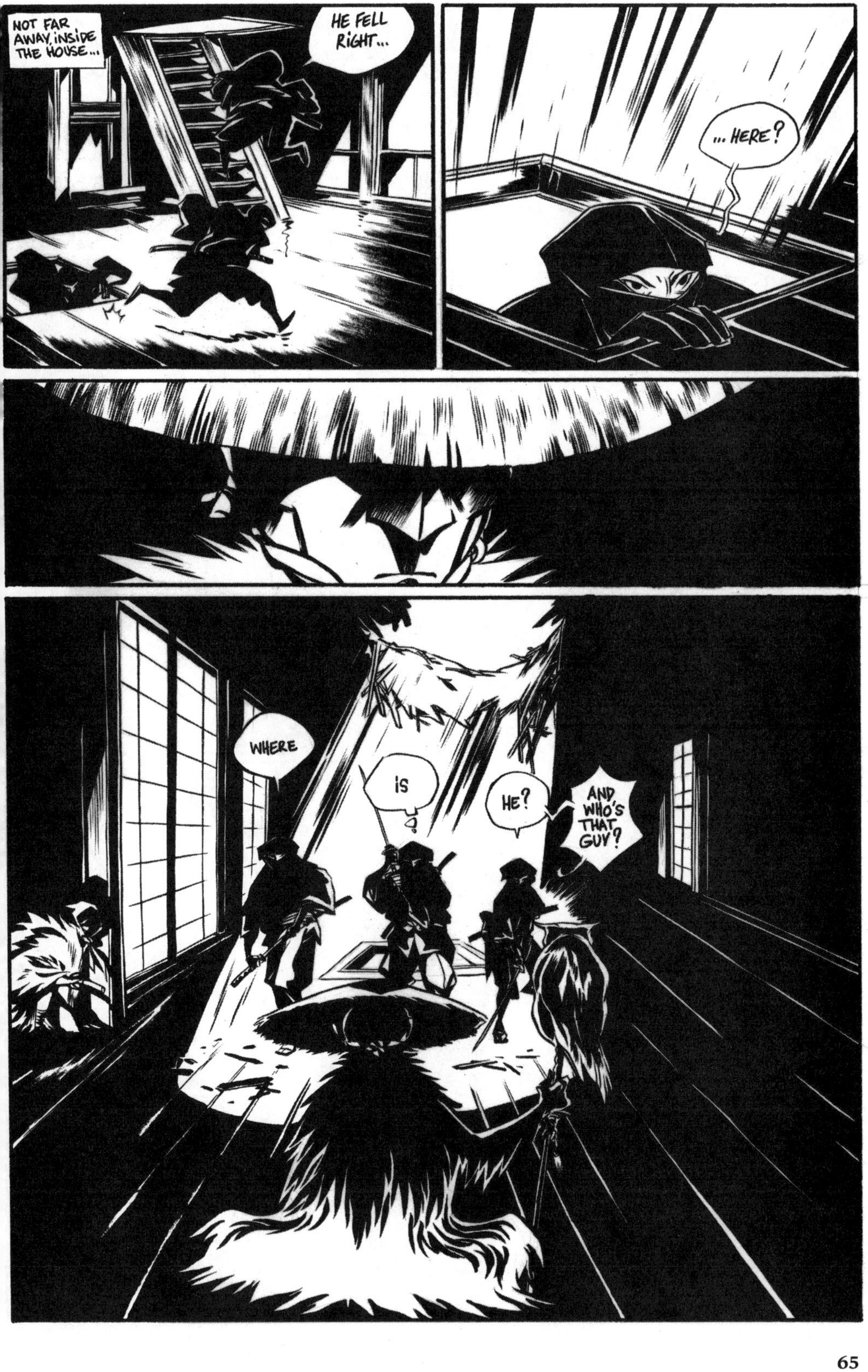
NOT FAR AWAY, INSIDE THE HOUSE...
HE FELL RIGHT...
... HERE?
WHERE
IS
HE?
AND WHO'S THAT GUY?

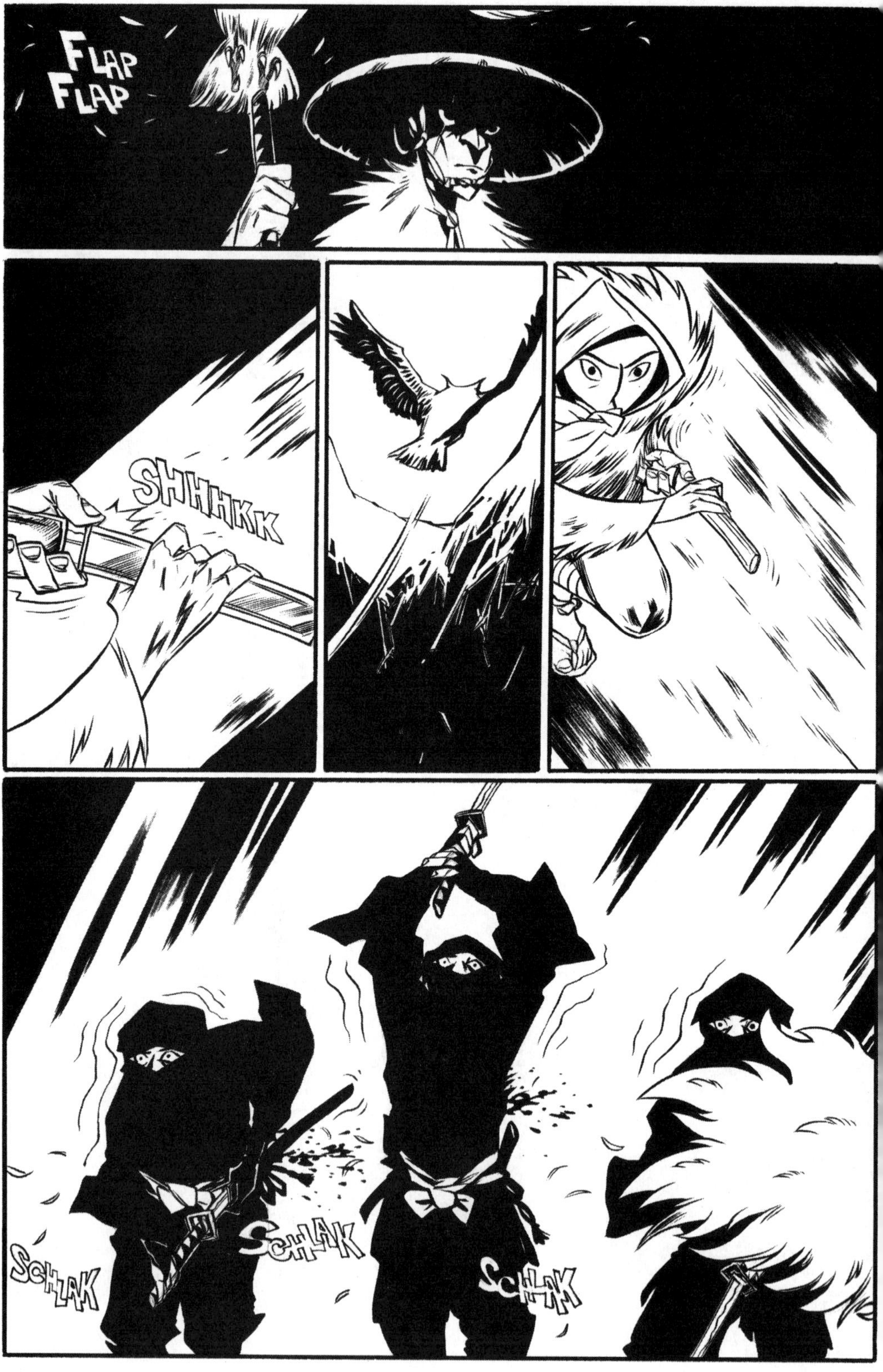
FLAP
FLAP
SHHHKK
SCHLAK
SCHLAK
SCHLAK

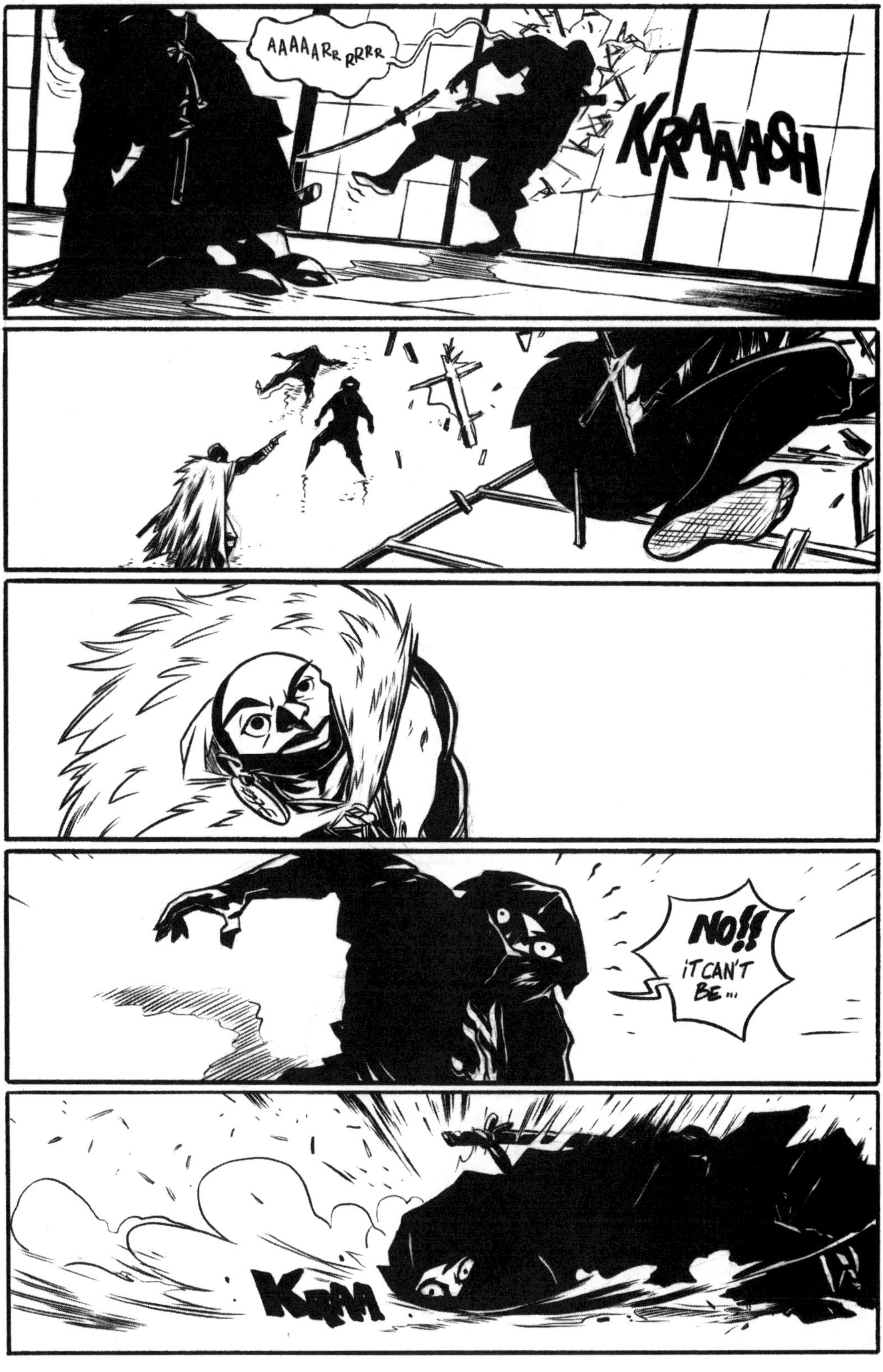
AAAAARRRRRR
KRAAAASH
NO!!
IT CAN'T BE...
KRAM

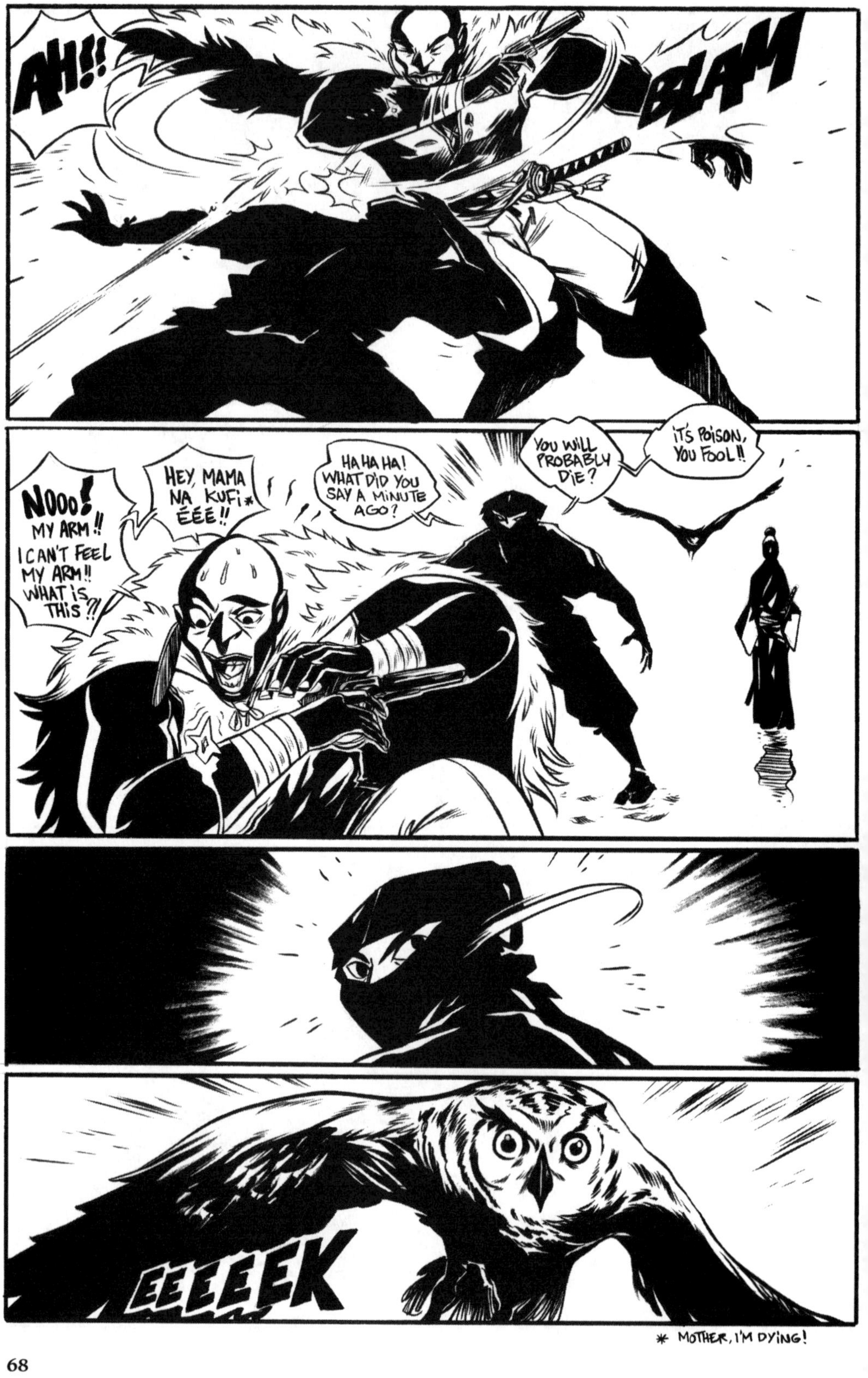
AH!!
BLAM
NOOO! MY ARM!! I CAN'T FEEL MY ARM!! WHAT IS THIS?!!
HEY, MAMA NA KUFI* ÉÉÉ!!
HA HA HA! WHAT DID YOU SAY A MINUTE AGO?
YOU WILL PROBABLY DIE?
IT'S POISON, YOU FOOL!!
EEEEEK

* MOTHER, I'M DYING!

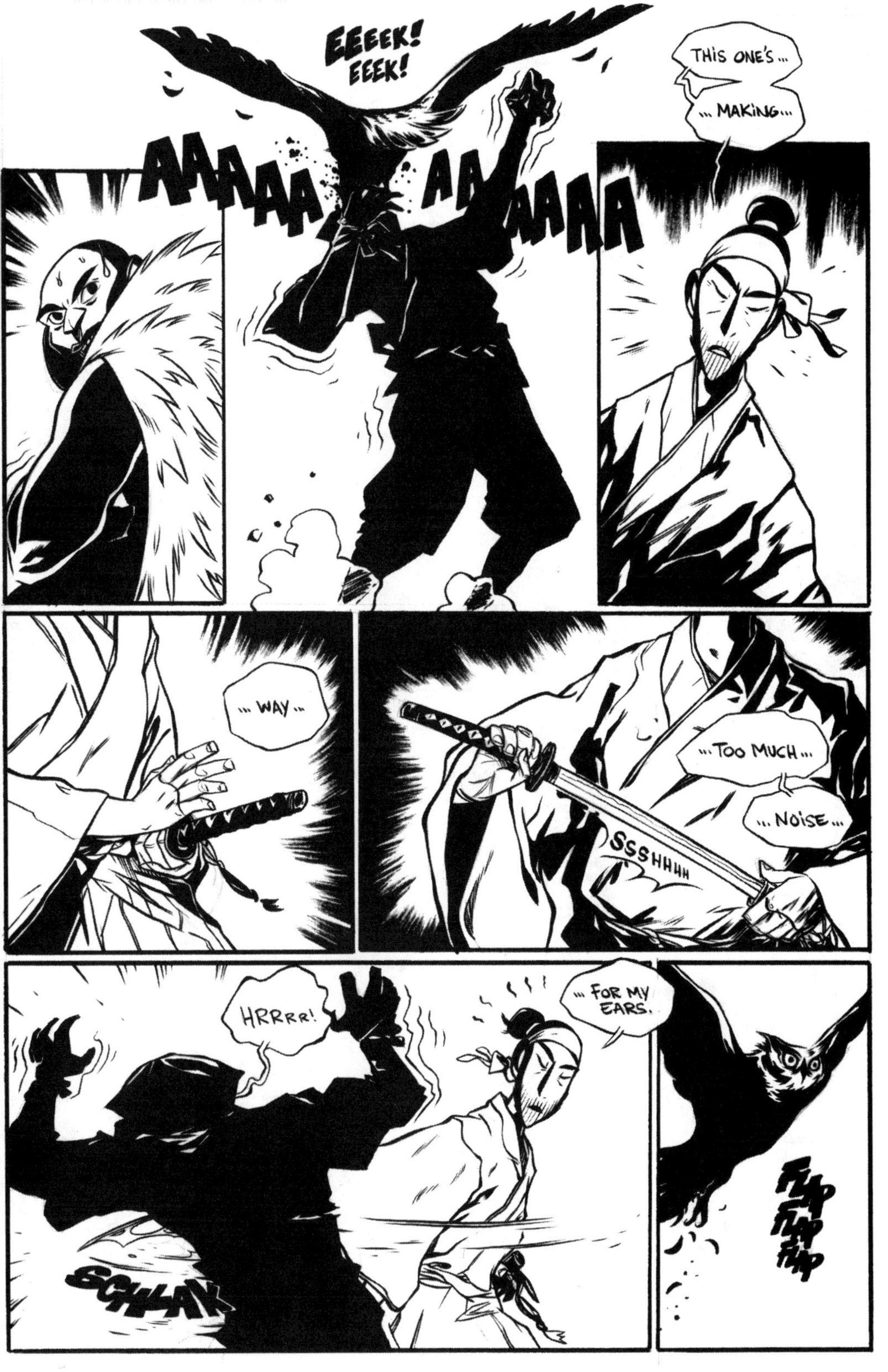
EEEEK! EEEK!
AAAAAAAAAAAAA
THIS ONE'S...
...MAKING...
...WAY...
...TOO MUCH...
...NOISE...
SSSHHHH
HRRRR!
...FOR MY EARS.
SCHLAK
FLAP FLAP FLAP

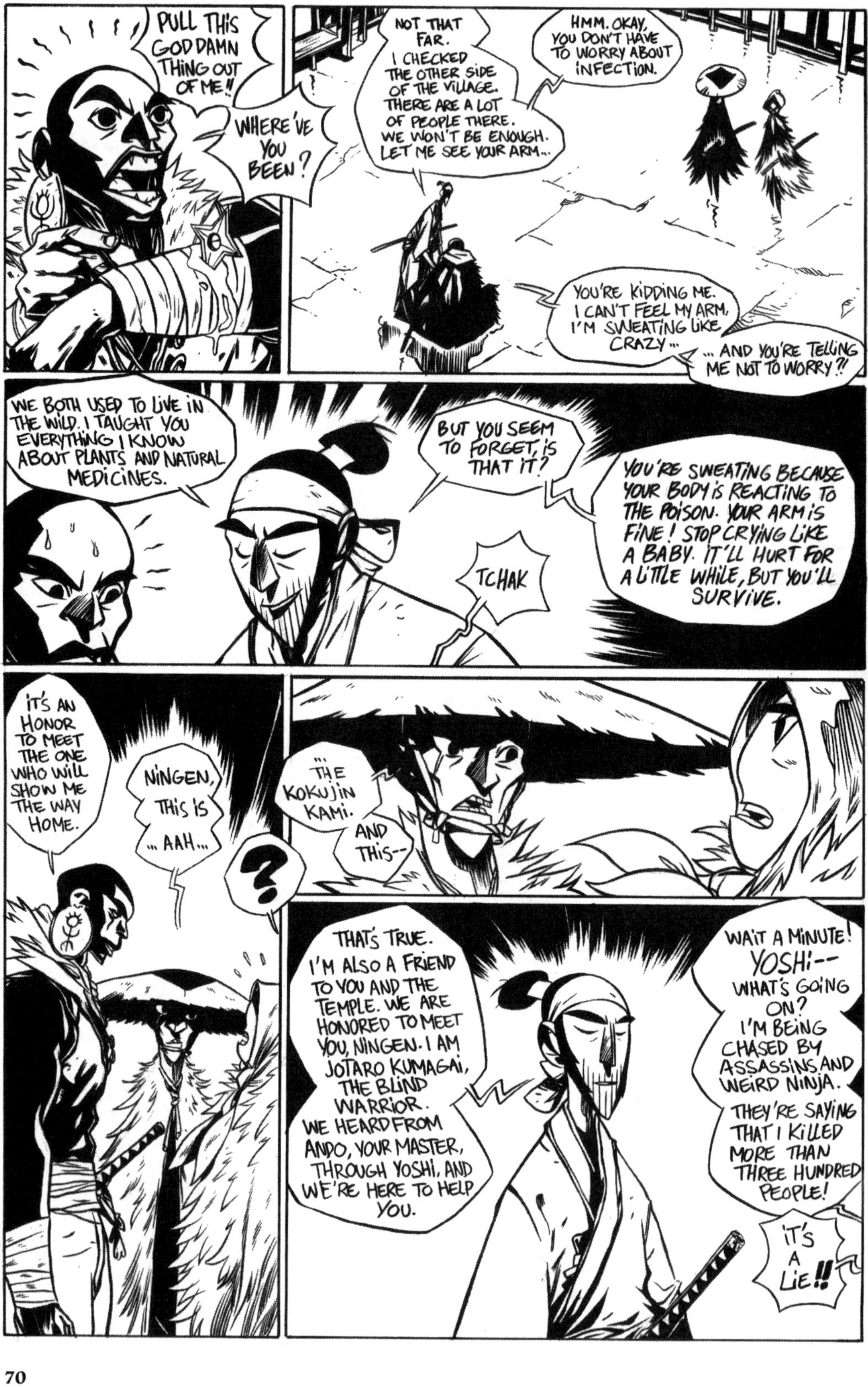
PULL THIS GOD DAMN THING OUT OF ME!!
WHERE'VE YOU BEEN?
NOT THAT FAR. I CHECKED THE OTHER SIDE OF THE VILLAGE. THERE ARE A LOT OF PEOPLE THERE. WE WON'T BE ENOUGH. LET ME SEE YOUR ARM...
HMM. OKAY, YOU DON'T HAVE TO WORRY ABOUT INFECTION.
YOU'RE KIDDING ME. I CAN'T FEEL MY ARM, I'M SWEATING LIKE CRAZY...
... AND YOU'RE TELLING ME NOT TO WORRY?!
WE BOTH USED TO LIVE IN THE WILD. I TAUGHT YOU EVERYTHING I KNOW ABOUT PLANTS AND NATURAL MEDICINES.
BUT YOU SEEM TO FORGET, IS THAT IT?
YOU'RE SWEATING BECAUSE YOUR BODY IS REACTING TO THE POISON. YOUR ARM IS FINE! STOP CRYING LIKE A BABY. IT'LL HURT FOR A LITTLE WHILE, BUT YOU'LL SURVIVE.
TCHAK
IT'S AN HONOR TO MEET THE ONE WHO WILL SHOW ME THE WAY HOME.
NINGEN, THIS IS ... AAH...
?
... THE KOKUJIN KAMI.
AND THIS--
THAT'S TRUE. I'M ALSO A FRIEND TO YOU AND THE TEMPLE. WE ARE HONORED TO MEET YOU, NINGEN. I AM JOTARO KUMAGAI, THE BLIND WARRIOR. WE HEARD FROM ANDO, YOUR MASTER, THROUGH YOSHI, AND WE'RE HERE TO HELP YOU.
WAIT A MINUTE! YOSHI-- WHAT'S GOING ON? I'M BEING CHASED BY ASSASSINS AND WEIRD NINJA.
THEY'RE SAYING THAT I KILLED MORE THAN THREE HUNDRED PEOPLE!
IT'S A LIE!!

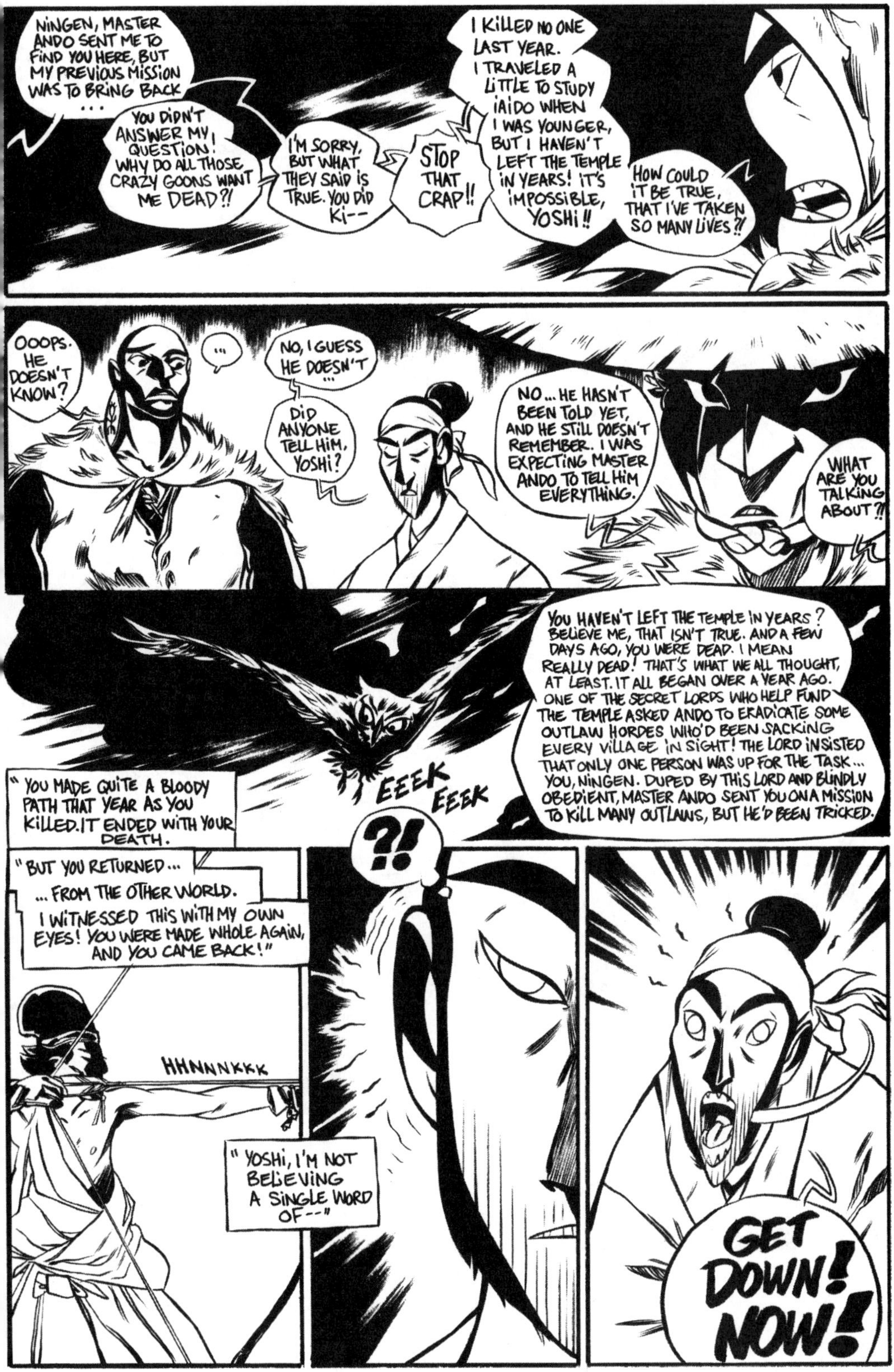
NINGEN, MASTER ANDO SENT ME TO FIND YOU HERE, BUT MY PREVIOUS MISSION WAS TO BRING BACK ...
YOU DIDN'T ANSWER MY QUESTION! WHY DO ALL THOSE CRAZY GOONS WANT ME DEAD?!
I'M SORRY, BUT WHAT THEY SAID IS TRUE. YOU DID KI--
STOP THAT CRAP!!
I KILLED NO ONE LAST YEAR. I TRAVELED A LITTLE TO STUDY IAIDO WHEN I WAS YOUNGER, BUT I HAVEN'T LEFT THE TEMPLE IN YEARS! IT'S IMPOSSIBLE, YOSHI!!
HOW COULD IT BE TRUE, THAT I'VE TAKEN SO MANY LIVES?!
OOOPS. HE DOESN'T KNOW?
...
NO, I GUESS HE DOESN'T ...
DID ANYONE TELL HIM, YOSHI?
NO... HE HASN'T BEEN TOLD YET, AND HE STILL DOESN'T REMEMBER. I WAS EXPECTING MASTER ANDO TO TELL HIM EVERYTHING.
WHAT ARE YOU TALKING ABOUT?!
YOU HAVEN'T LEFT THE TEMPLE IN YEARS? BELIEVE ME, THAT ISN'T TRUE. AND A FEW DAYS AGO, YOU WERE DEAD. I MEAN REALLY DEAD! THAT'S WHAT WE ALL THOUGHT, AT LEAST. IT ALL BEGAN OVER A YEAR AGO. ONE OF THE SECRET LORDS WHO HELP FUND THE TEMPLE ASKED ANDO TO ERADICATE SOME OUTLAW HORDES WHO'D BEEN SACKING EVERY VILLAGE IN SIGHT! THE LORD INSISTED THAT ONLY ONE PERSON WAS UP FOR THE TASK... YOU, NINGEN. DUPED BY THIS LORD AND BLINDLY OBEDIENT, MASTER ANDO SENT YOU ON A MISSION TO KILL MANY OUTLAWS, BUT HE'D BEEN TRICKED.
"YOU MADE QUITE A BLOODY PATH THAT YEAR AS YOU KILLED. IT ENDED WITH YOUR DEATH.
EEEK EEEK
"BUT YOU RETURNED ...
... FROM THE OTHER WORLD.
I WITNESSED THIS WITH MY OWN EYES! YOU WERE MADE WHOLE AGAIN, AND YOU CAME BACK!"
HHNNNKKK
"YOSHI, I'M NOT BELIEVING A SINGLE WORD OF--"
?!
GET DOWN! NOW!

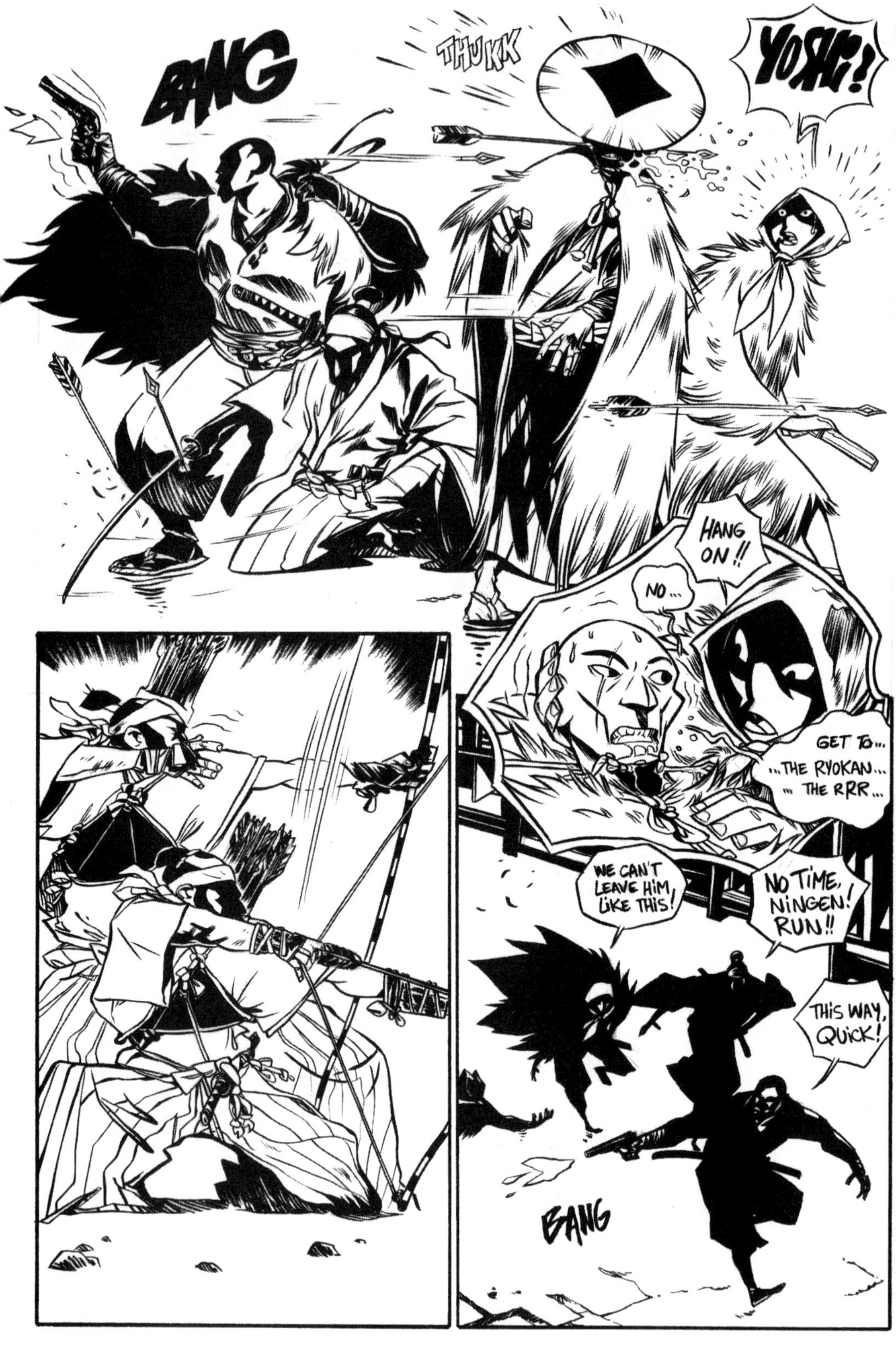
BANG
THUKK
YOSHI?!
HANG ON!!
NO...
GET TO...
...THE RYOKAN...
... THE RRR...
WE CAN'T LEAVE HIM LIKE THIS!
NO TIME, NINGEN! RUN!!
THIS WAY, QUICK!
BANG

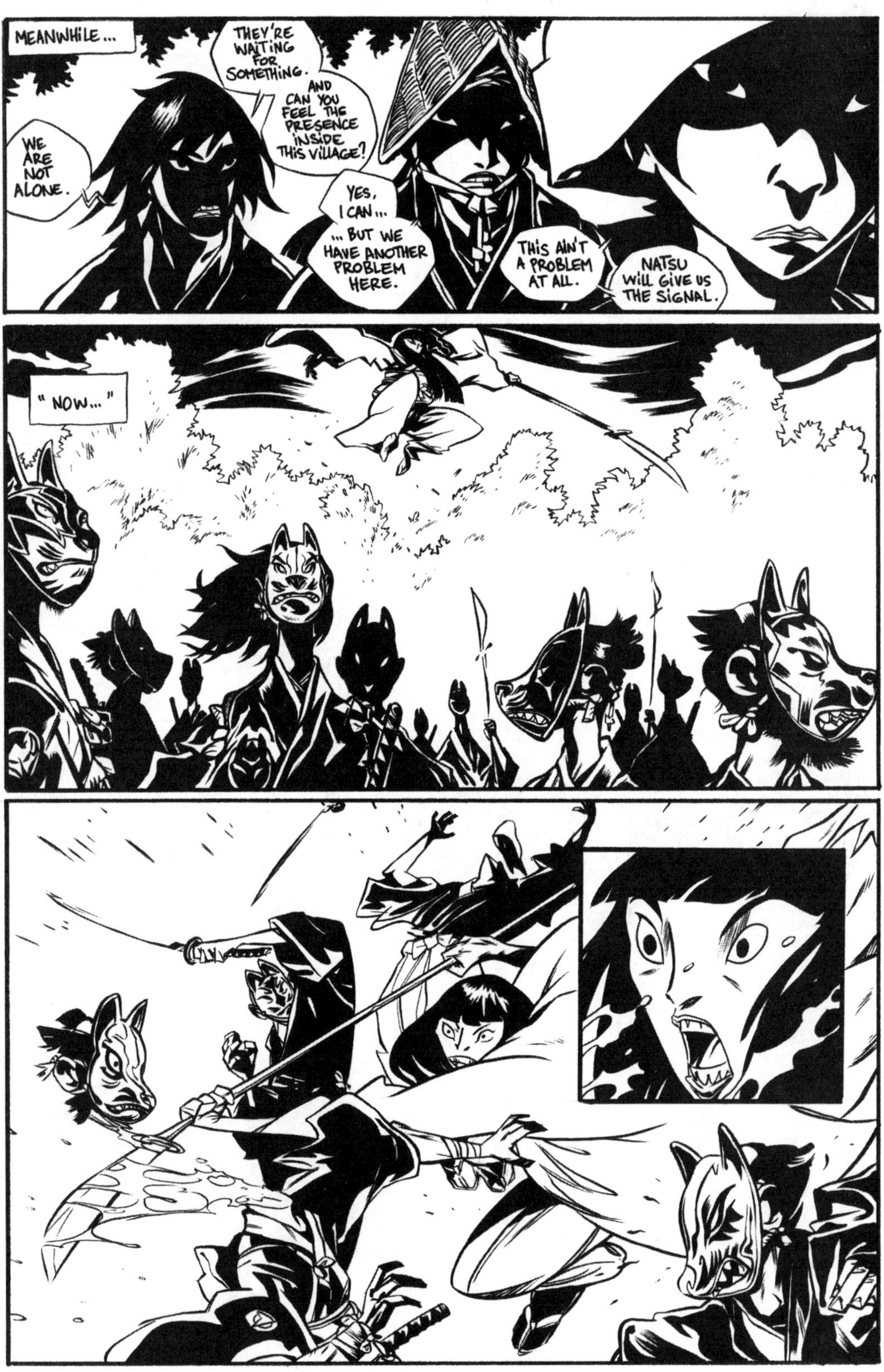
MEANWHILE...
WE ARE NOT ALONE.
THEY'RE WAITING FOR SOMETHING.
AND CAN YOU FEEL THE PRESENCE INSIDE THIS VILLAGE?
YES, I CAN...
... BUT WE HAVE ANOTHER PROBLEM HERE.
THIS AIN'T A PROBLEM AT ALL.
NATSU WILL GIVE US THE SIGNAL.
" NOW... "

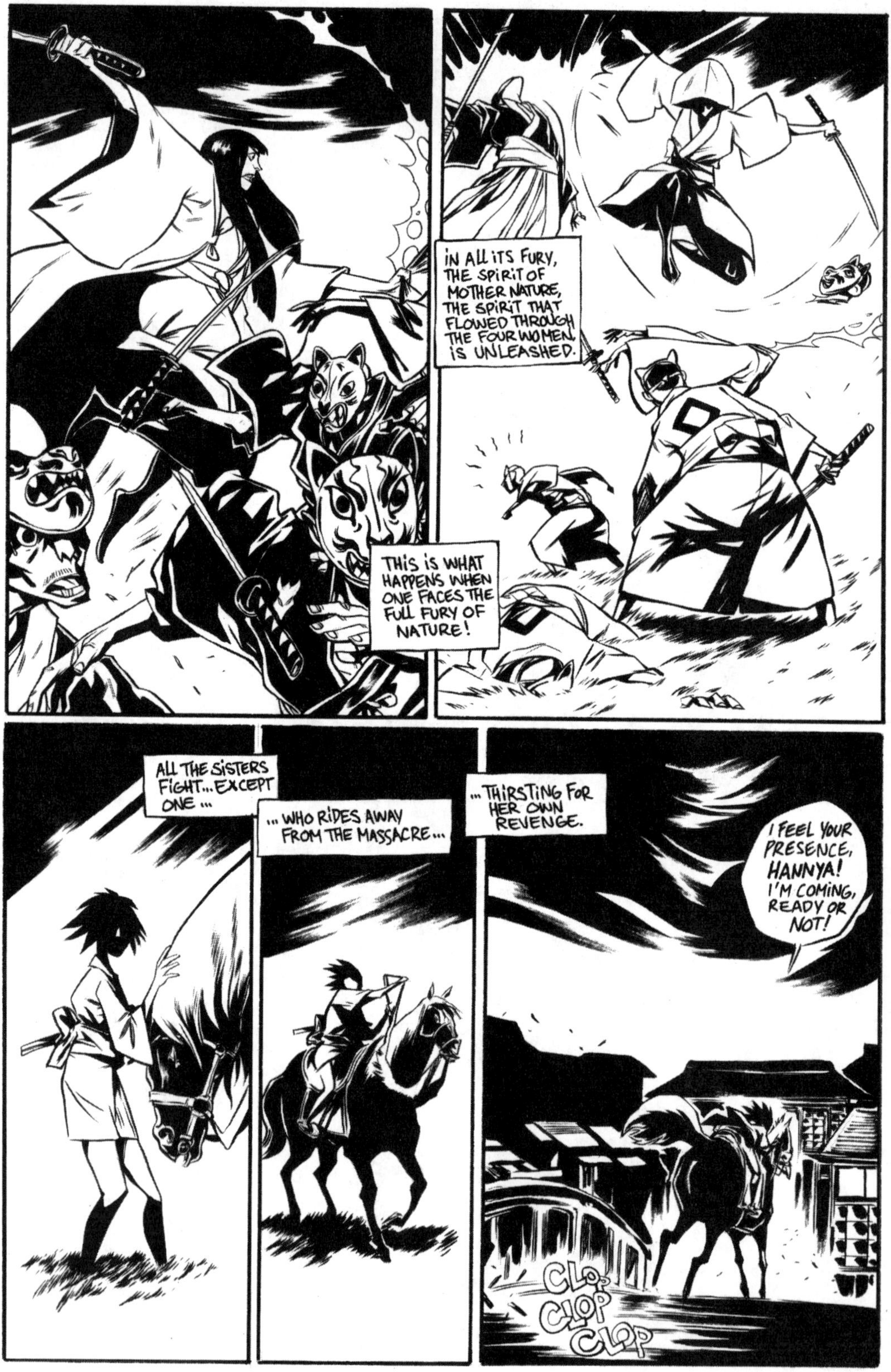
IN ALL ITS FURY, THE SPIRIT OF MOTHER NATURE, THE SPIRIT THAT FLOWED THROUGH THE FOUR WOMEN, IS UNLEASHED.
THIS IS WHAT HAPPENS WHEN ONE FACES THE FULL FURY OF NATURE!
ALL THE SISTERS FIGHT... EXCEPT ONE...
...WHO RIDES AWAY FROM THE MASSACRE...
...THIRSTING FOR HER OWN REVENGE.
I FEEL YOUR PRESENCE, HANNYA! I'M COMING, READY OR NOT!
CLOP CLOP CLOP

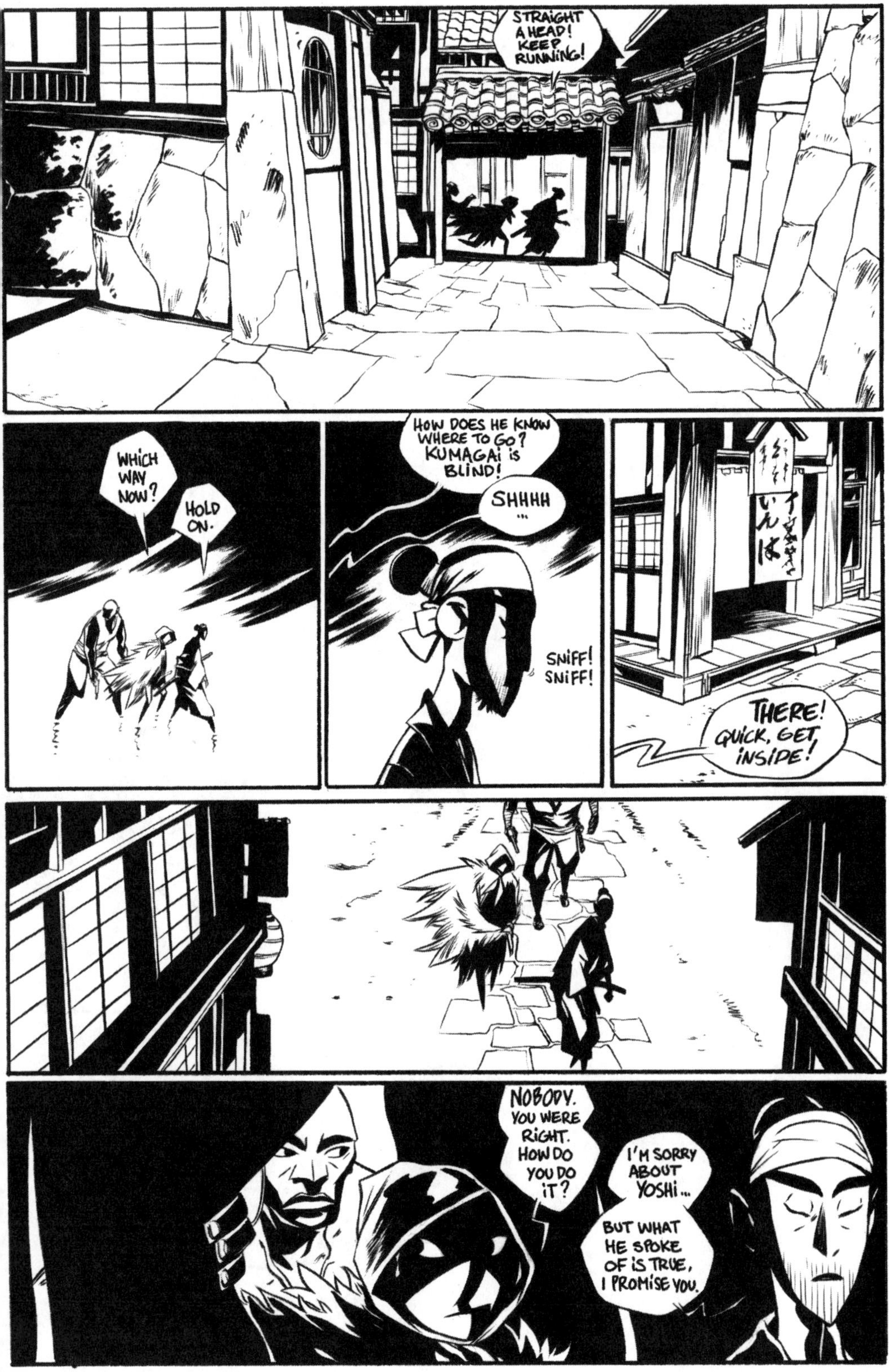
STRAIGHT A HEAD! KEEP RUNNING!
WHICH WAY NOW?
HOLD ON.
HOW DOES HE KNOW WHERE TO GO? KUMAGAI IS BLIND!
SHHHH ...
SNIFF! SNIFF!
THERE! QUICK, GET INSIDE!
NOBODY. YOU WERE RIGHT. HOW DO YOU DO IT?
I'M SORRY ABOUT YOSHI...
BUT WHAT HE SPOKE OF IS TRUE, I PROMISE YOU.

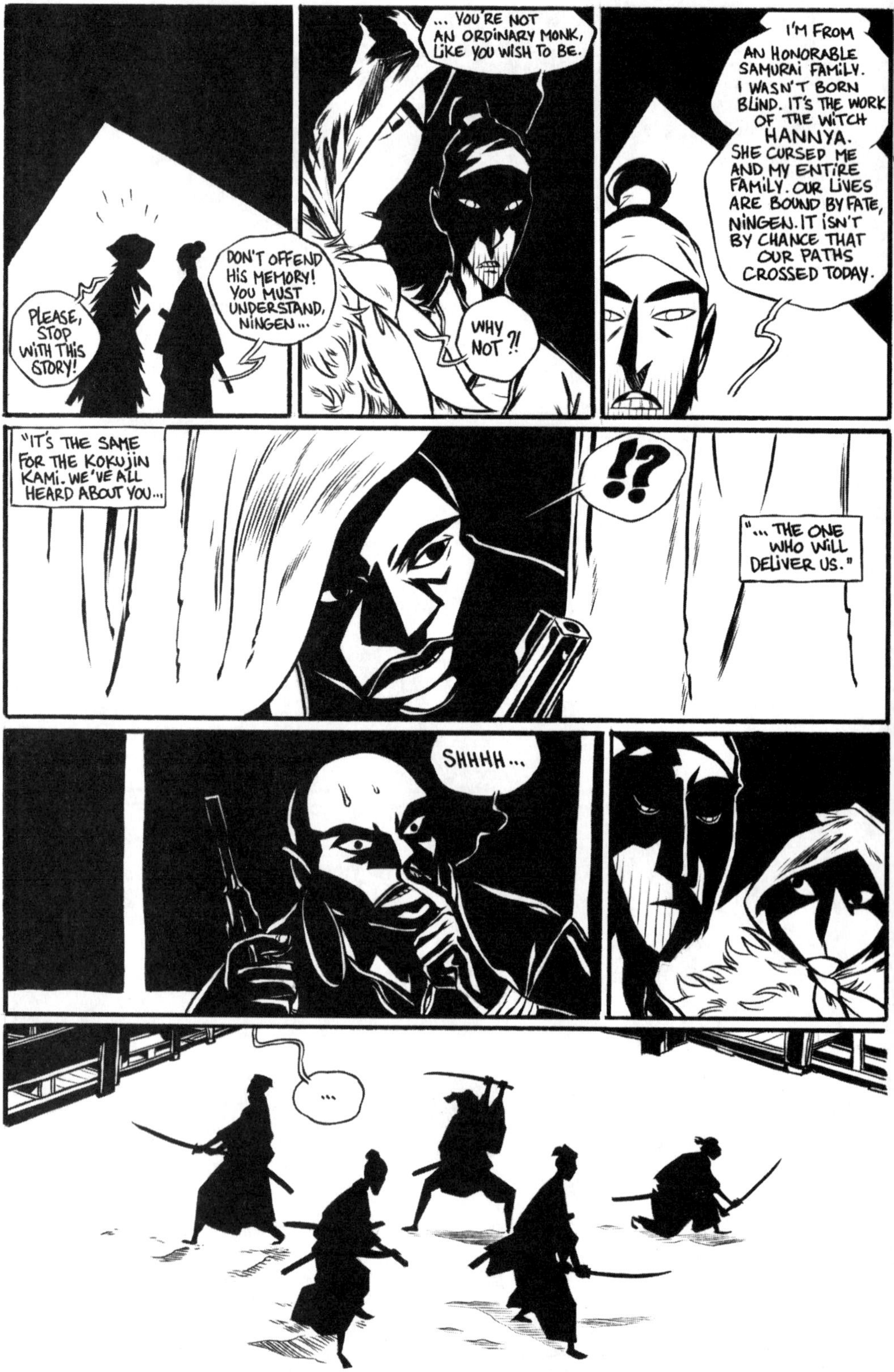
... YOU'RE NOT AN ORDINARY MONK, LIKE YOU WISH TO BE.
PLEASE, STOP WITH THIS STORY!
DON'T OFFEND HIS MEMORY! YOU MUST UNDERSTAND, NINGEN...
WHY NOT ?!
I'M FROM AN HONORABLE SAMURAI FAMILY. I WASN'T BORN BLIND. IT'S THE WORK OF THE WITCH HANNYA. SHE CURSED ME AND MY ENTIRE FAMILY. OUR LIVES ARE BOUND BY FATE, NINGEN. IT ISN'T BY CHANCE THAT OUR PATHS CROSSED TODAY.
"IT'S THE SAME FOR THE KOKUJIN KAMI. WE'VE ALL HEARD ABOUT YOU...
!?
"... THE ONE WHO WILL DELIVER US."
SHHHH...
...

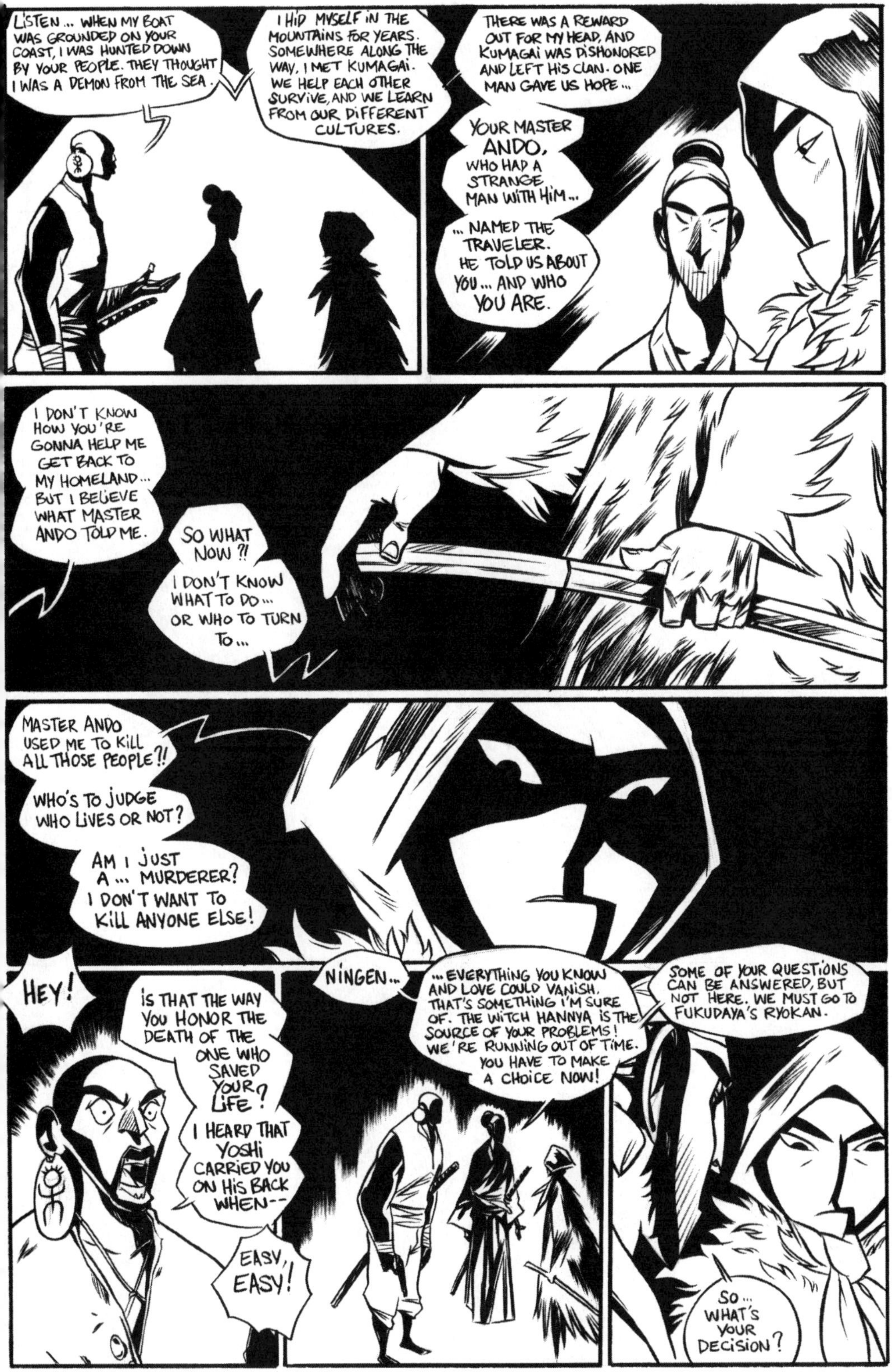
LISTEN... WHEN MY BOAT WAS GROUNDED ON YOUR COAST, I WAS HUNTED DOWN BY YOUR PEOPLE. THEY THOUGHT I WAS A DEMON FROM THE SEA.
I HID MYSELF IN THE MOUNTAINS FOR YEARS. SOMEWHERE ALONG THE WAY, I MET KUMAGAI. WE HELP EACH OTHER SURVIVE, AND WE LEARN FROM OUR DIFFERENT CULTURES.
THERE WAS A REWARD OUT FOR MY HEAD, AND KUMAGAI WAS DISHONORED AND LEFT HIS CLAN. ONE MAN GAVE US HOPE...
YOUR MASTER ANDO, WHO HAD A STRANGE MAN WITH HIM...
... NAMED THE TRAVELER. HE TOLD US ABOUT YOU... AND WHO YOU ARE.
I DON'T KNOW HOW YOU'RE GONNA HELP ME GET BACK TO MY HOMELAND... BUT I BELIEVE WHAT MASTER ANDO TOLD ME.
SO WHAT NOW?!
I DON'T KNOW WHAT TO DO... OR WHO TO TURN TO...
MASTER ANDO USED ME TO KILL ALL THOSE PEOPLE?!
WHO'S TO JUDGE WHO LIVES OR NOT?
AM I JUST A... MURDERER? I DON'T WANT TO KILL ANYONE ELSE!
HEY!
IS THAT THE WAY YOU HONOR THE DEATH OF THE ONE WHO SAVED YOUR LIFE?
I HEARD THAT YOSHI CARRIED YOU ON HIS BACK WHEN--
EASY, EASY!
NINGEN...
... EVERYTHING YOU KNOW AND LOVE COULD VANISH. THAT'S SOMETHING I'M SURE OF. THE WITCH HANNYA IS THE SOURCE OF YOUR PROBLEMS! WE'RE RUNNING OUT OF TIME. YOU HAVE TO MAKE A CHOICE NOW!
SOME OF YOUR QUESTIONS CAN BE ANSWERED, BUT NOT HERE. WE MUST GO TO FUKUDAYA'S RYOKAN.
SO... WHAT'S YOUR DECISION?

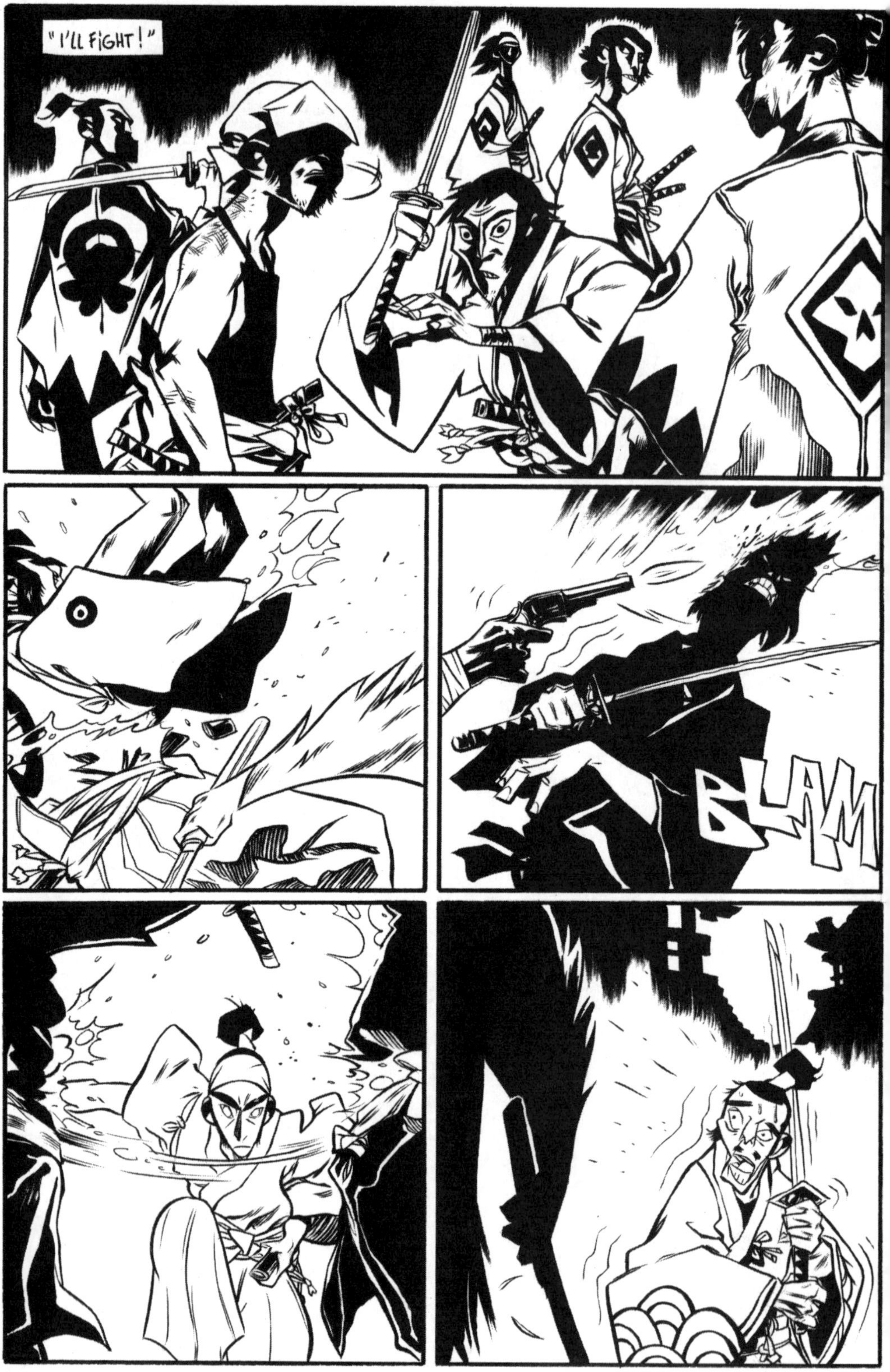
"I'LL FIGHT!"
BLAM

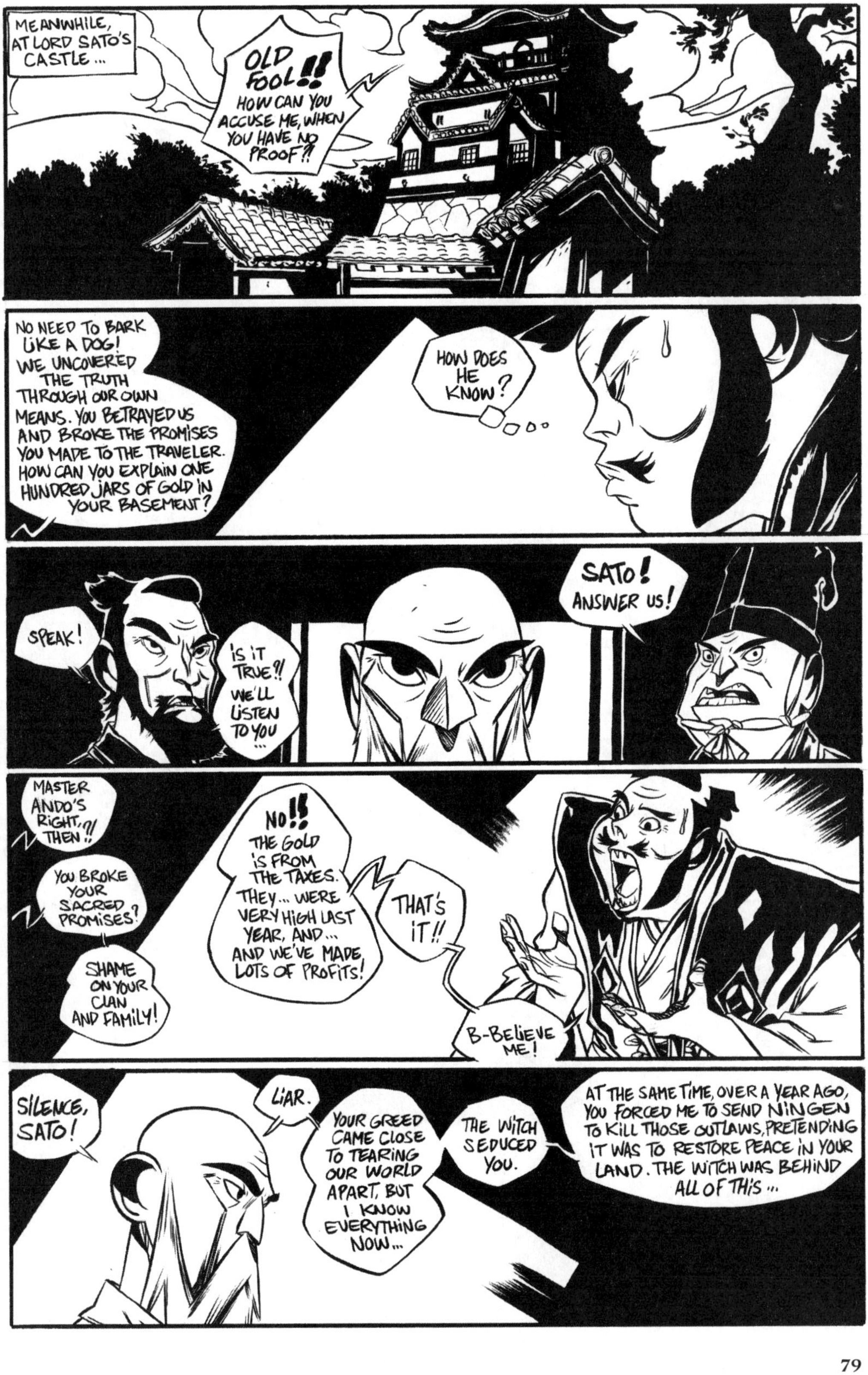
MEANWHILE, AT LORD SATO'S CASTLE ...
OLD FOOL!! HOW CAN YOU ACCUSE ME, WHEN YOU HAVE NO PROOF?!
NO NEED TO BARK LIKE A DOG! WE UNCOVERED THE TRUTH THROUGH OUR OWN MEANS. YOU BETRAYED US AND BROKE THE PROMISES YOU MADE TO THE TRAVELER. HOW CAN YOU EXPLAIN ONE HUNDRED JARS OF GOLD IN YOUR BASEMENT?
HOW DOES HE KNOW?
SPEAK!
IS IT TRUE?! WE'LL LISTEN TO YOU ...
SATO! ANSWER US!
MASTER ANDO'S RIGHT, THEN?!
YOU BROKE YOUR SACRED PROMISES?
SHAME ON YOUR CLAN AND FAMILY!
NO!! THE GOLD IS FROM THE TAXES. THEY... WERE VERY HIGH LAST YEAR, AND... AND WE'VE MADE LOTS OF PROFITS!
THAT'S IT!!
B-BELIEVE ME!
SILENCE, SATO!
LIAR.
YOUR GREED CAME CLOSE TO TEARING OUR WORLD APART, BUT I KNOW EVERYTHING NOW...
THE WITCH SEDUCED YOU.
AT THE SAME TIME, OVER A YEAR AGO, YOU FORCED ME TO SEND NINGEN TO KILL THOSE OUTLAWS, PRETENDING IT WAS TO RESTORE PEACE IN YOUR LAND. THE WITCH WAS BEHIND ALL OF THIS ...

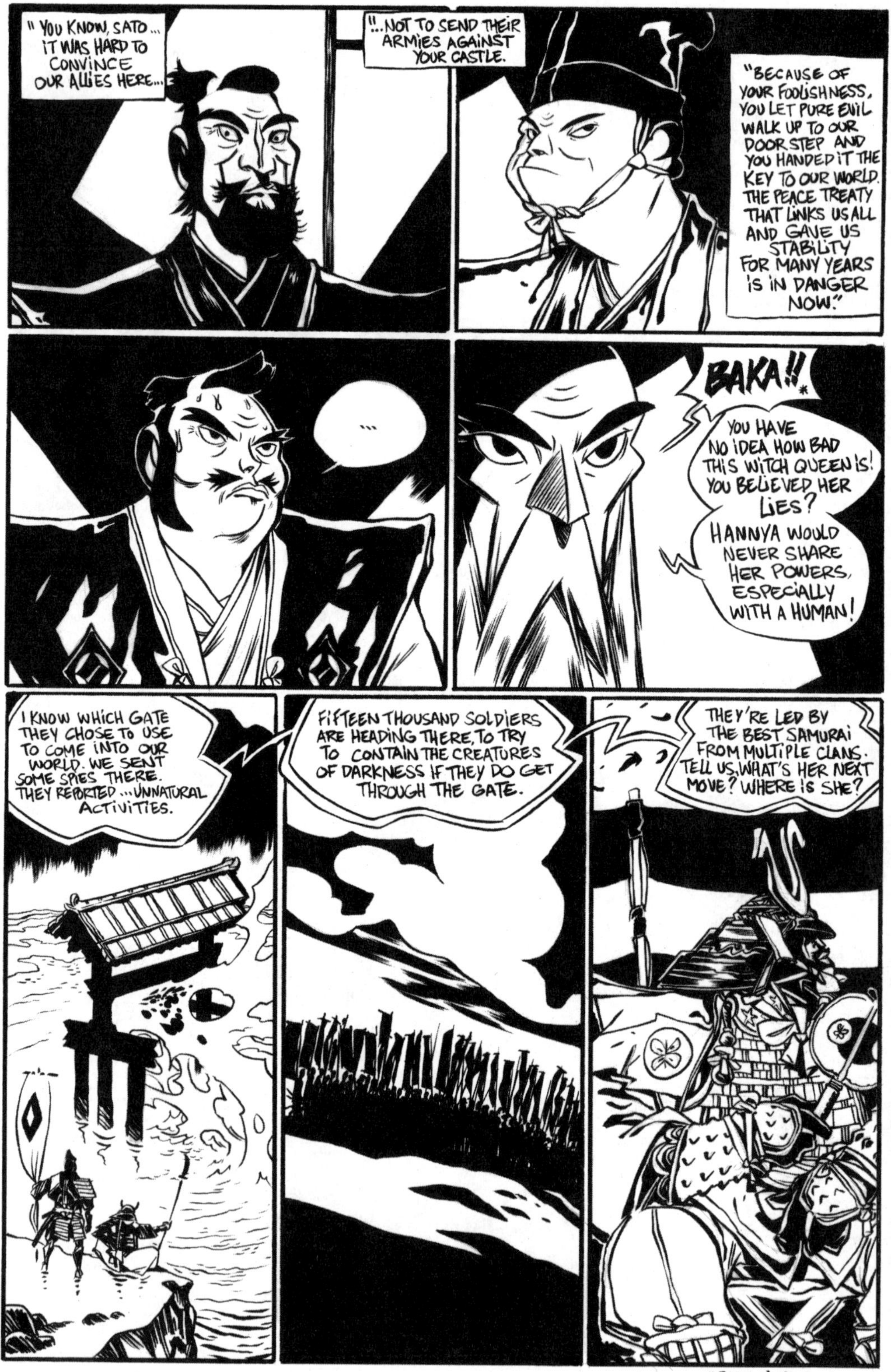
"YOU KNOW, SATO... IT WAS HARD TO CONVINCE OUR ALLIES HERE...
"...NOT TO SEND THEIR ARMIES AGAINST YOUR CASTLE.
"BECAUSE OF YOUR FOOLISHNESS, YOU LET PURE EVIL WALK UP TO OUR DOORSTEP AND YOU HANDED IT THE KEY TO OUR WORLD. THE PEACE TREATY THAT LINKS US ALL AND GAVE US STABILITY FOR MANY YEARS IS IN DANGER NOW."
...
BAKA!!*
YOU HAVE NO IDEA HOW BAD THIS WITCH QUEEN IS! YOU BELIEVED HER LIES?
HANNYA WOULD NEVER SHARE HER POWERS, ESPECIALLY WITH A HUMAN!
I KNOW WHICH GATE THEY CHOSE TO USE TO COME INTO OUR WORLD. WE SENT SOME SPIES THERE. THEY REPORTED ...UNNATURAL ACTIVITIES.
FIFTEEN THOUSAND SOLDIERS ARE HEADING THERE, TO TRY TO CONTAIN THE CREATURES OF DARKNESS IF THEY DO GET THROUGH THE GATE.
THEY'RE LED BY THE BEST SAMURAI FROM MULTIPLE CLANS. TELL US, WHAT'S HER NEXT MOVE? WHERE IS SHE?

*BAKA: IDIOT

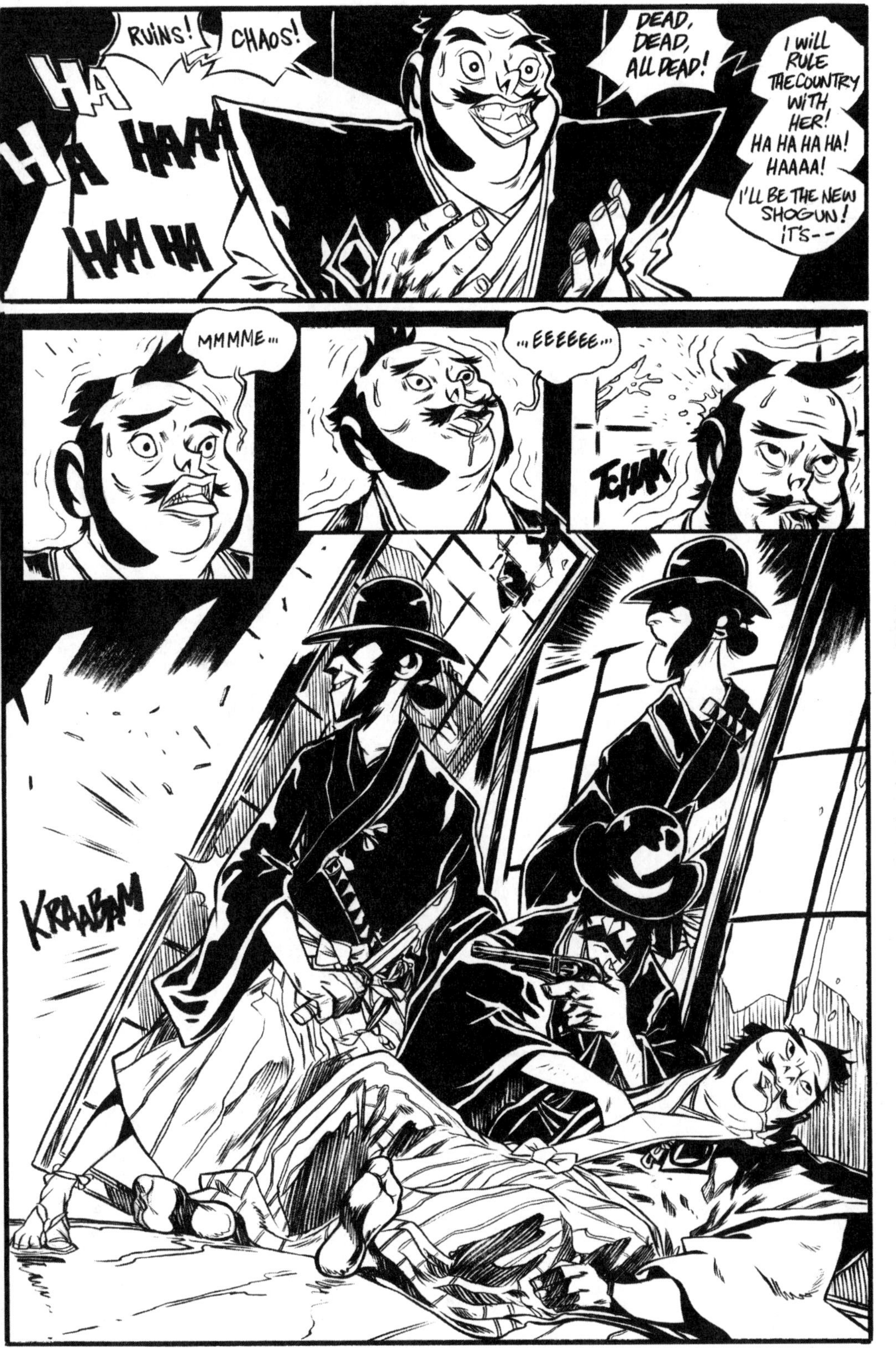
HA HA HAAA HAA HA
RUINS!
CHAOS!
DEAD, DEAD, ALL DEAD!
I WILL RULE THE COUNTRY WITH HER! HA HA HA HA! HAAAA!
I'LL BE THE NEW SHOGUN! IT'S--
MMMME...
...EEEEEE...
TCHAK
KRAABAM

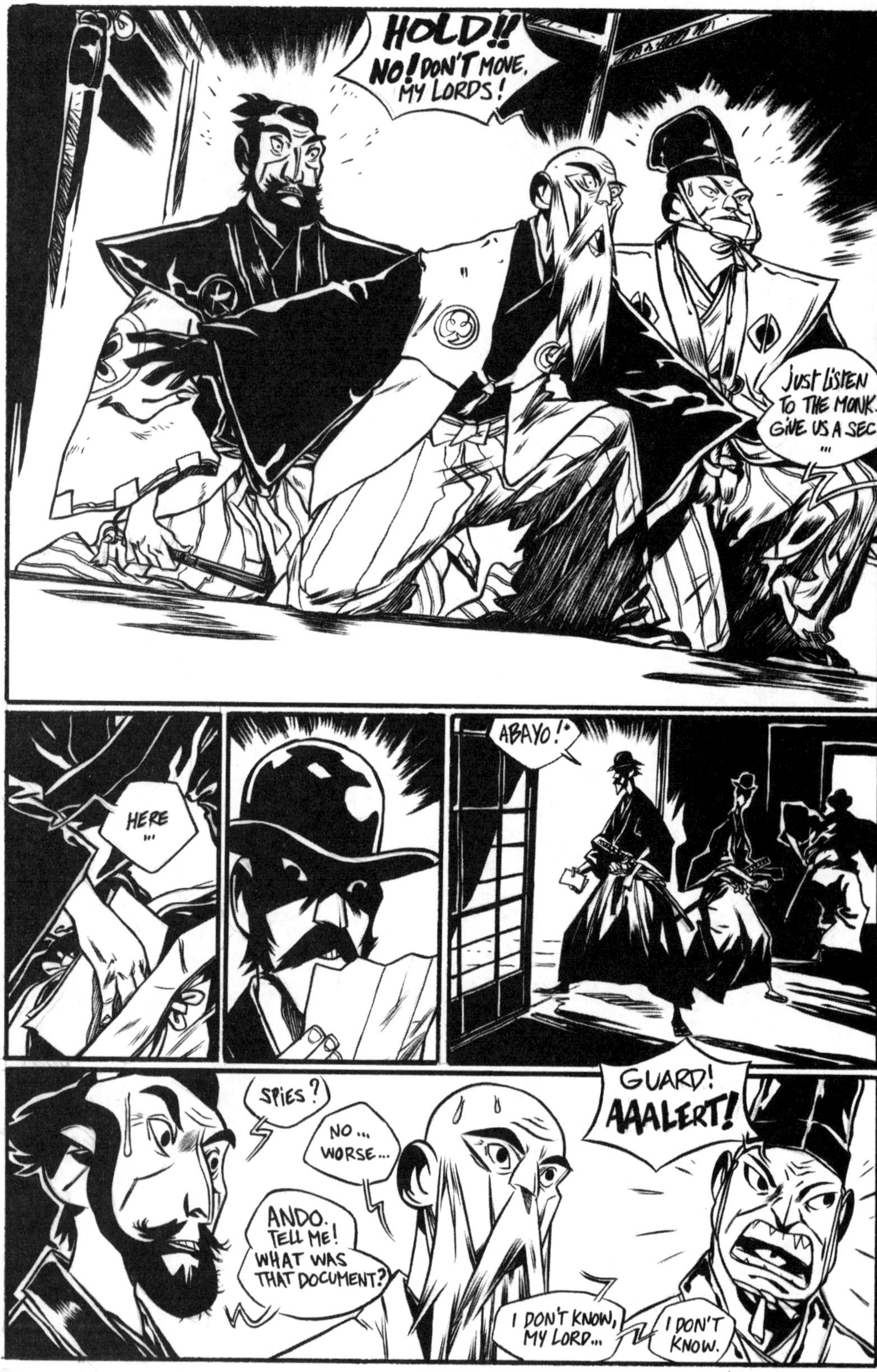
HOLD!! NO! DON'T MOVE, MY LORDS!
JUST LISTEN TO THE MONK. GIVE US A SEC ...
HERE ...
ABAYO!*
SPIES?
NO ... WORSE...
GUARD! AAALERT!
ANDO. TELL ME! WHAT WAS THAT DOCUMENT?
I DON'T KNOW, MY LORD...
I DON'T KNOW.

* ABAYO: FAREWELL

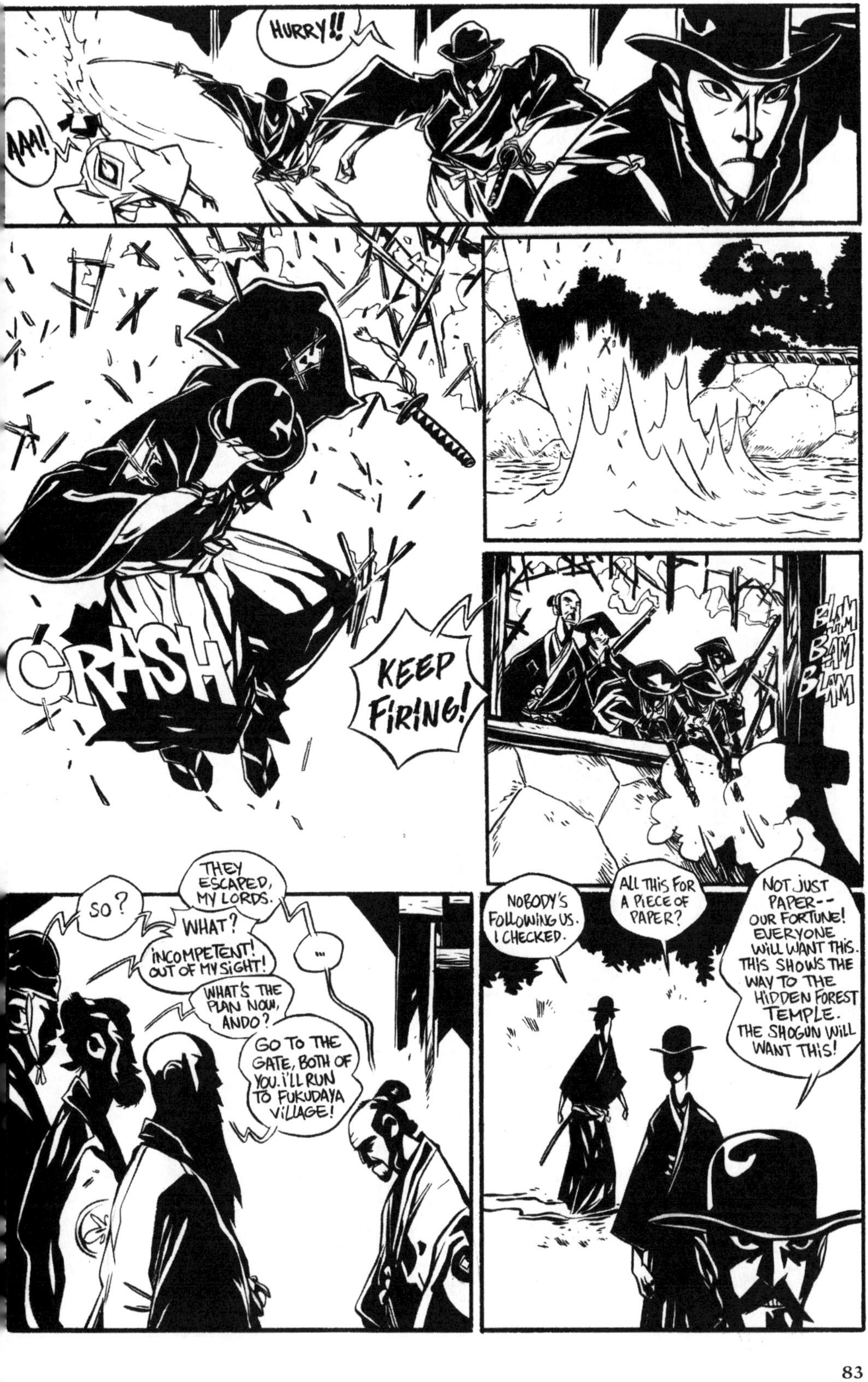
HURRY!!
AAA!
CRASH
KEEP FIRING!
BLAM BAM BLAM
SO?
THEY ESCAPED, MY LORDS.
WHAT?
INCOMPETENT! OUT OF MY SIGHT!
...
WHAT'S THE PLAN NOW, ANDO?
GO TO THE GATE, BOTH OF YOU. I'LL RUN TO FUKUDAYA VILLAGE!
NOBODY'S FOLLOWING US. I CHECKED.
ALL THIS FOR A PIECE OF PAPER?
NOT JUST PAPER-- OUR FORTUNE! EVERYONE WILL WANT THIS. THIS SHOWS THE WAY TO THE HIDDEN FOREST TEMPLE. THE SHOGUN WILL WANT THIS!

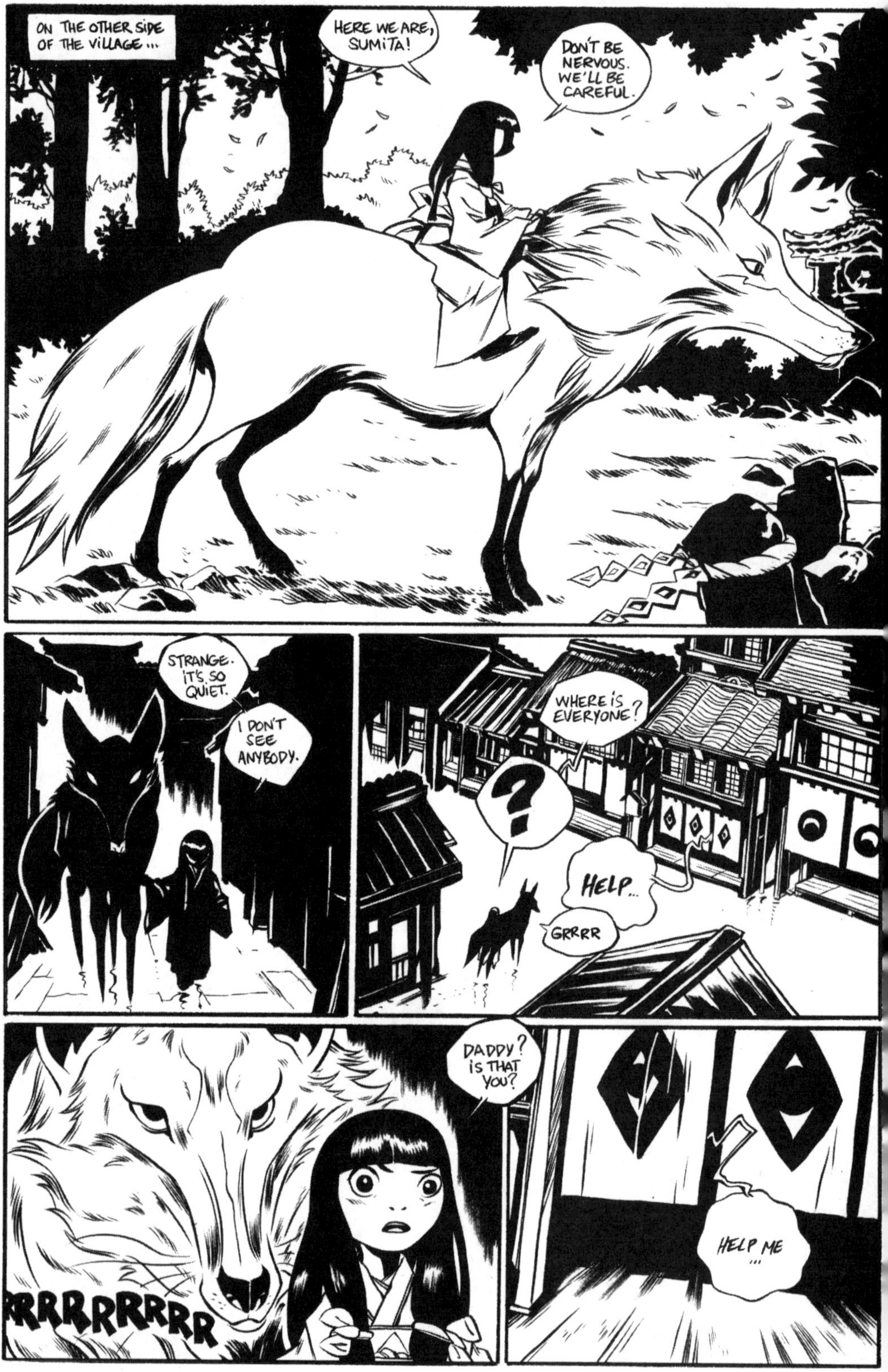
ON THE OTHER SIDE OF THE VILLAGE...
HERE WE ARE, SUMITA!
DON'T BE NERVOUS. WE'LL BE CAREFUL.
STRANGE. IT'S SO QUIET.
I DON'T SEE ANYBODY.
WHERE IS EVERYONE?
?
HELP...
GRRRR
DADDY? IS THAT YOU?
HELP ME ...
RRRRRRRRRR

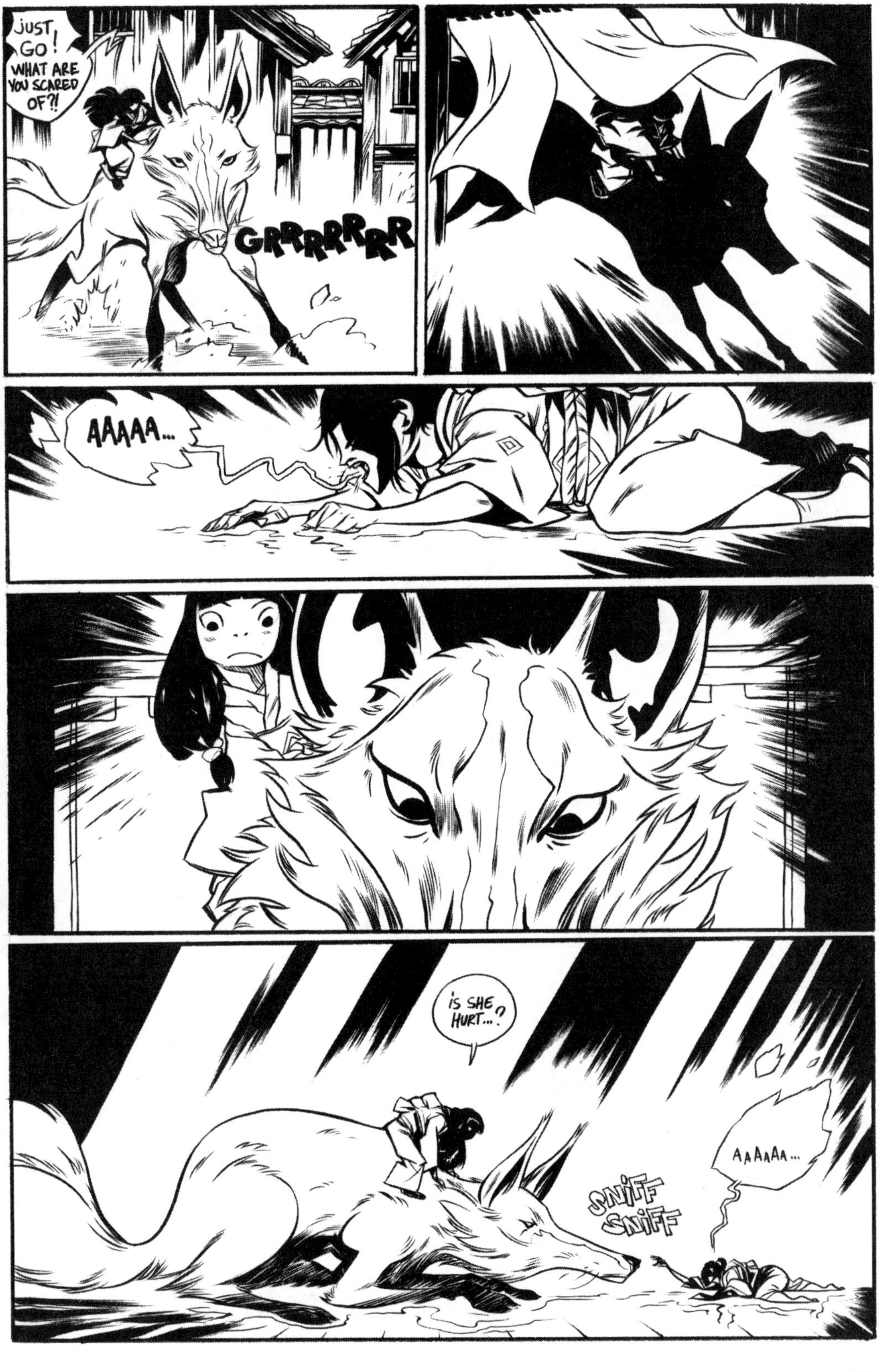
JUST GO! WHAT ARE YOU SCARED OF?!
GRRRRRRR
AAAAA...
IS SHE HURT...?
AAAAAA...
SNIFF SNIFF

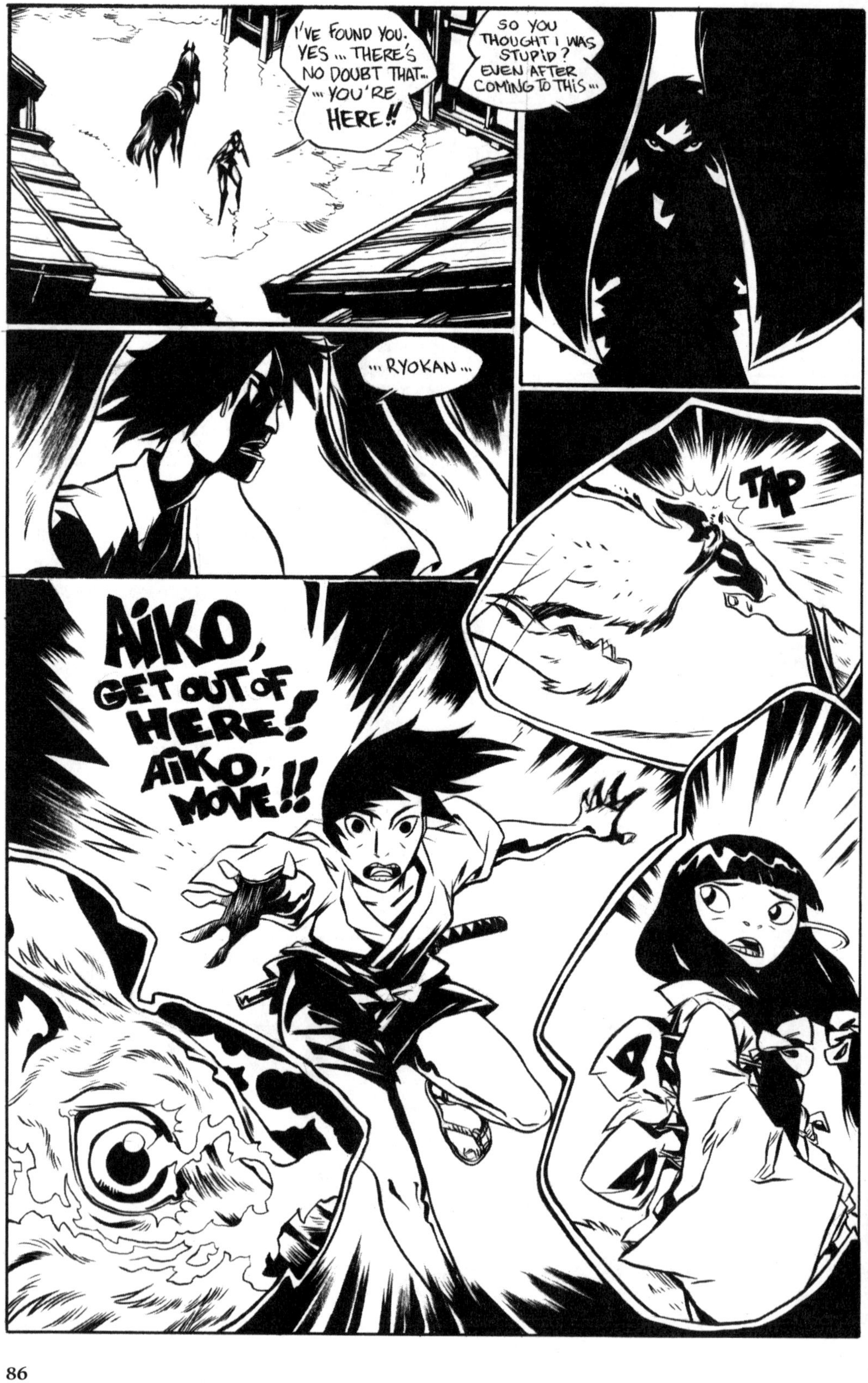

I'VE FOUND YOU. YES ... THERE'S NO DOUBT THAT... ... YOU'RE HERE!!
SO YOU THOUGHT I WAS STUPID? EVEN AFTER COMING TO THIS ...
... RYOKAN ...
TAP
AIKO, GET OUT OF HERE! AIKO, MOVE!!

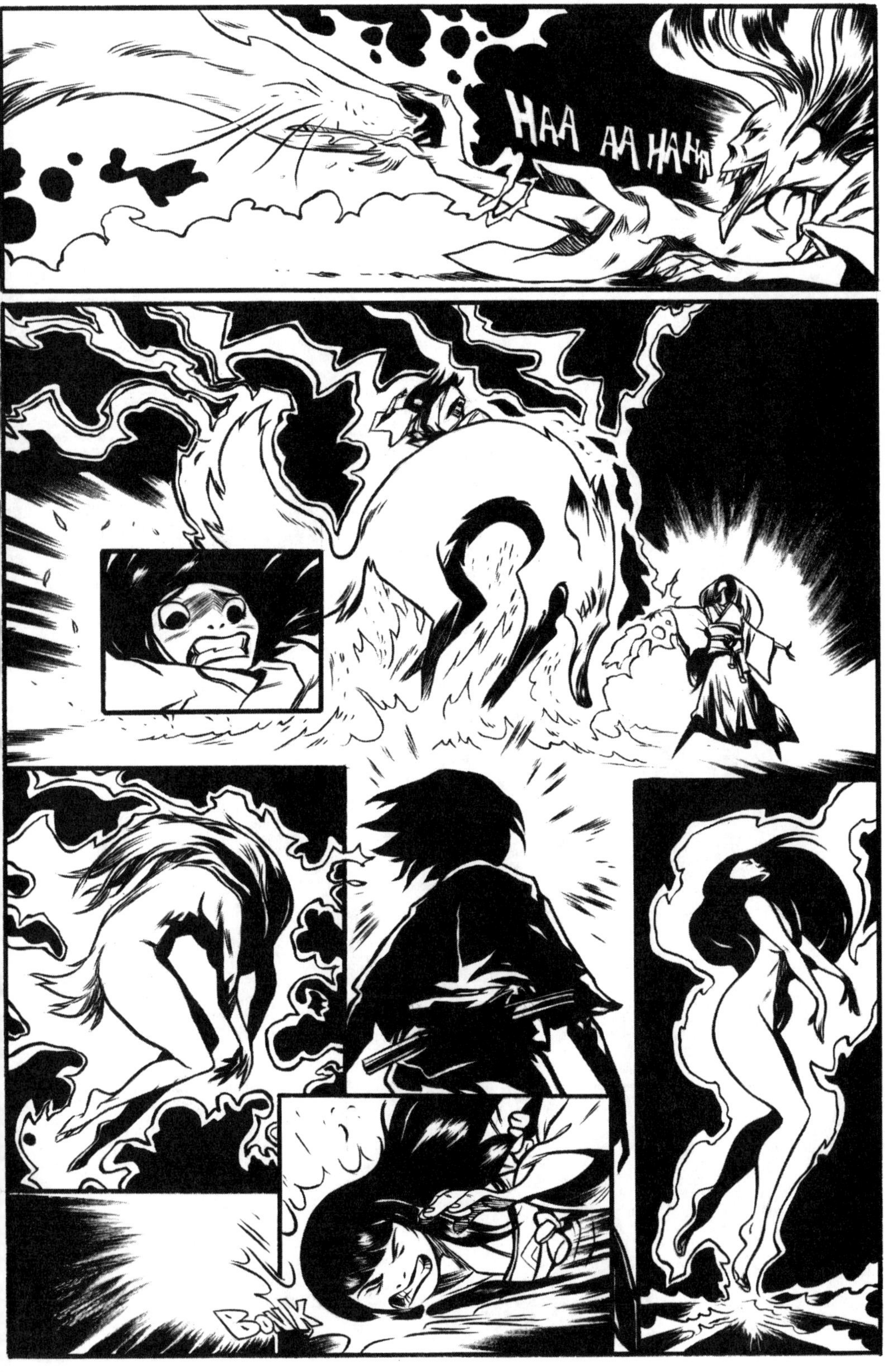
HAA AA HAHA
BONK

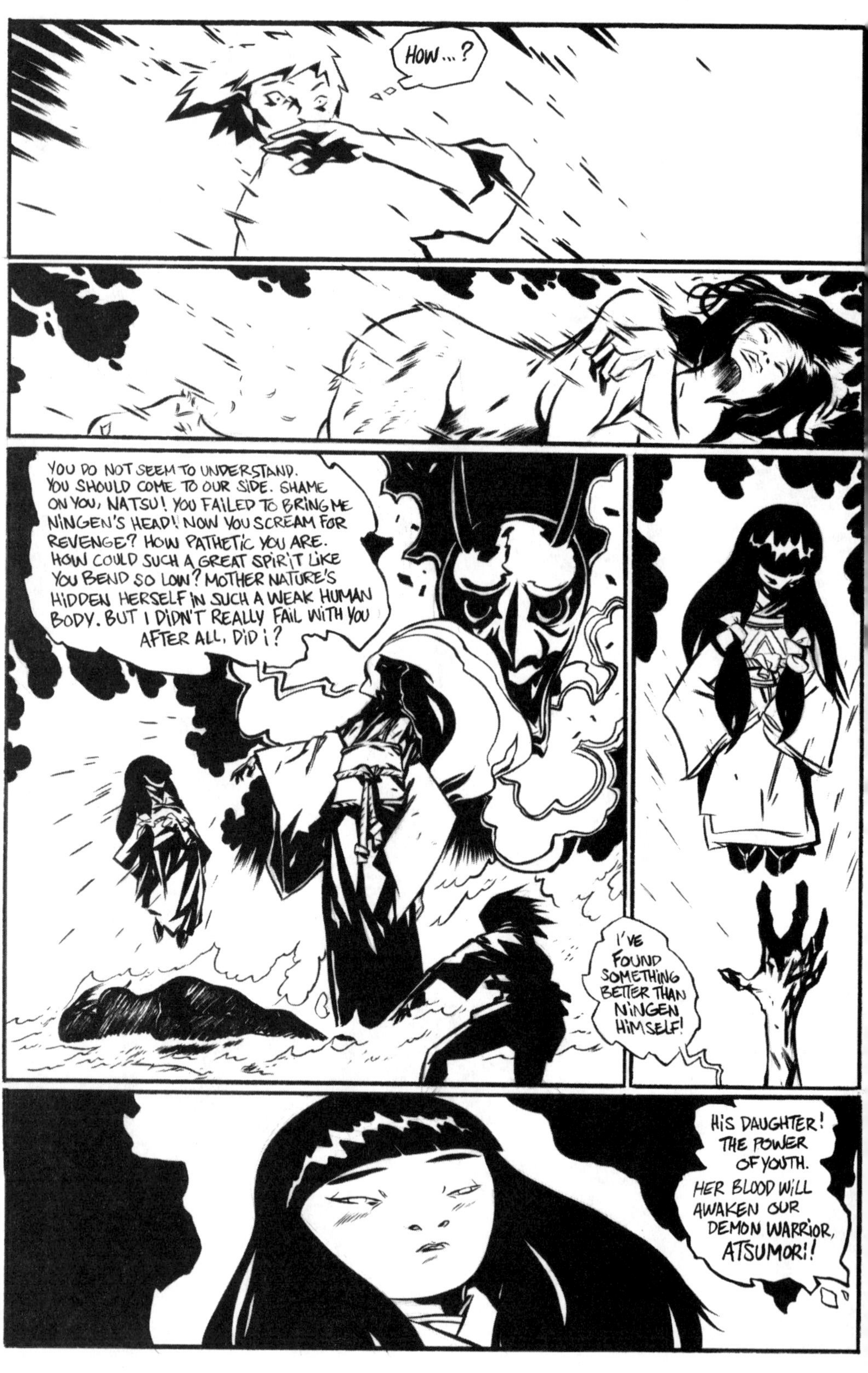
HOW...?
YOU DO NOT SEEM TO UNDERSTAND. YOU SHOULD COME TO OUR SIDE. SHAME ON YOU, NATSU! YOU FAILED TO BRING ME NINGEN'S HEAD! NOW YOU SCREAM FOR REVENGE? HOW PATHETIC YOU ARE. HOW COULD SUCH A GREAT SPIRIT LIKE YOU BEND SO LOW? MOTHER NATURE'S HIDDEN HERSELF IN SUCH A WEAK HUMAN BODY. BUT I DIDN'T REALLY FAIL WITH YOU AFTER ALL, DID I?
I'VE FOUND SOMETHING BETTER THAN NINGEN HIMSELF!
HIS DAUGHTER! THE POWER OF YOUTH. HER BLOOD WILL AWAKEN OUR DEMON WARRIOR, ATSUMORI!

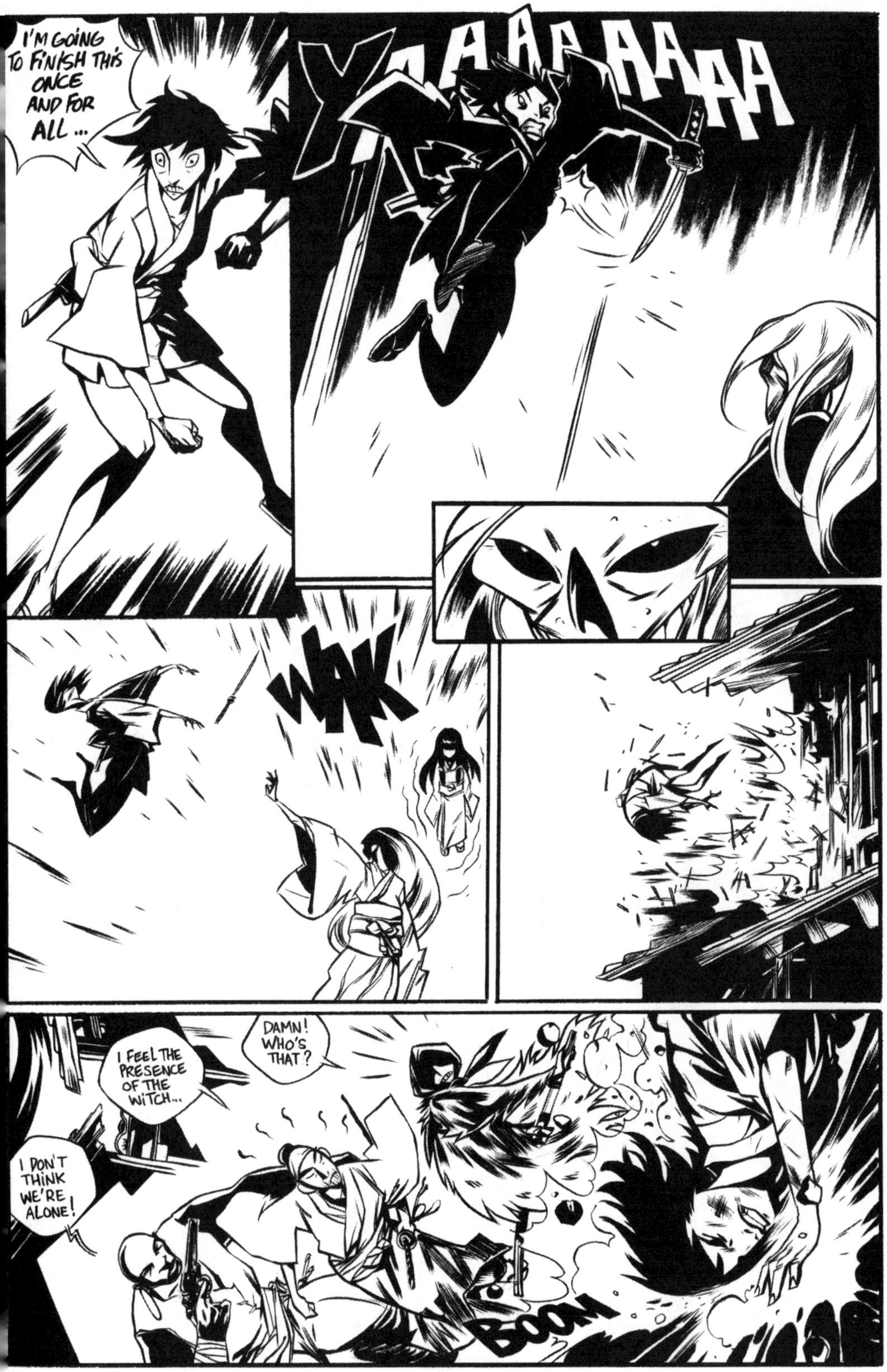
I'M GOING TO FINISH THIS ONCE AND FOR ALL...
YAAAAAAAAA
WAK
I FEEL THE PRESENCE OF THE WITCH...
DAMN! WHO'S THAT?
I DON'T THINK WE'RE ALONE!
BOOM

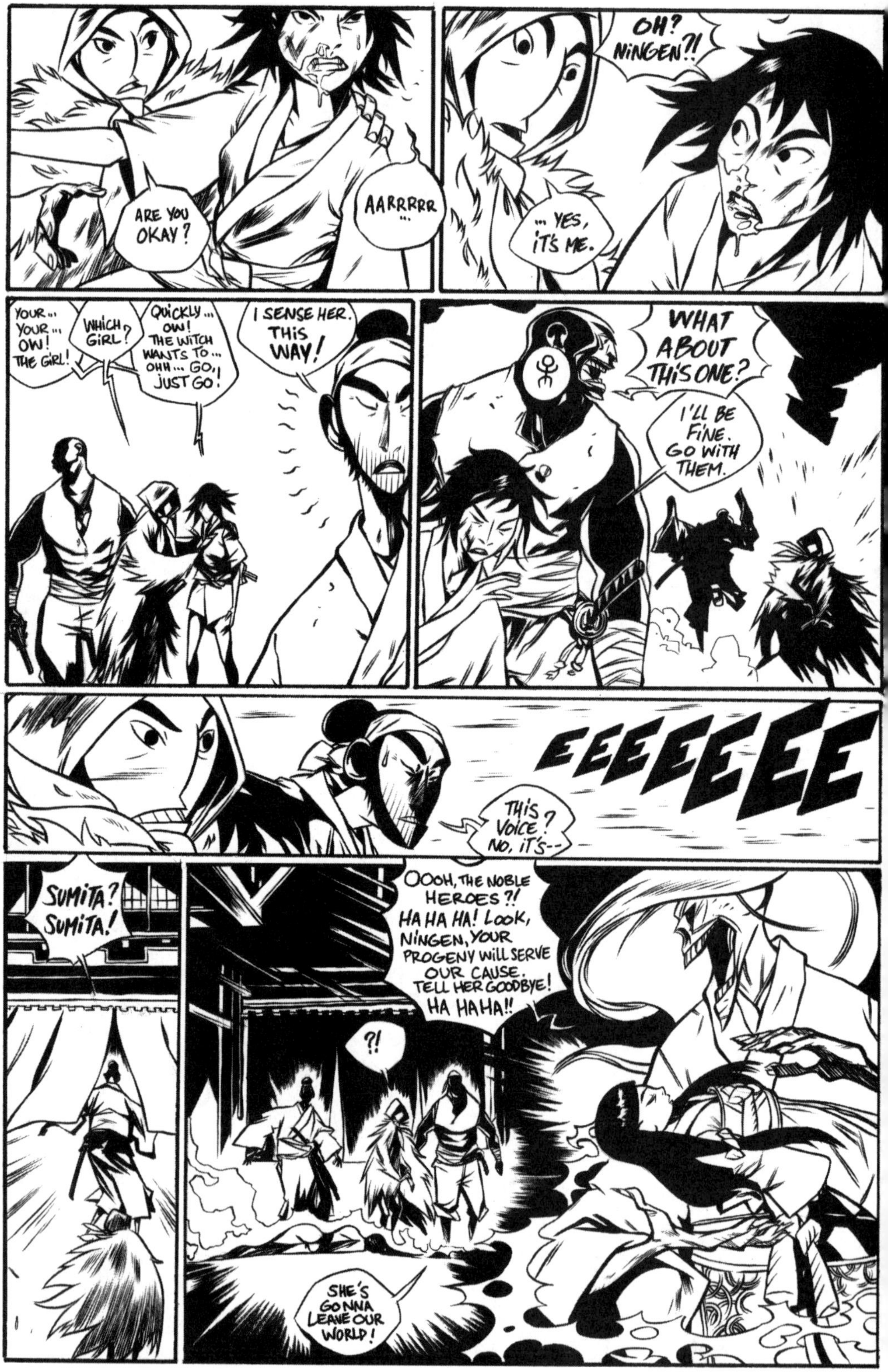

ARE YOU OKAY?
AARRRRR...
OH? NINGEN?!
... YES, IT'S ME.
YOUR... YOUR... OW! THE GIRL!
WHICH GIRL?
QUICKLY... OW! THE WITCH WANTS TO... OHH... GO, JUST GO!
I SENSE HER. THIS WAY!
WHAT ABOUT THIS ONE?
I'LL BE FINE. GO WITH THEM.
EEEEEEE
THIS VOICE? NO, IT'S--
SUMITA? SUMITA!
OOOH, THE NOBLE HEROES?! HA HA HA! LOOK, NINGEN, YOUR PROGENY WILL SERVE OUR CAUSE. TELL HER GOODBYE! HA HAHA!!
?!
SHE'S GONNA LEAVE OUR WORLD!

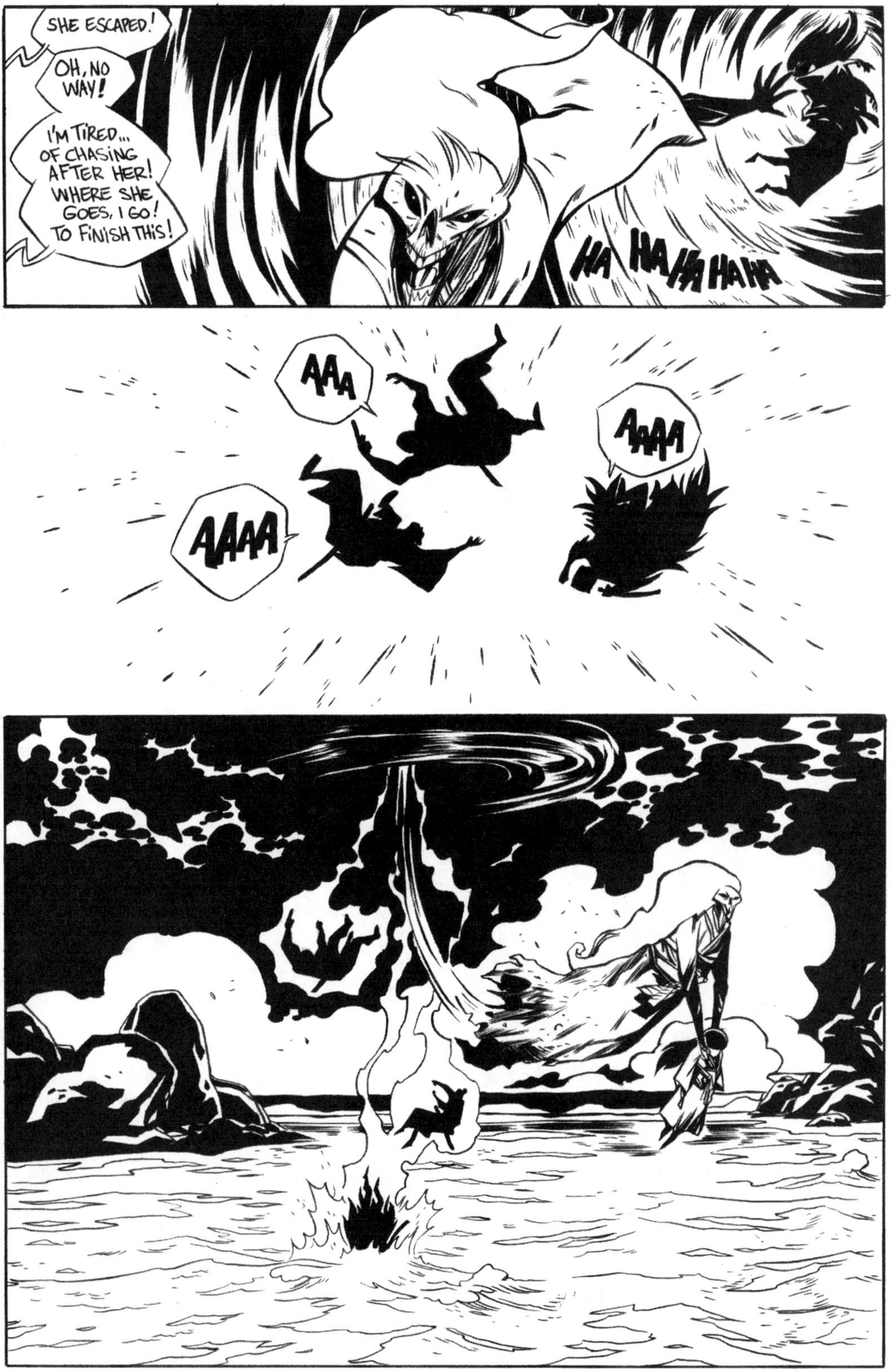
SHE ESCAPED!
OH, NO WAY!
I'M TIRED... OF CHASING AFTER HER! WHERE SHE GOES, I GO! TO FINISH THIS!
HA HA HA HA HA HA
AAA
AAAA
AAAA

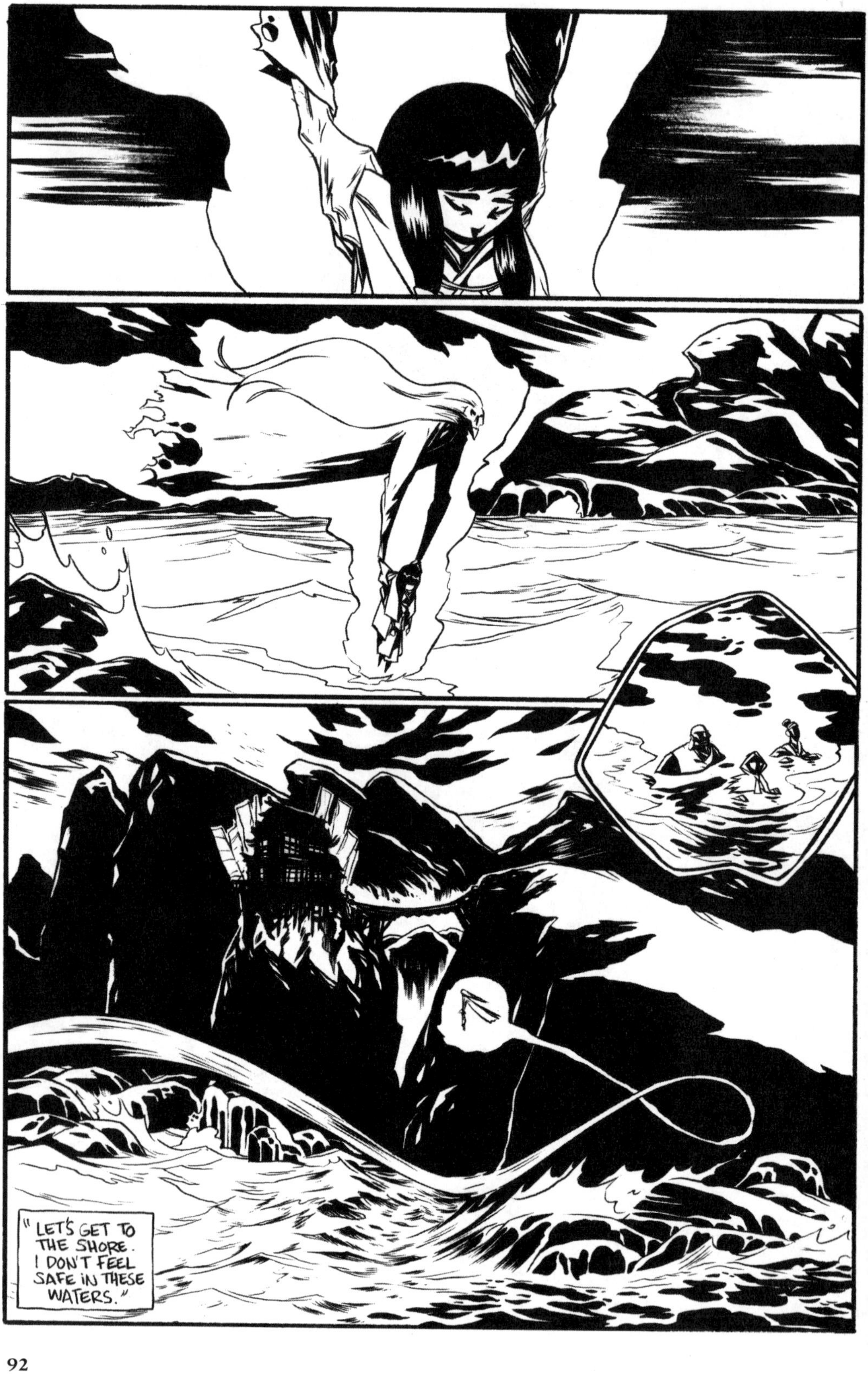
"LET'S GET TO THE SHORE. I DON'T FEEL SAFE IN THESE WATERS."

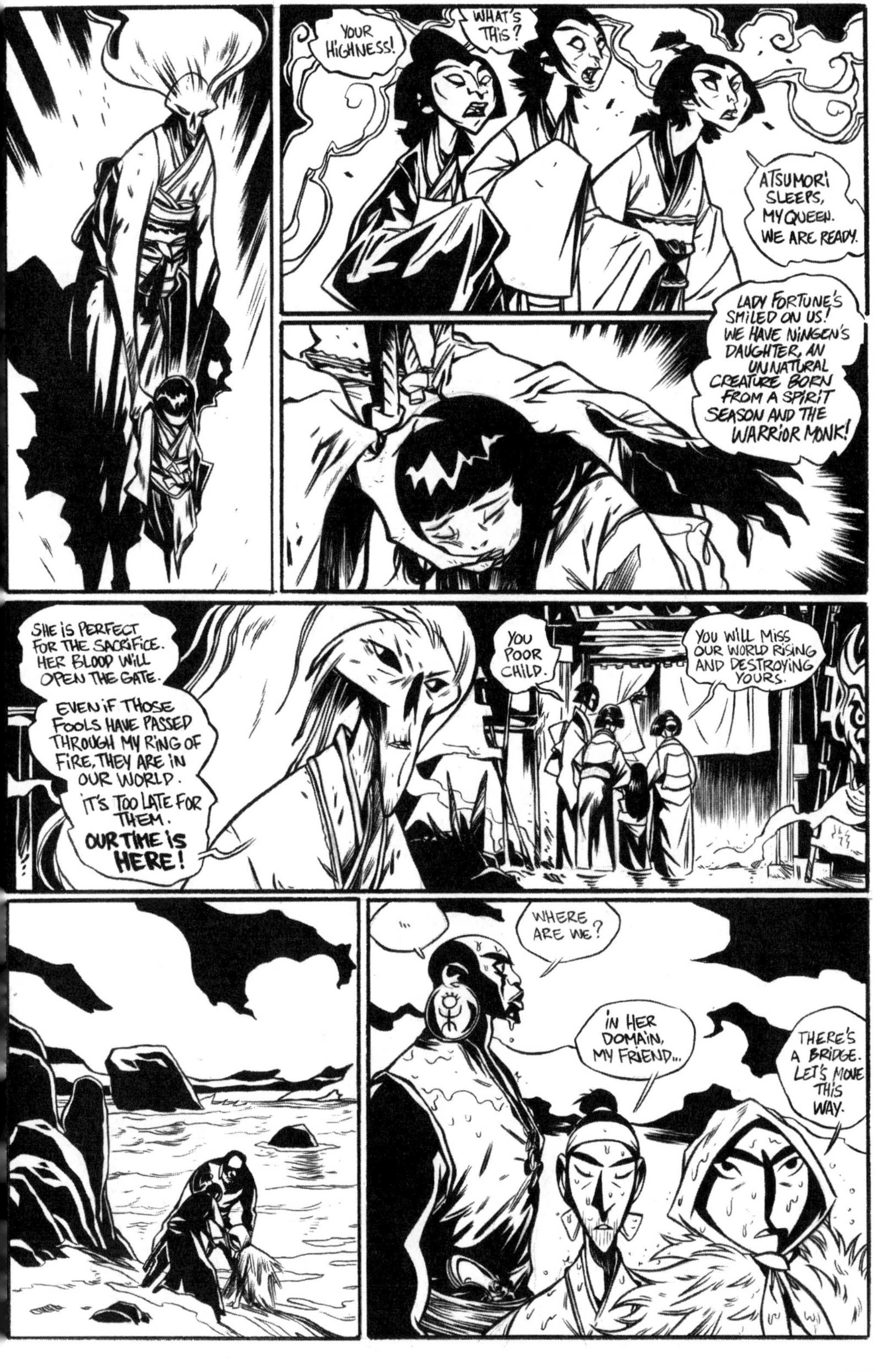
YOUR HIGHNESS!
WHAT'S THIS?
ATSUMORI SLEEPS, MY QUEEN. WE ARE READY.
LADY FORTUNE'S SMILED ON US! WE HAVE NINGEN'S DAUGHTER, AN UNNATURAL CREATURE BORN FROM A SPIRIT SEASON AND THE WARRIOR MONK!
SHE IS PERFECT FOR THE SACRIFICE. HER BLOOD WILL OPEN THE GATE.
EVEN IF THOSE FOOLS HAVE PASSED THROUGH MY RING OF FIRE, THEY ARE IN OUR WORLD.
IT'S TOO LATE FOR THEM.
OUR TIME IS HERE!
YOU POOR CHILD.
YOU WILL MISS OUR WORLD RISING AND DESTROYING YOURS.
...
WHERE ARE WE?
IN HER DOMAIN, MY FRIEND...
THERE'S A BRIDGE. LET'S MOVE THIS WAY.

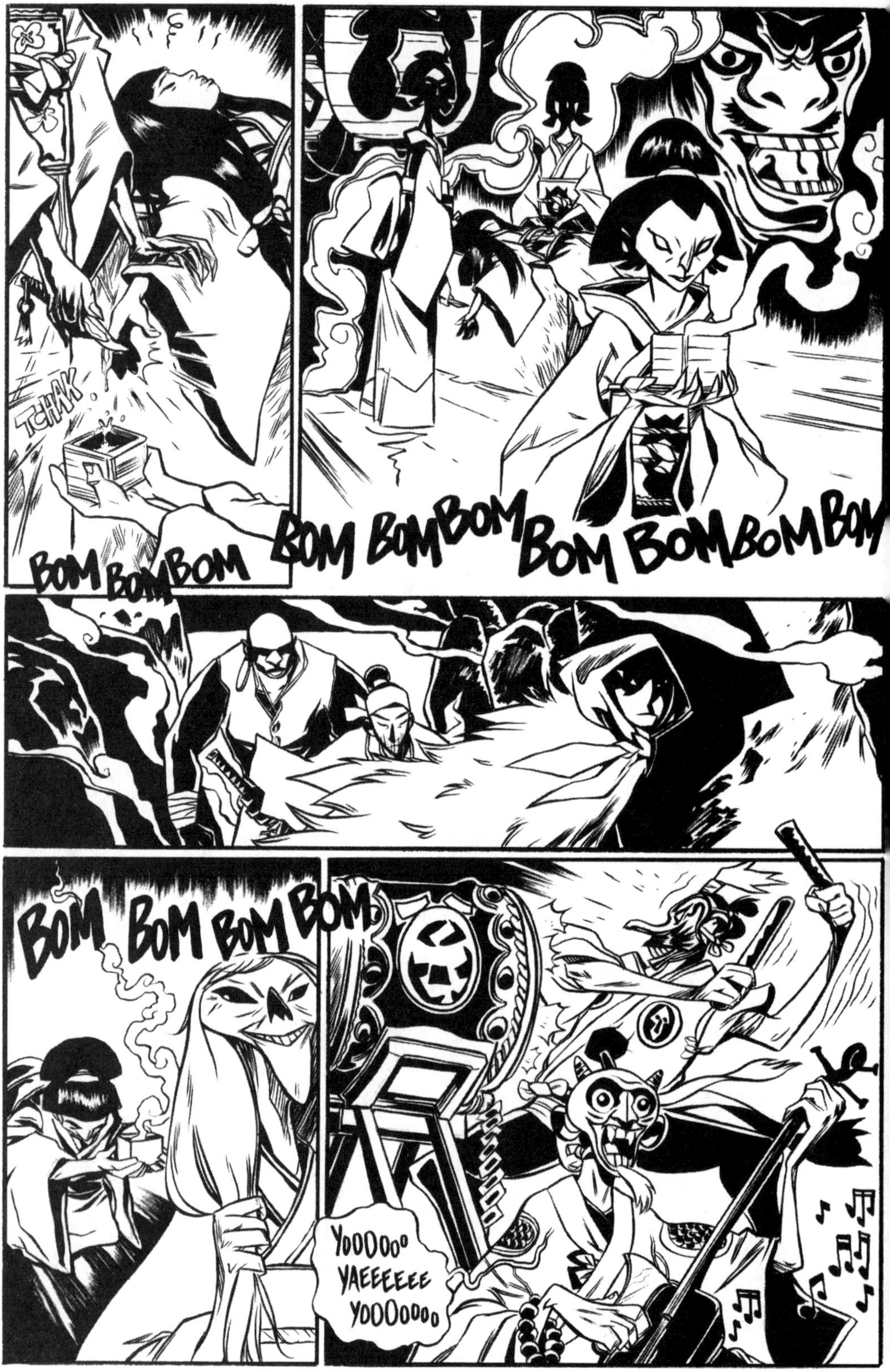
TCHAK
BOM BOM BOM
BOM BOM BOM BOM BOM BOM BOM BOM
BOM BOM BOM BOM
YOODOoo
YAEEEEEE
YOOOoooo

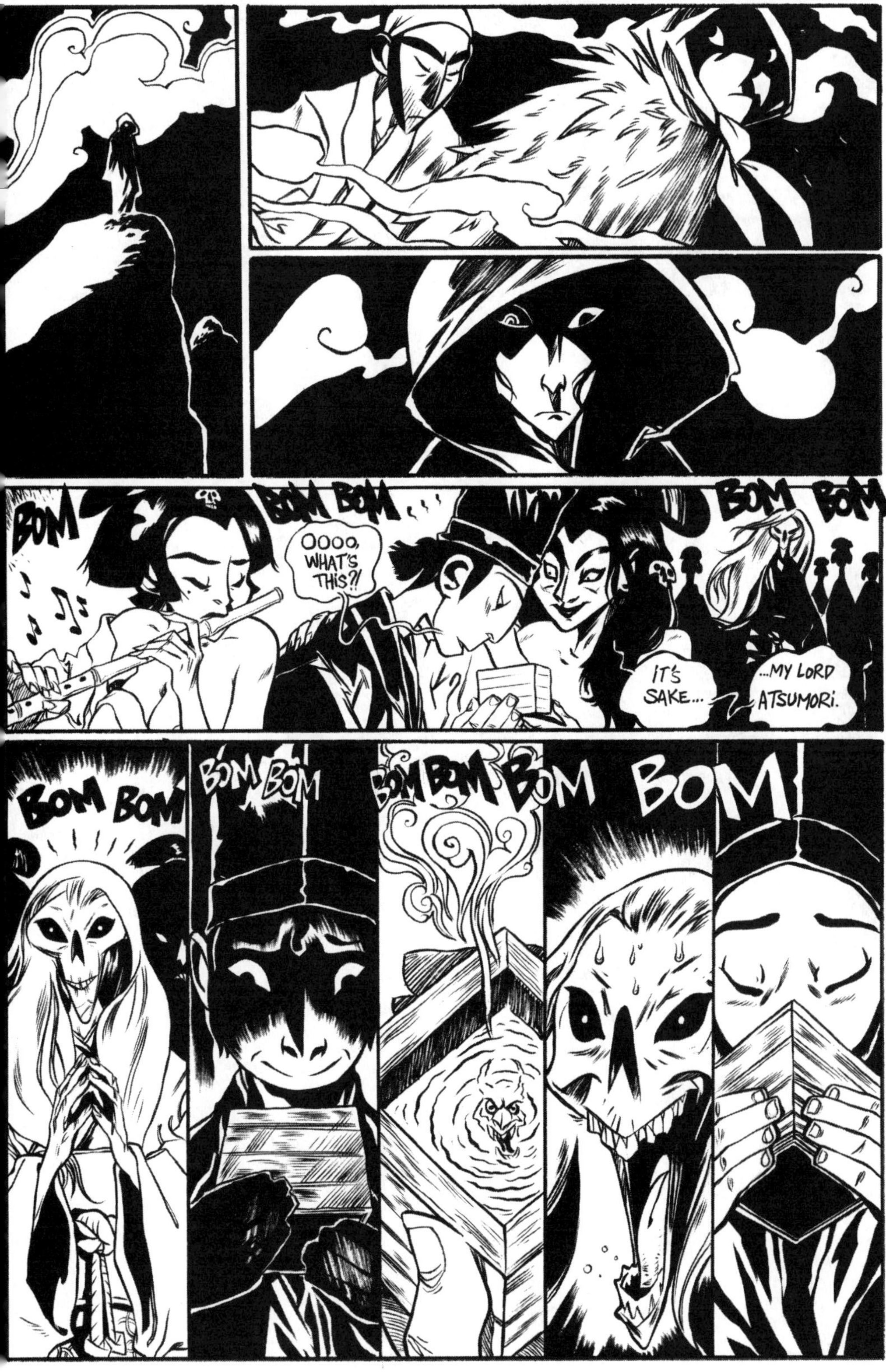
BOM
BOM BOM
OOOO, WHAT'S THIS?!
BOM BOM
IT'S SAKE...
...MY LORD ATSUMORI.
BOM BOM
BOM BOM
BOM BOM BOM BOM

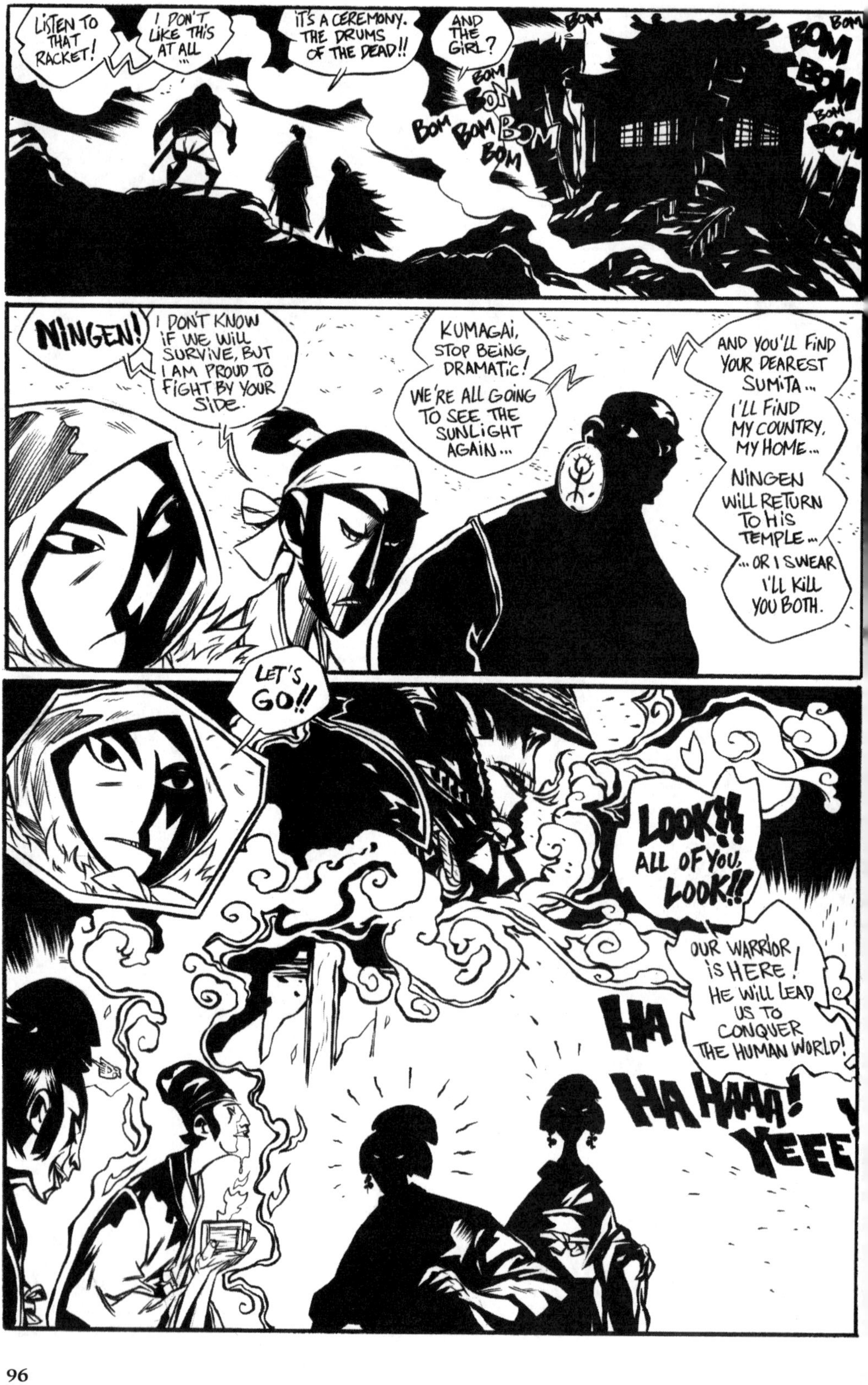

LISTEN TO THAT RACKET!
I DON'T LIKE THIS AT ALL ...
IT'S A CEREMONY. THE DRUMS OF THE DEAD!!
AND THE GIRL?
BOM BOM BOM BOM BOM BOM BOM
BOM BOM BOM BOM BOM BOM
NINGEN!
I DON'T KNOW IF WE WILL SURVIVE, BUT I AM PROUD TO FIGHT BY YOUR SIDE.
KUMAGAI, STOP BEING DRAMATIC!
WE'RE ALL GOING TO SEE THE SUNLIGHT AGAIN...
AND YOU'LL FIND YOUR DEAREST SUMITA...
I'LL FIND MY COUNTRY, MY HOME...
NINGEN WILL RETURN TO HIS TEMPLE...
...OR I SWEAR I'LL KILL YOU BOTH.
LET'S GO!!
LOOK!! ALL OF YOU, LOOK!!
OUR WARRIOR IS HERE! HE WILL LEAD US TO CONQUER THE HUMAN WORLD!
HA HA HAAA! YEEE

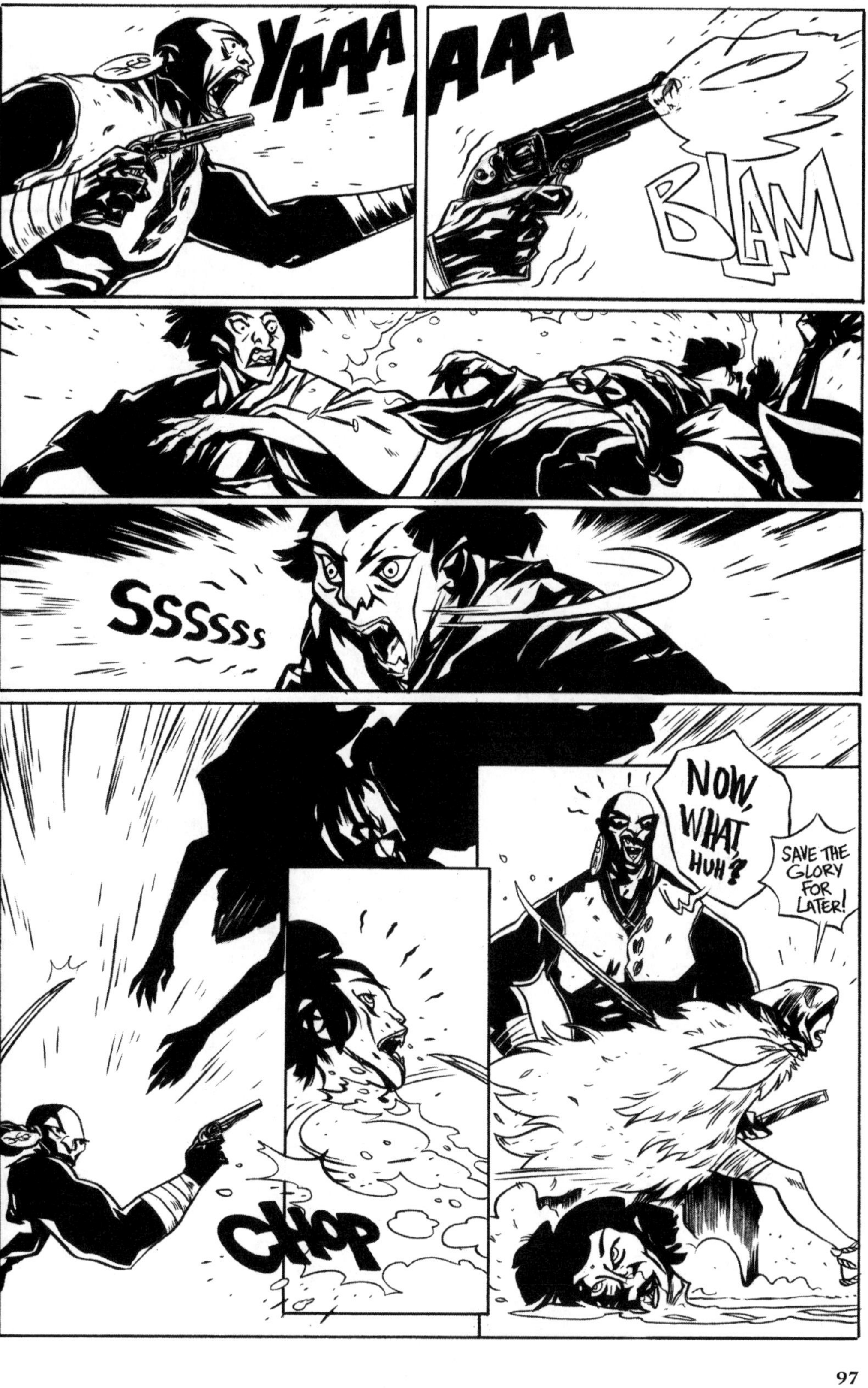
YAAAAAA
BLAM
SSSSSS
NOW, WHAT, HUH?
SAVE THE GLORY FOR LATER!
CHOP

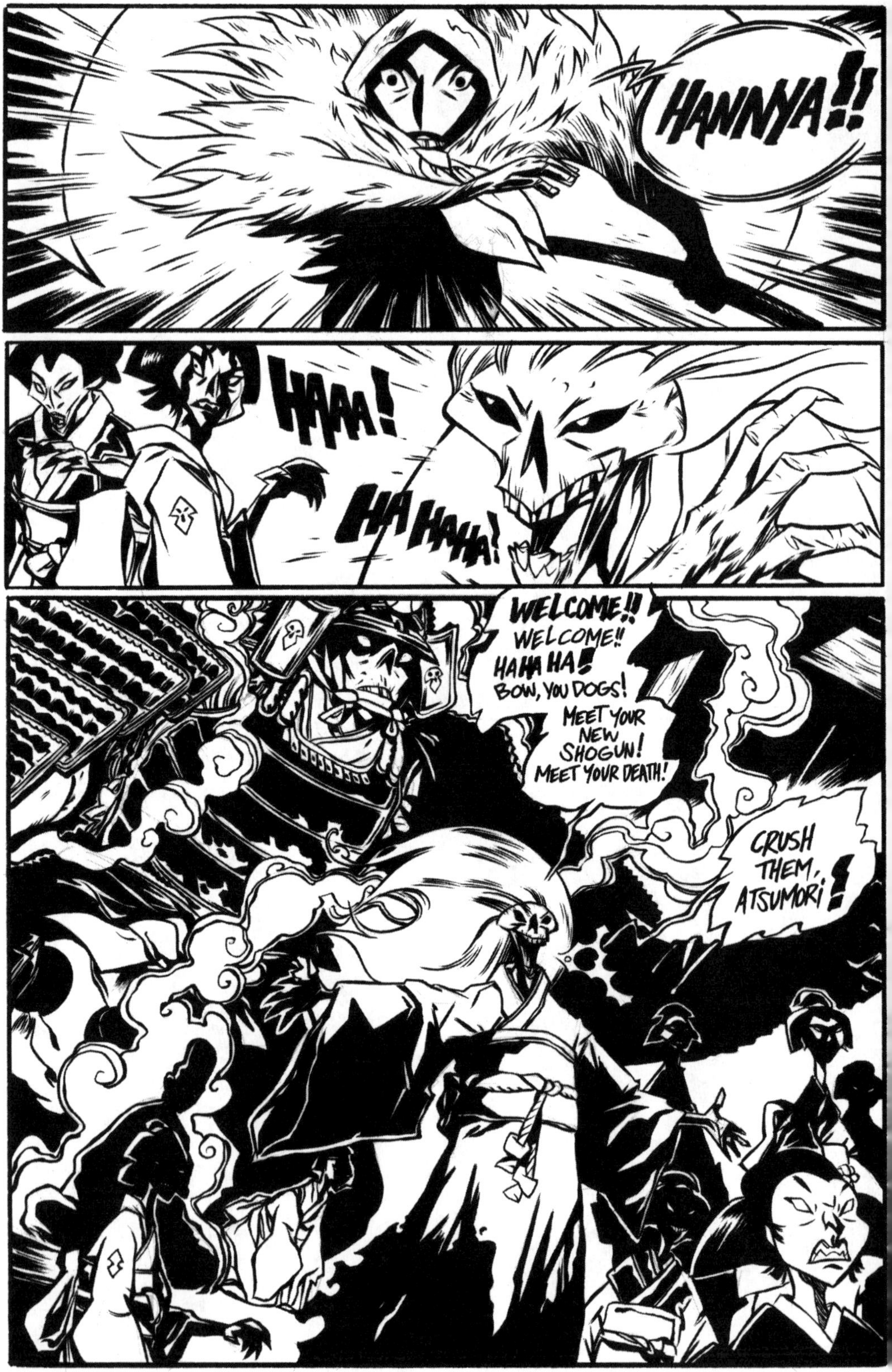
HANNYA!!
HAAA!
HA HAHA!
WELCOME!! WELCOME!! HA HA HA!
BOW, YOU DOGS!
MEET YOUR NEW SHOGUN! MEET YOUR DEATH!
CRUSH THEM, ATSUMORI!

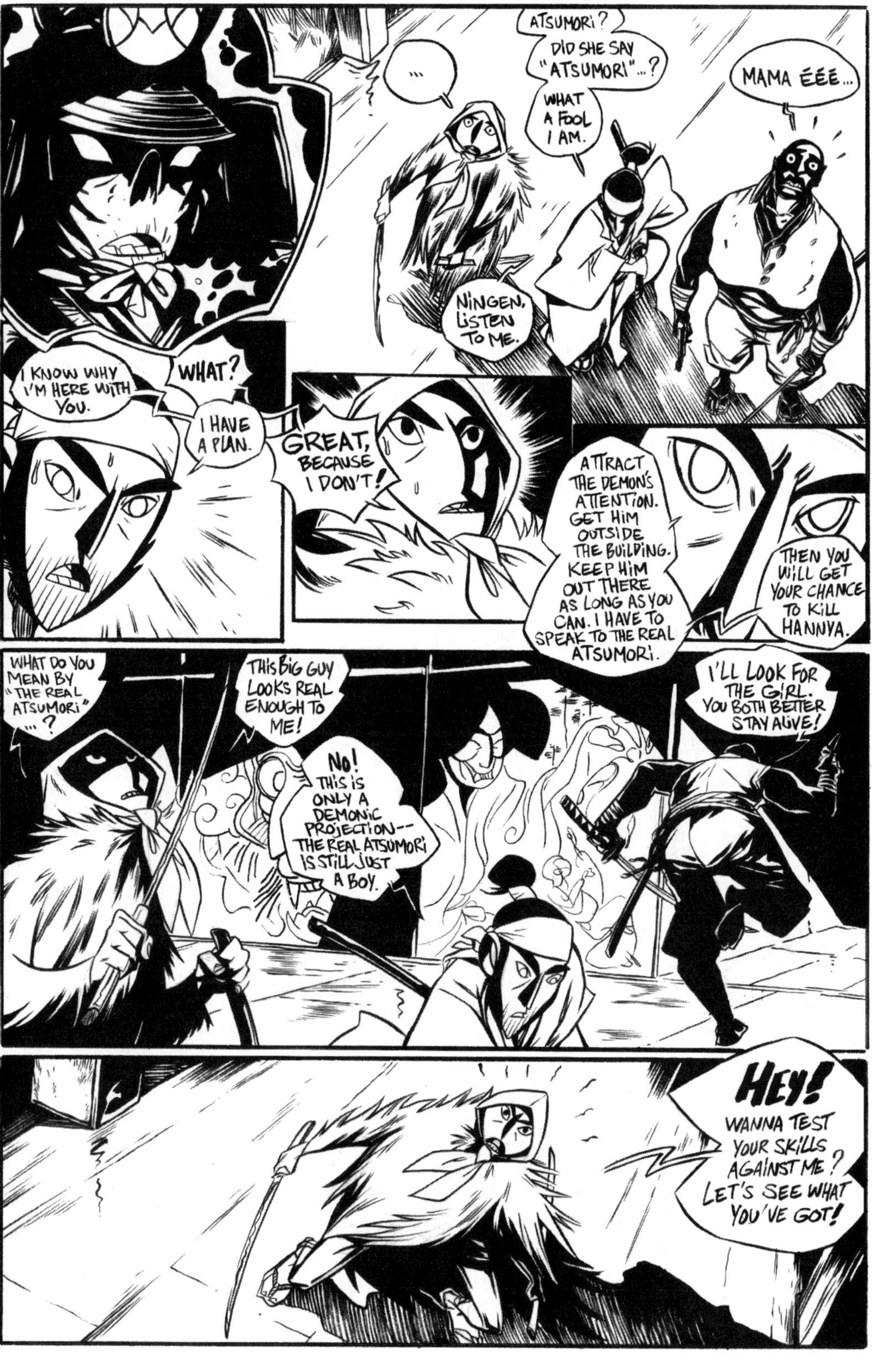
...
ATSUMORI? DID SHE SAY "ATSUMORI"...?
WHAT A FOOL I AM.
MAMA ÉÉÉ...
NINGEN, LISTEN TO ME.
I KNOW WHY I'M HERE WITH YOU.
WHAT?
I HAVE A PLAN.
GREAT, BECAUSE I DON'T!
ATTRACT THE DEMON'S ATTENTION. GET HIM OUTSIDE THE BUILDING. KEEP HIM OUT THERE AS LONG AS YOU CAN. I HAVE TO SPEAK TO THE REAL ATSUMORI.
THEN YOU WILL GET YOUR CHANCE TO KILL HANNYA.
WHAT DO YOU MEAN BY "THE REAL ATSUMORI"...?
THIS BIG GUY LOOKS REAL ENOUGH TO ME!
NO! THIS IS ONLY A DEMONIC PROJECTION-- THE REAL ATSUMORI IS STILL JUST A BOY.
I'LL LOOK FOR THE GIRL. YOU BOTH BETTER STAY ALIVE!
HEY!
WANNA TEST YOUR SKILLS AGAINST ME? LET'S SEE WHAT YOU'VE GOT!

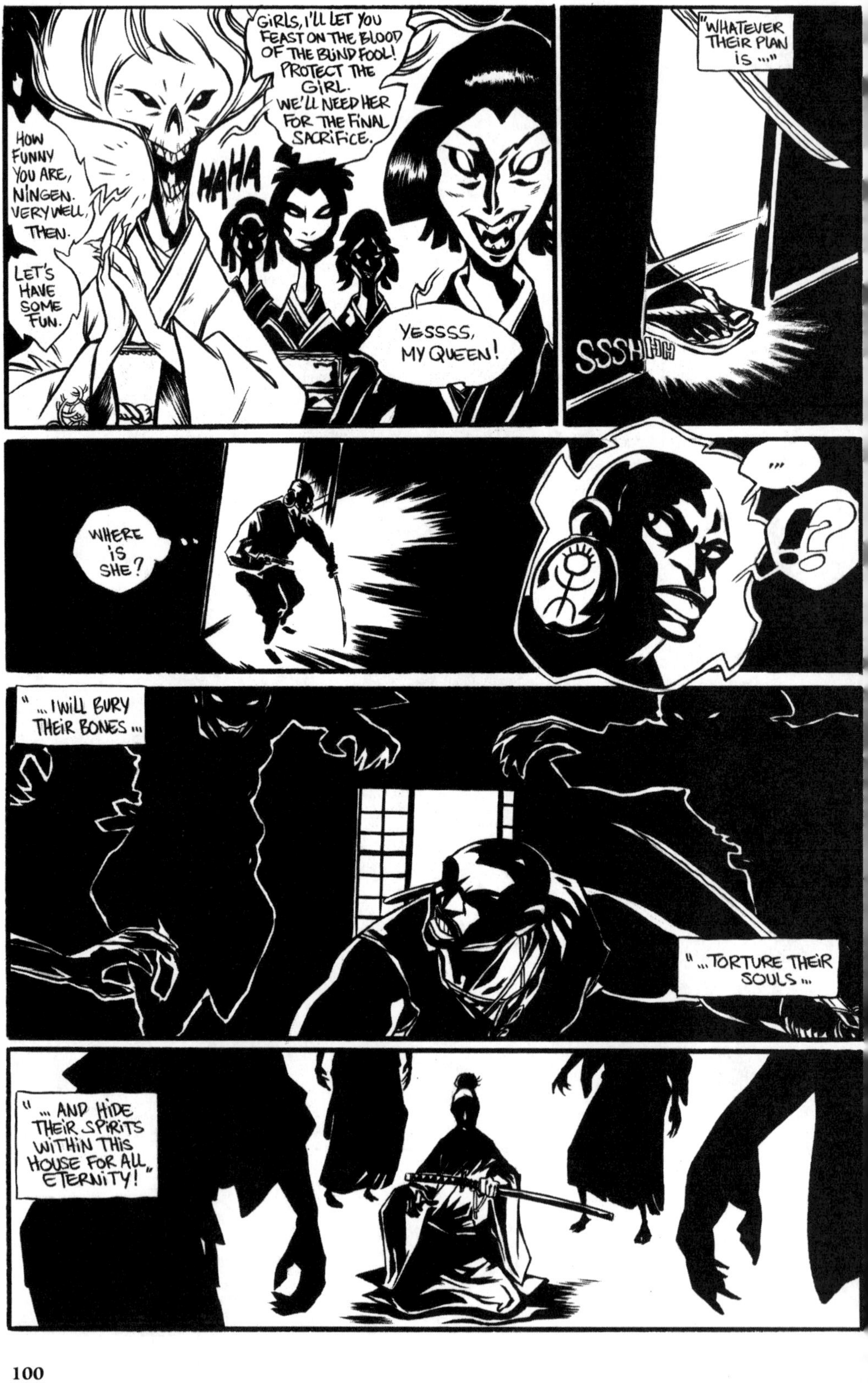
GIRLS, I'LL LET YOU FEAST ON THE BLOOD OF THE BLIND FOOL! PROTECT THE GIRL. WE'LL NEED HER FOR THE FINAL SACRIFICE.
HOW FUNNY YOU ARE, NINGEN. VERY WELL, THEN.
LET'S HAVE SOME FUN.
HAHA
YESSSS, MY QUEEN!
"WHATEVER THEIR PLAN IS ..."
SSSHHH
WHERE IS SHE?
...
!?
"... I WILL BURY THEIR BONES ...
"... TORTURE THEIR SOULS ...
"... AND HIDE THEIR SPIRITS WITHIN THIS HOUSE FOR ALL ETERNITY!"

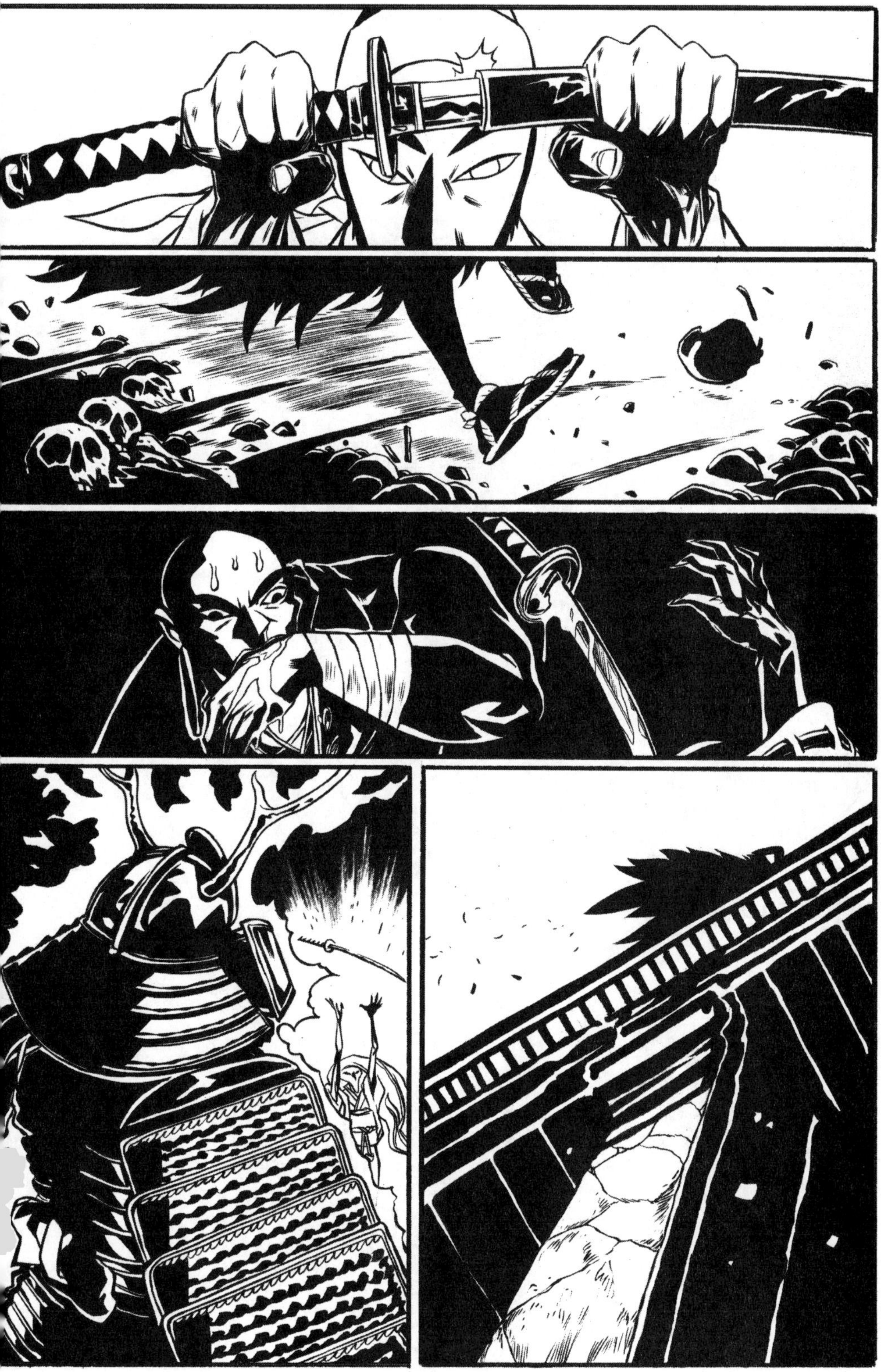

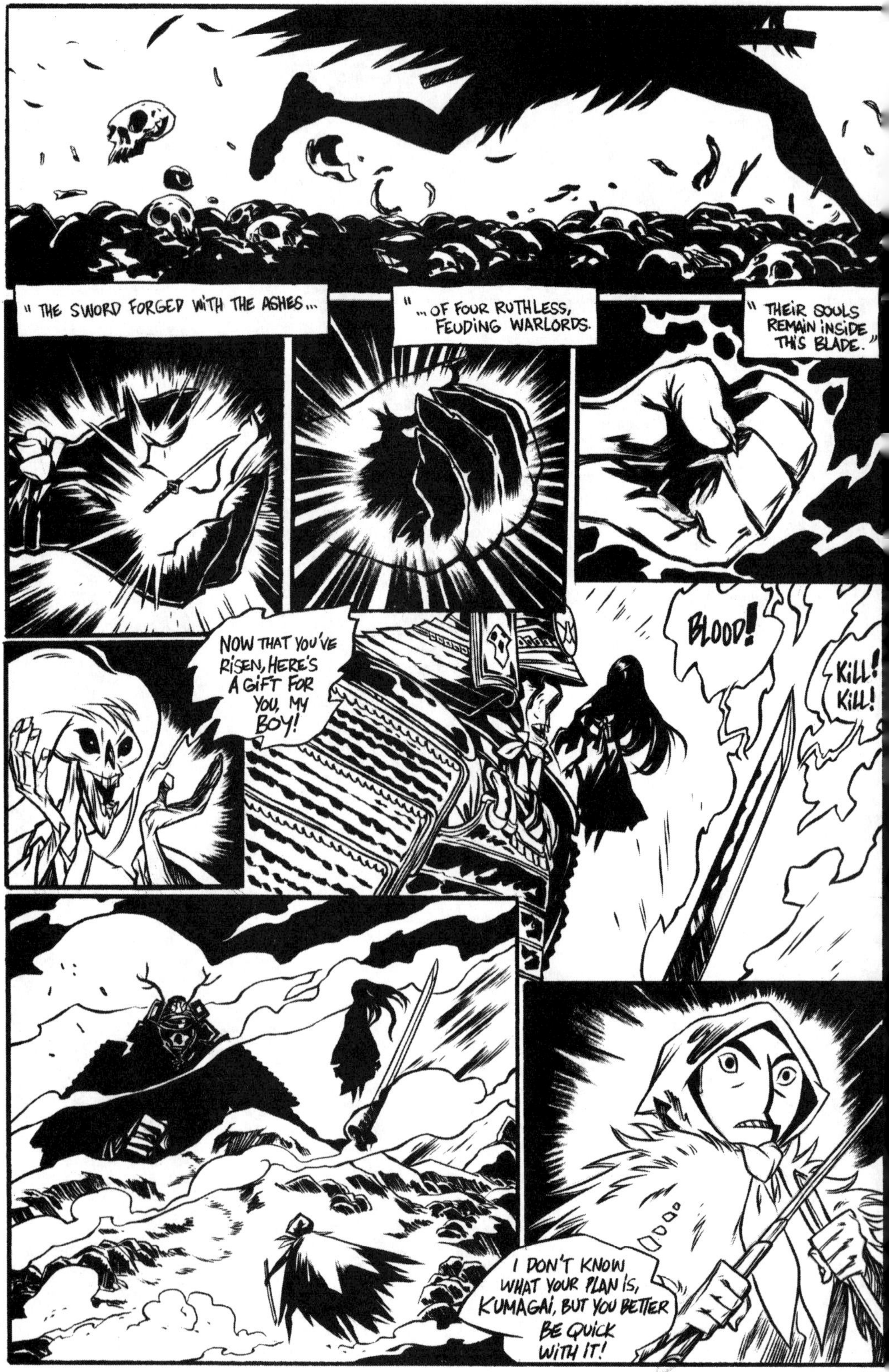
"THE SWORD FORGED WITH THE ASHES...
"...OF FOUR RUTHLESS, FEUDING WARLORDS.
"THEIR SOULS REMAIN INSIDE THIS BLADE."
NOW THAT YOU'VE RISEN, HERE'S A GIFT FOR YOU, MY BOY!
BLOOD!
KILL! KILL!
I DON'T KNOW WHAT YOUR PLAN IS, KUMAGAI, BUT YOU BETTER BE QUICK WITH IT!

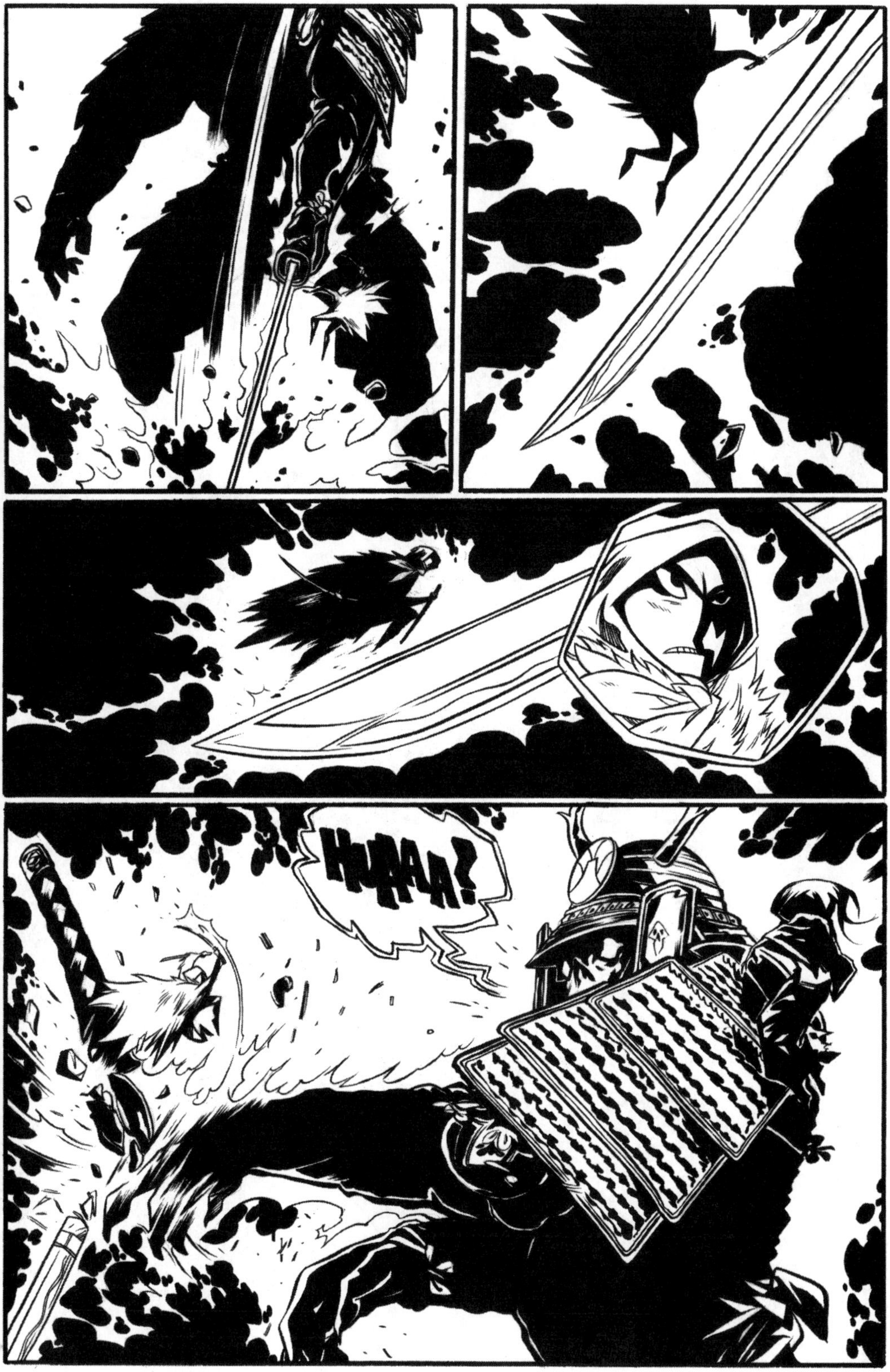
HUAAA?!

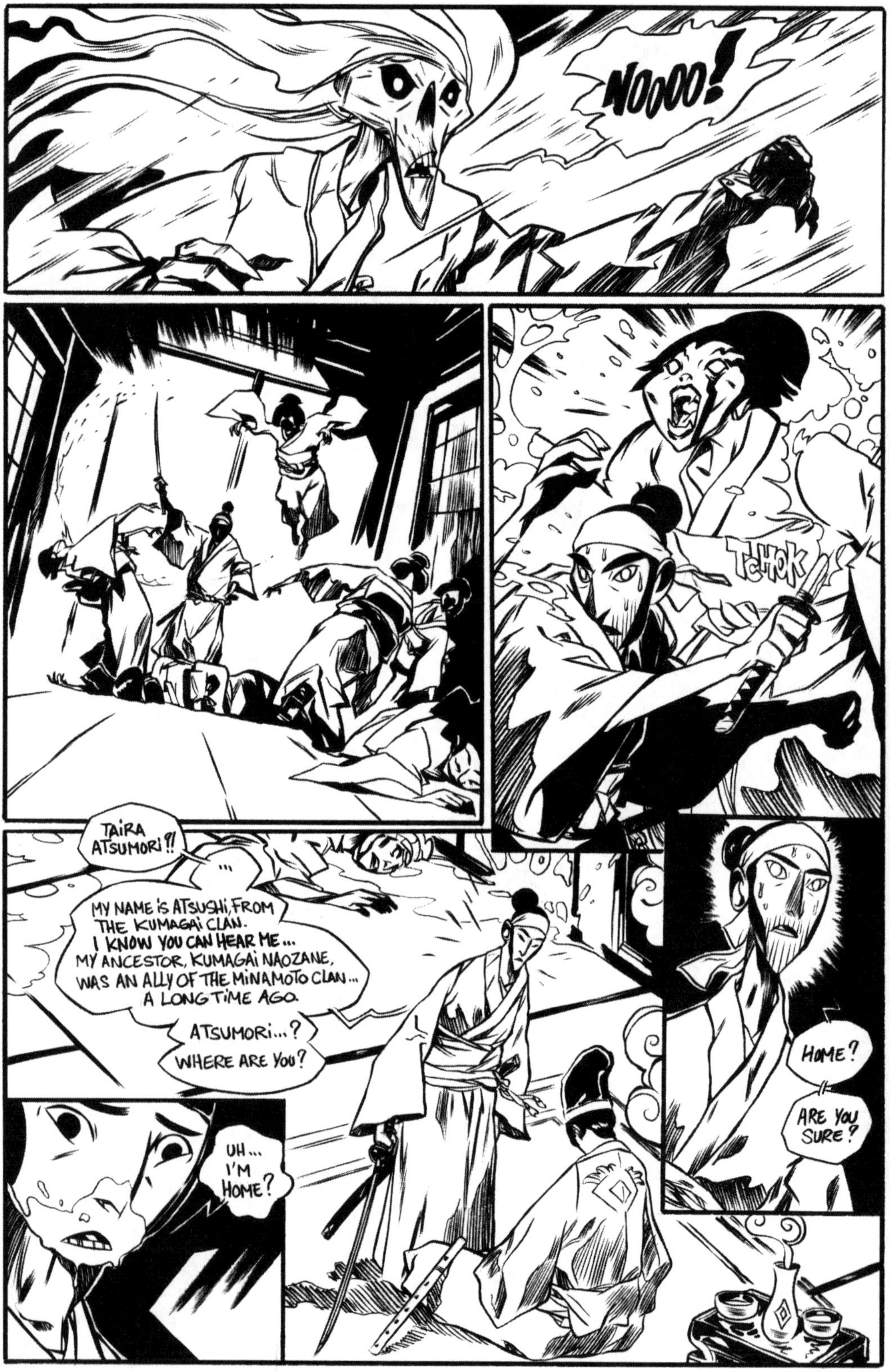
NOOOO!
TCHOK
TAIRA ATSUMORI?!
...
MY NAME IS ATSUSHI, FROM THE KUMAGAI CLAN.
I KNOW YOU CAN HEAR ME...
MY ANCESTOR, KUMAGAI NAOZANE, WAS AN ALLY OF THE MINAMOTO CLAN... A LONG TIME AGO.
ATSUMORI...?
WHERE ARE YOU?
HOME?
ARE YOU SURE?
UH... I'M HOME?

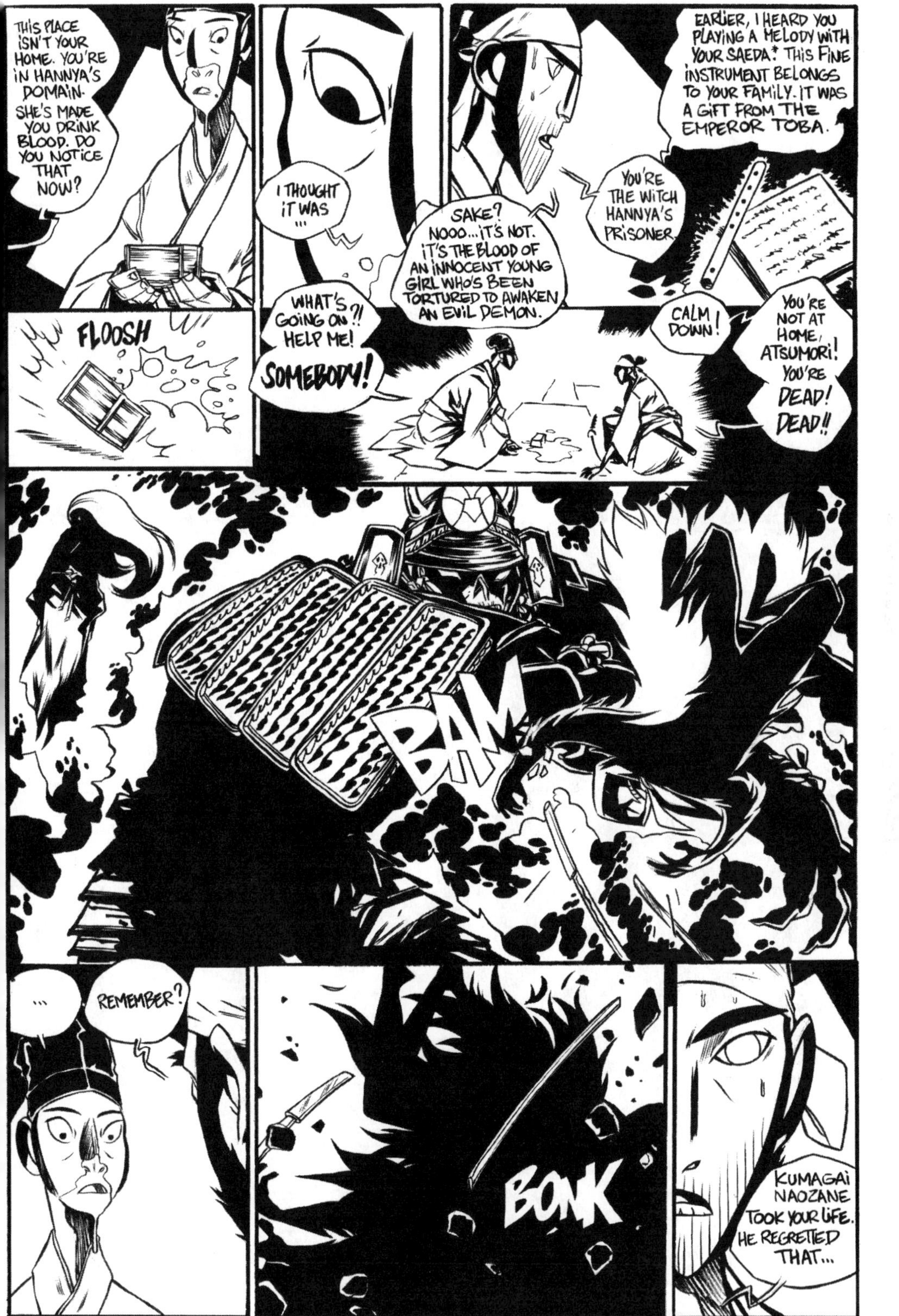
THIS PLACE ISN'T YOUR HOME. YOU'RE IN HANNYA'S DOMAIN.
SHE'S MADE YOU DRINK BLOOD. DO YOU NOTICE THAT NOW?
I THOUGHT IT WAS ...
SAKE? NOOO... IT'S NOT. IT'S THE BLOOD OF AN INNOCENT YOUNG GIRL WHO'S BEEN TORTURED TO AWAKEN AN EVIL DEMON.
EARLIER, I HEARD YOU PLAYING A MELODY WITH YOUR SAEDA.* THIS FINE INSTRUMENT BELONGS TO YOUR FAMILY. IT WAS A GIFT FROM THE EMPEROR TOBA.
YOU'RE THE WITCH HANNYA'S PRISONER.
FLOOSH
WHAT'S GOING ON?! HELP ME!
SOMEBODY!
CALM DOWN!
YOU'RE NOT AT HOME, ATSUMORI! YOU'RE DEAD! DEAD!!
BAM
...
REMEMBER?
BONK
KUMAGAI NAOZANE TOOK YOUR LIFE. HE REGRETTED THAT...

* SAEDA: FLUTE

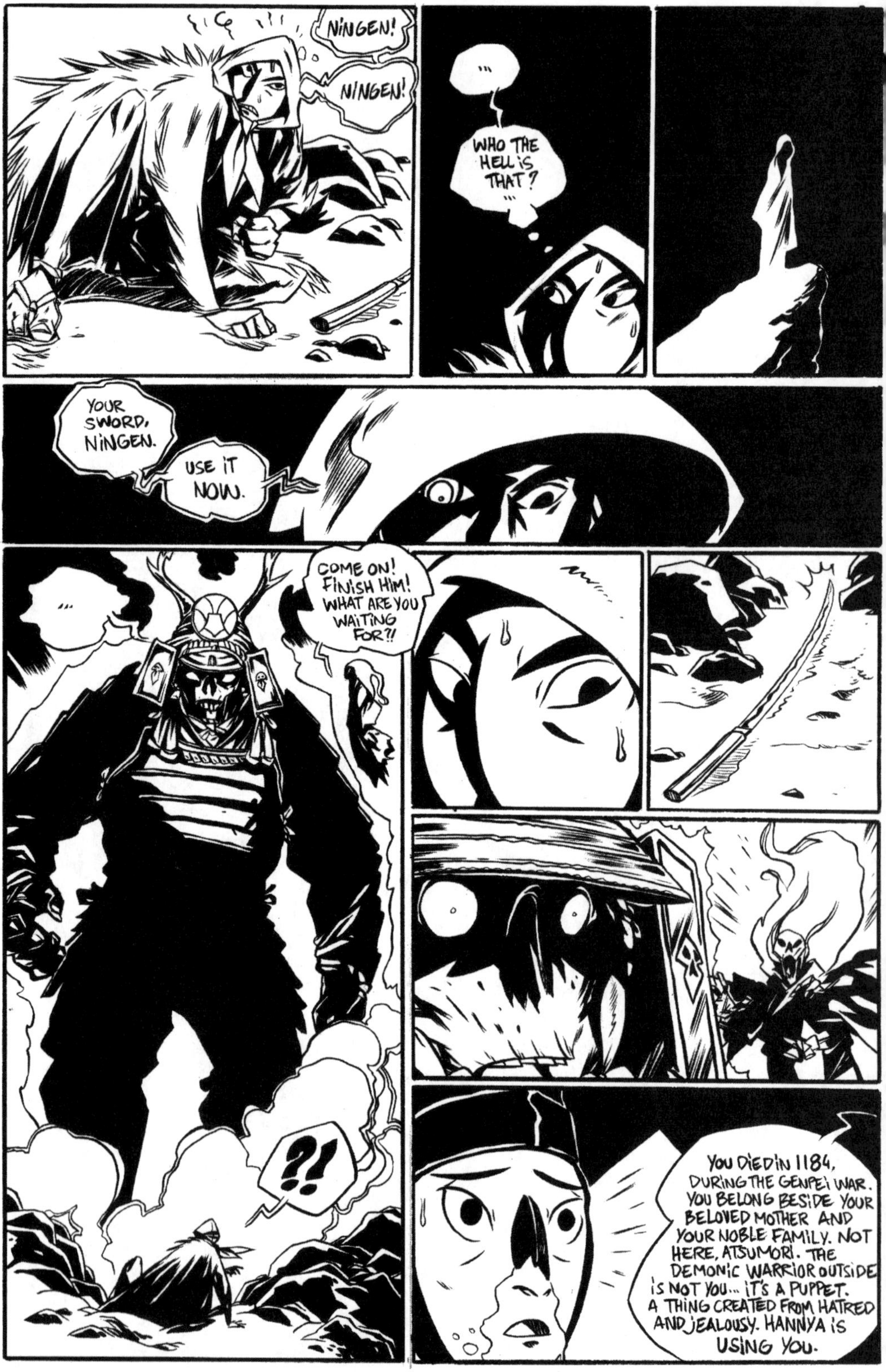
NINGEN!
NINGEN!
...
WHO THE HELL IS THAT? ...
YOUR SWORD, NINGEN.
USE IT NOW.
COME ON! FINISH HIM! WHAT ARE YOU WAITING FOR?!
?!
YOU DIED IN 1184, DURING THE GENPEI WAR. YOU BELONG BESIDE YOUR BELOVED MOTHER AND YOUR NOBLE FAMILY. NOT HERE, ATSUMORI. THE DEMONIC WARRIOR OUTSIDE IS NOT YOU... IT'S A PUPPET. A THING CREATED FROM HATRED AND JEALOUSY. HANNYA IS USING YOU.

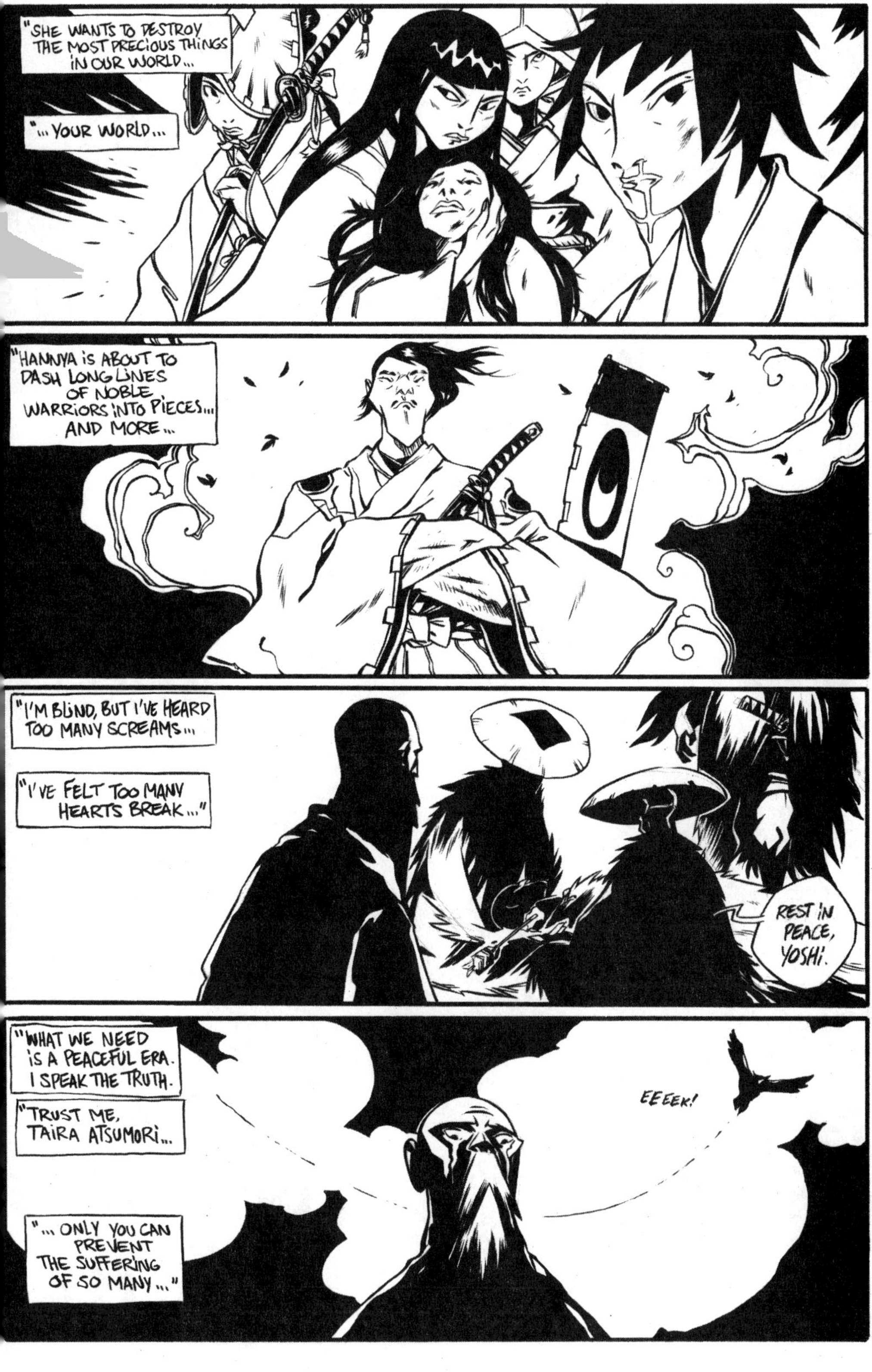
"SHE WANTS TO DESTROY THE MOST PRECIOUS THINGS IN OUR WORLD...
"...YOUR WORLD...
"HANNYA IS ABOUT TO DASH LONG LINES OF NOBLE WARRIORS INTO PIECES... AND MORE...
"I'M BLIND, BUT I'VE HEARD TOO MANY SCREAMS...
"I'VE FELT TOO MANY HEARTS BREAK..."
REST IN PEACE, YOSHI.
"WHAT WE NEED IS A PEACEFUL ERA. I SPEAK THE TRUTH.
"TRUST ME, TAIRA ATSUMORI...
EEEEK!
"...ONLY YOU CAN PREVENT THE SUFFERING OF SO MANY..."

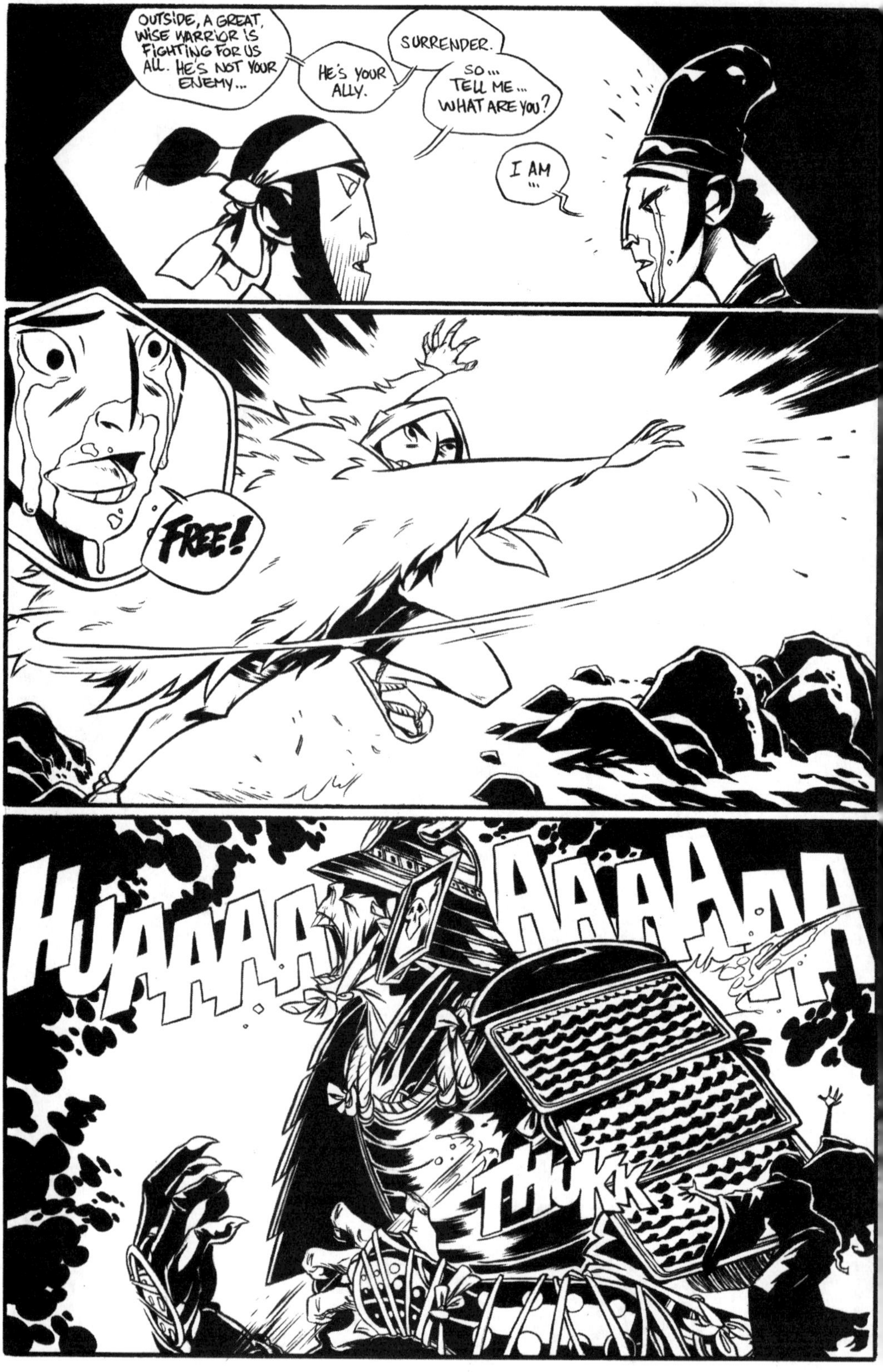
OUTSIDE, A GREAT, WISE WARRIOR IS FIGHTING FOR US ALL. HE'S NOT YOUR ENEMY...
HE'S YOUR ALLY.
SURRENDER.
SO... TELL ME... WHAT ARE YOU?
I AM ...
FREE!
HUAAAAAAAAAAA
THUKK

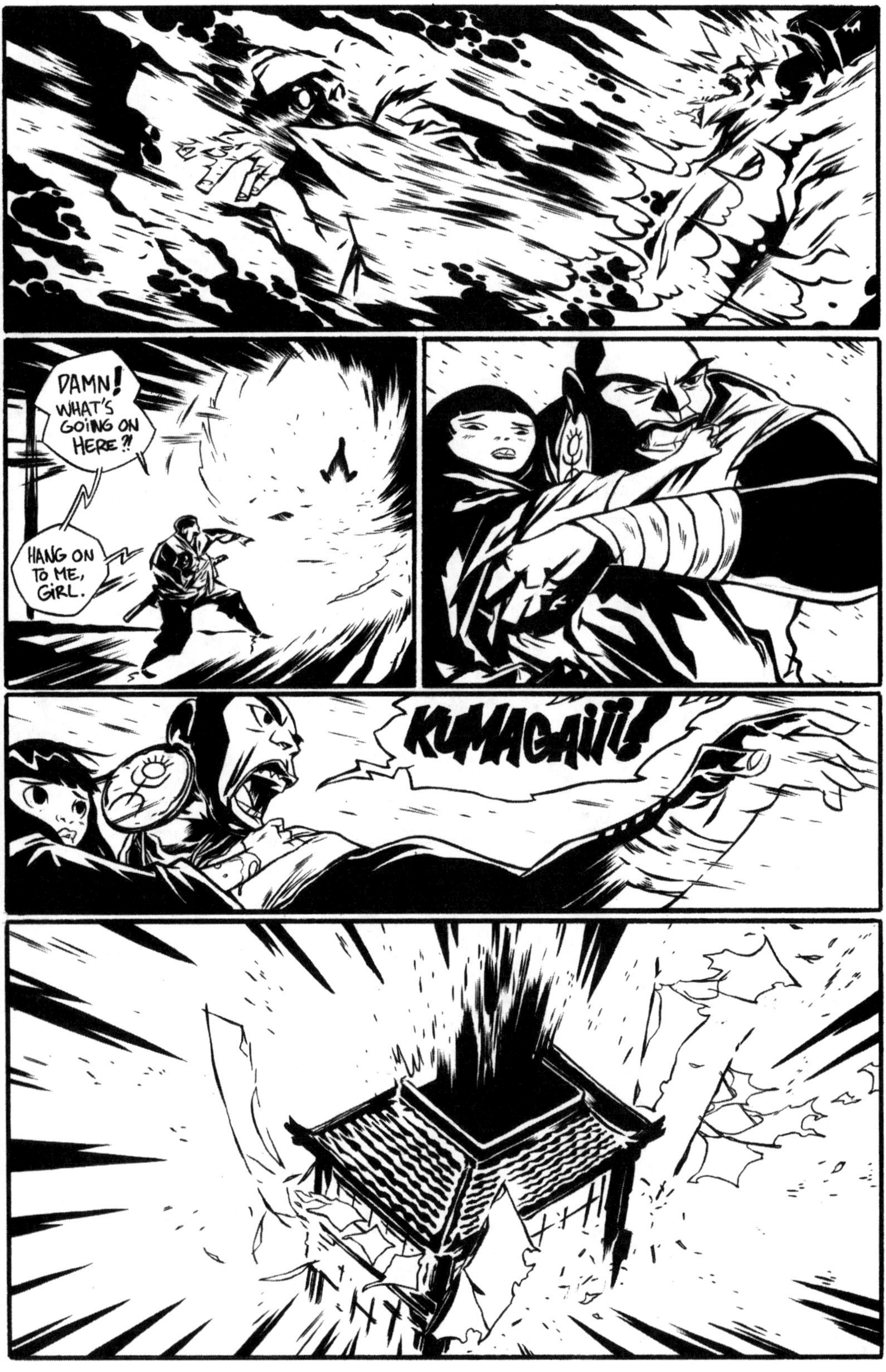
DAMN! WHAT'S GOING ON HERE?!
HANG ON TO ME, GIRL.
KUMAGAIII!

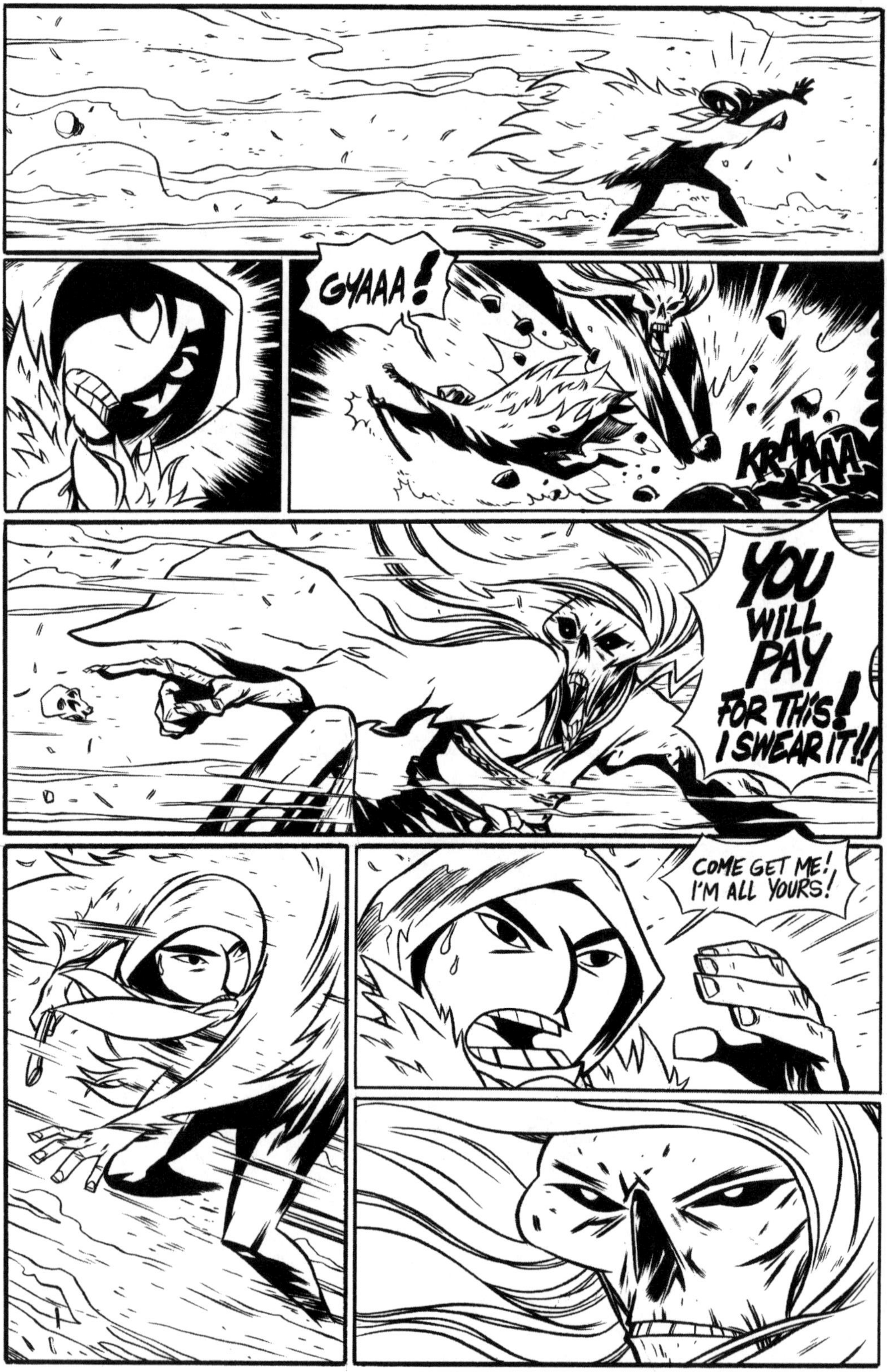
GYAAA!
KRAAAAA
YOU WILL PAY FOR THIS! I SWEAR IT!!
COME GET ME! I'M ALL YOURS!

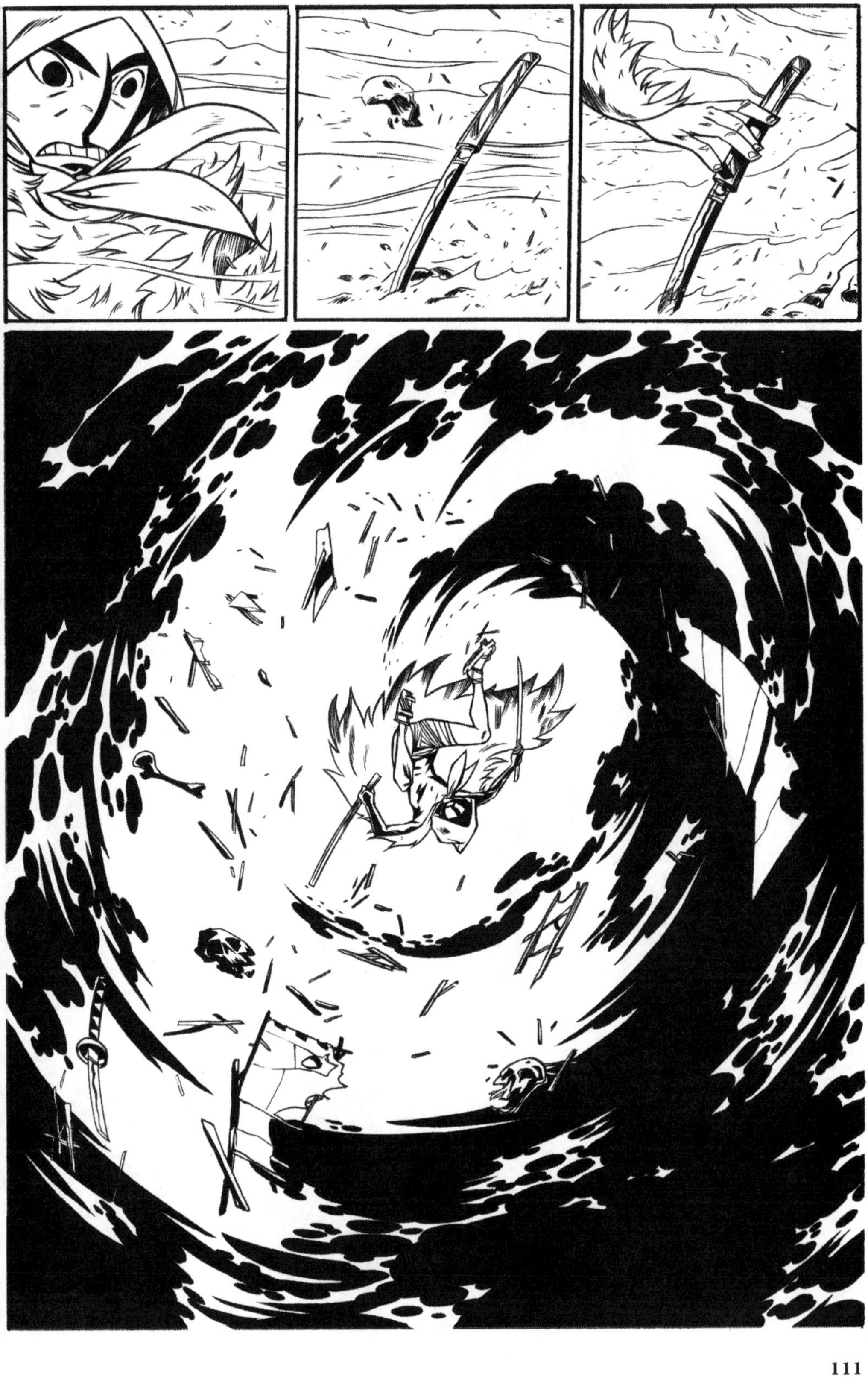

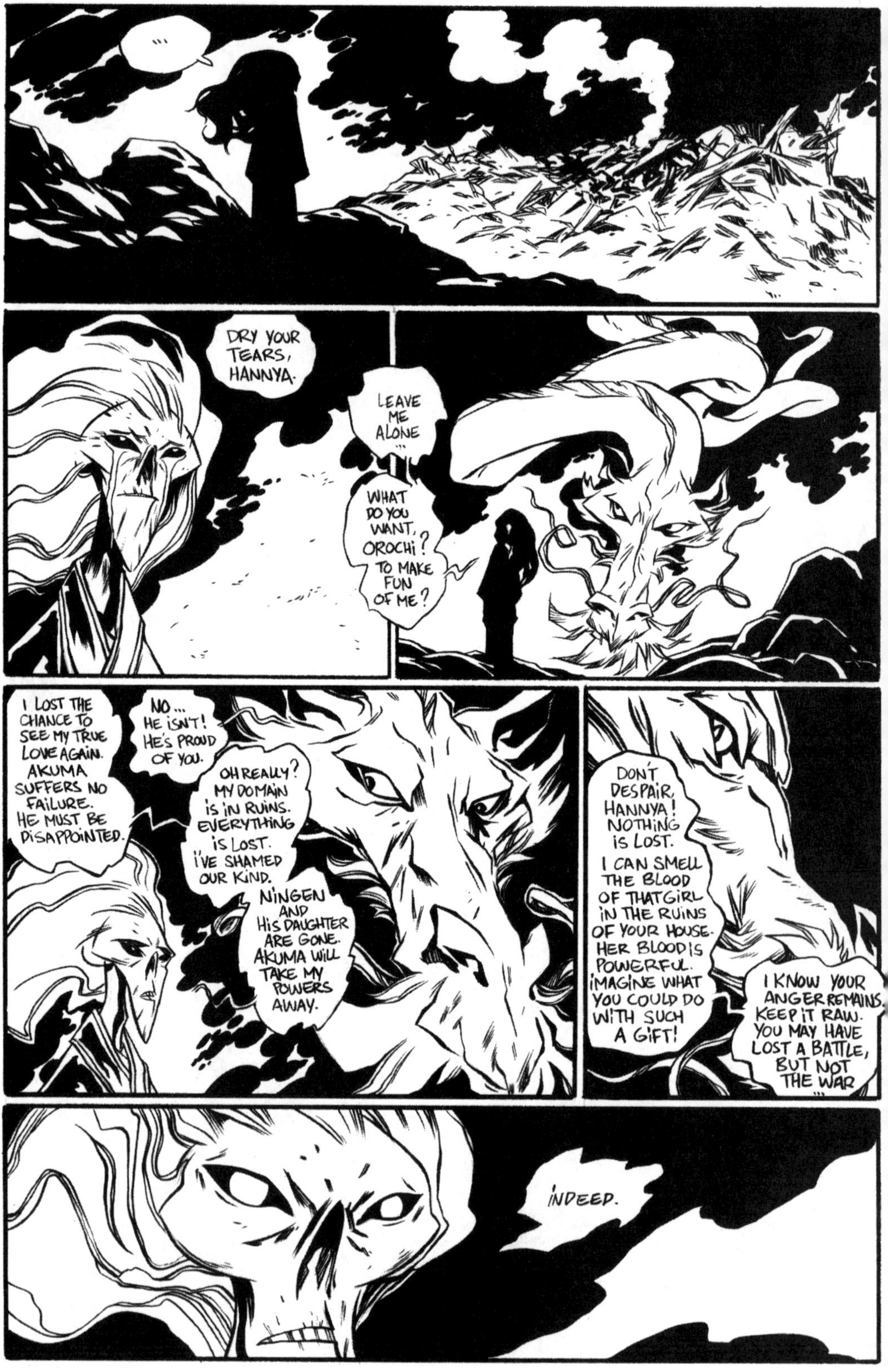
...
DRY YOUR TEARS, HANNYA.
LEAVE ME ALONE ...
WHAT DO YOU WANT, OROCHI? TO MAKE FUN OF ME?
I LOST THE CHANCE TO SEE MY TRUE LOVE AGAIN. AKUMA SUFFERS NO FAILURE. HE MUST BE DISAPPOINTED.
NO... HE ISN'T! HE'S PROUD OF YOU.
OH REALLY? MY DOMAIN IS IN RUINS. EVERYTHING IS LOST. I'VE SHAMED OUR KIND.
NINGEN AND HIS DAUGHTER ARE GONE. AKUMA WILL TAKE MY POWERS AWAY.
DON'T DESPAIR, HANNYA! NOTHING IS LOST.
I CAN SMELL THE BLOOD OF THAT GIRL IN THE RUINS OF YOUR HOUSE. HER BLOOD IS POWERFUL. IMAGINE WHAT YOU COULD DO WITH SUCH A GIFT!
I KNOW YOUR ANGER REMAINS. KEEP IT RAW. YOU MAY HAVE LOST A BATTLE, BUT NOT THE WAR ...
INDEED.

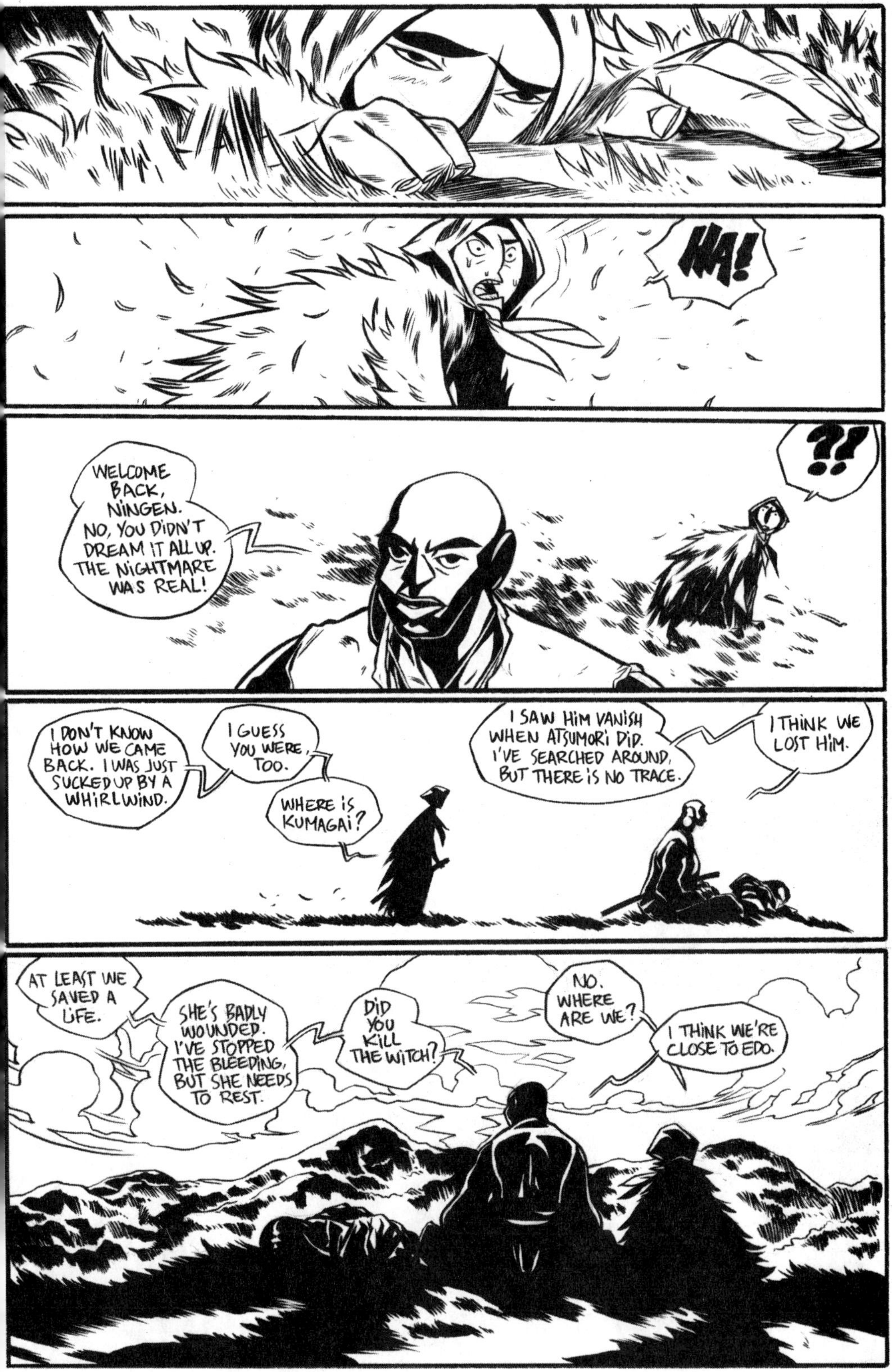
HA!
??
WELCOME BACK, NINGEN. NO, YOU DIDN'T DREAM IT ALL UP. THE NIGHTMARE WAS REAL!
I DON'T KNOW HOW WE CAME BACK. I WAS JUST SUCKED UP BY A WHIRLWIND.
I GUESS YOU WERE, TOO.
WHERE IS KUMAGAI?
I SAW HIM VANISH WHEN ATSUMORI DID. I'VE SEARCHED AROUND, BUT THERE IS NO TRACE.
I THINK WE LOST HIM.
AT LEAST WE SAVED A LIFE.
SHE'S BADLY WOUNDED. I'VE STOPPED THE BLEEDING, BUT SHE NEEDS TO REST.
DID YOU KILL THE WITCH?
NO. WHERE ARE WE?
I THINK WE'RE CLOSE TO EDO.

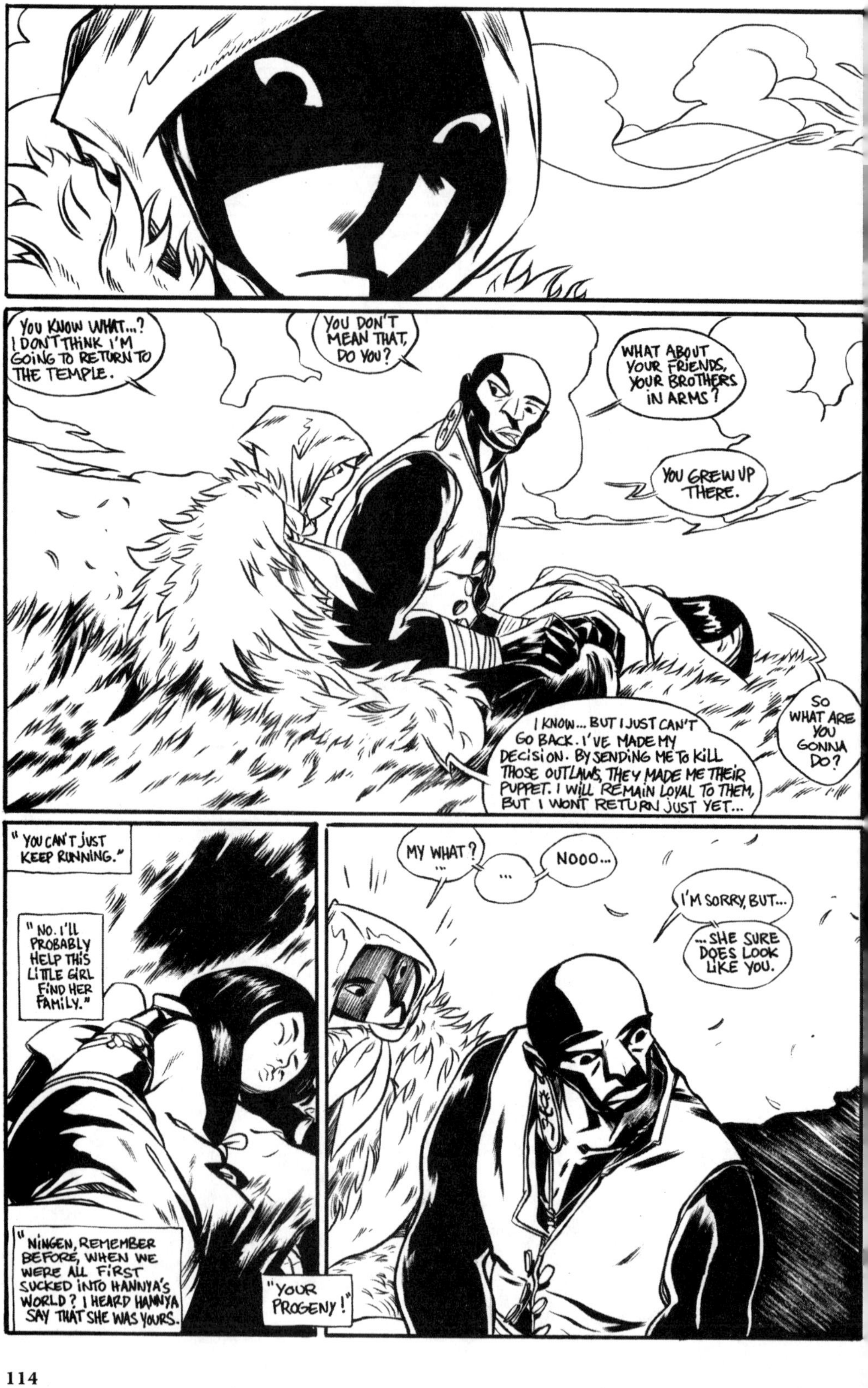

YOU KNOW WHAT...? I DON'T THINK I'M GOING TO RETURN TO THE TEMPLE.
YOU DON'T MEAN THAT, DO YOU?
WHAT ABOUT YOUR FRIENDS, YOUR BROTHERS IN ARMS?
YOU GREW UP THERE.
I KNOW... BUT I JUST CAN'T GO BACK. I'VE MADE MY DECISION. BY SENDING ME TO KILL THOSE OUTLAWS, THEY MADE ME THEIR PUPPET. I WILL REMAIN LOYAL TO THEM, BUT I WONT RETURN JUST YET...
SO WHAT ARE YOU GONNA DO?
"YOU CAN'T JUST KEEP RUNNING."
"NO. I'LL PROBABLY HELP THIS LITTLE GIRL FIND HER FAMILY."
"NINGEN, REMEMBER BEFORE, WHEN WE WERE ALL FIRST SUCKED INTO HANNYA'S WORLD? I HEARD HANNYA SAY THAT SHE WAS YOURS.
"YOUR PROGENY!"
MY WHAT? ...
...
NOOO...
I'M SORRY, BUT...
...SHE SURE DOES LOOK LIKE YOU.

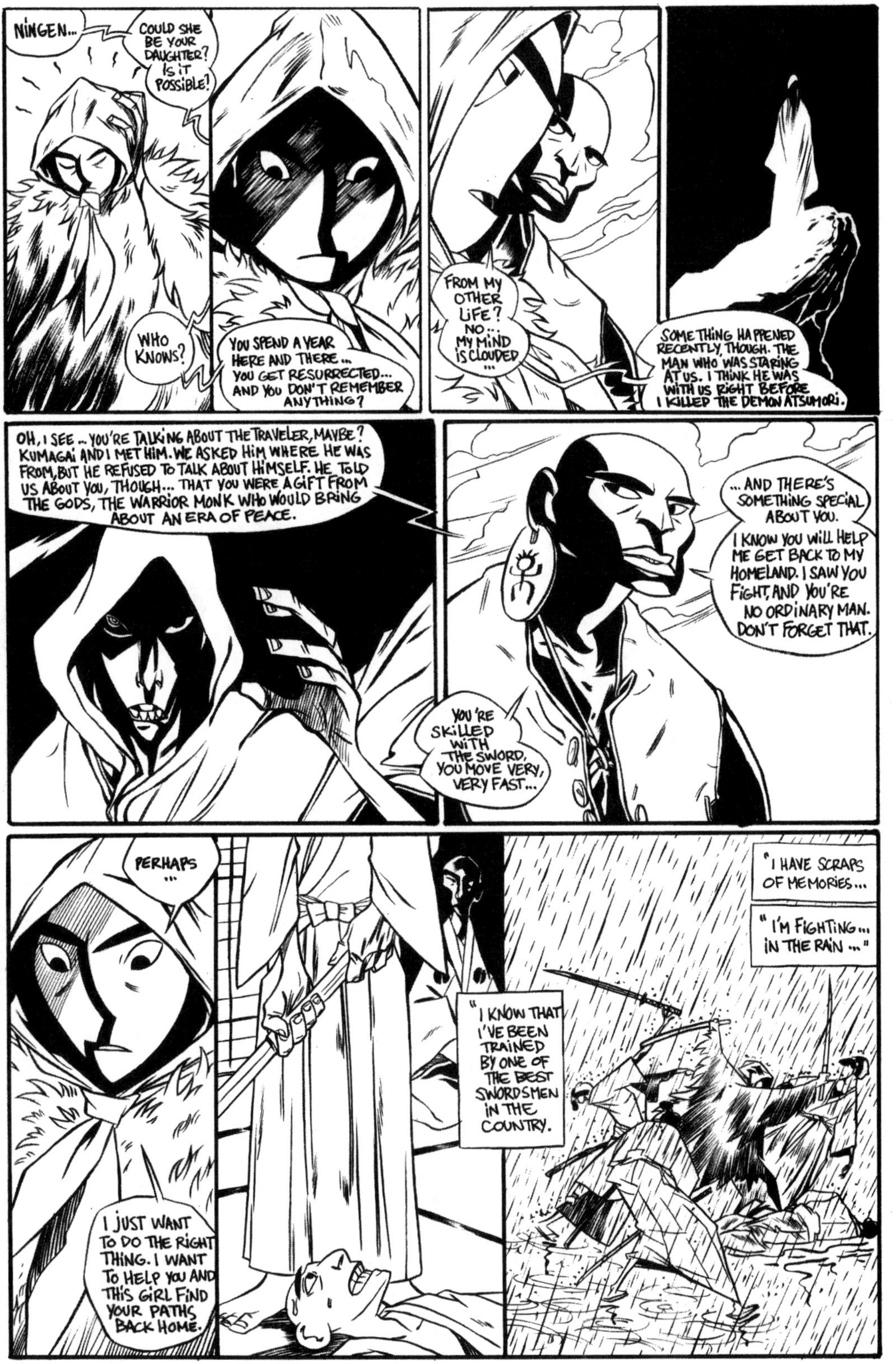
NINGEN...
COULD SHE BE YOUR DAUGHTER? IS IT POSSIBLE?
WHO KNOWS?
YOU SPEND A YEAR HERE AND THERE... YOU GET RESURRECTED... AND YOU DON'T REMEMBER ANYTHING?
FROM MY OTHER LIFE? NO... MY MIND IS CLOUDED...
SOMETHING HAPPENED RECENTLY, THOUGH. THE MAN WHO WAS STARING AT US. I THINK HE WAS WITH US RIGHT BEFORE I KILLED THE DEMON ATSUMORI.
OH, I SEE... YOU'RE TALKING ABOUT THE TRAVELER, MAYBE? KUMAGAI AND I MET HIM. WE ASKED HIM WHERE HE WAS FROM, BUT HE REFUSED TO TALK ABOUT HIMSELF. HE TOLD US ABOUT YOU, THOUGH... THAT YOU WERE A GIFT FROM THE GODS, THE WARRIOR MONK WHO WOULD BRING ABOUT AN ERA OF PEACE.
YOU'RE SKILLED WITH THE SWORD, YOU MOVE VERY, VERY FAST...
...AND THERE'S SOMETHING SPECIAL ABOUT YOU.
I KNOW YOU WILL HELP ME GET BACK TO MY HOMELAND. I SAW YOU FIGHT, AND YOU'RE NO ORDINARY MAN. DON'T FORGET THAT.
PERHAPS...
I JUST WANT TO DO THE RIGHT THING. I WANT TO HELP YOU AND THIS GIRL FIND YOUR PATHS BACK HOME.
"I KNOW THAT I'VE BEEN TRAINED BY ONE OF THE BEST SWORDSMEN IN THE COUNTRY.
"I HAVE SCRAPS OF MEMORIES...
"I'M FIGHTING... IN THE RAIN..."

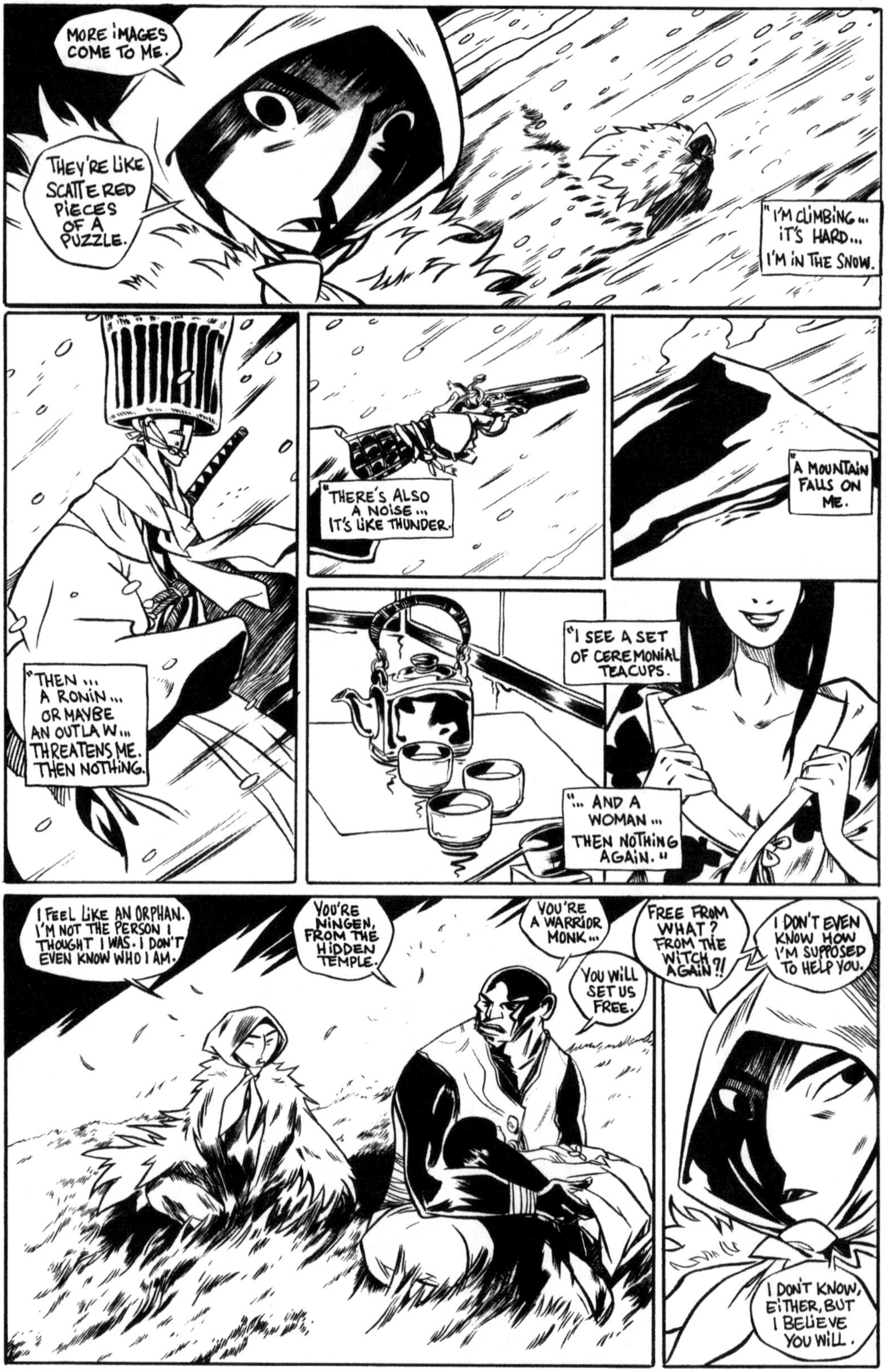
MORE IMAGES COME TO ME.
THEY'RE LIKE SCATTERED PIECES OF A PUZZLE.
"I'M CLIMBING... IT'S HARD... I'M IN THE SNOW.
"THERE'S ALSO A NOISE... IT'S LIKE THUNDER.
"A MOUNTAIN FALLS ON ME.
"THEN... A RONIN... OR MAYBE AN OUTLAW... THREATENS ME. THEN NOTHING.
"I SEE A SET OF CEREMONIAL TEACUPS.
"... AND A WOMAN... THEN NOTHING AGAIN."
I FEEL LIKE AN ORPHAN. I'M NOT THE PERSON I THOUGHT I WAS. I DON'T EVEN KNOW WHO I AM.
YOU'RE NINGEN, FROM THE HIDDEN TEMPLE.
YOU'RE A WARRIOR MONK...
YOU WILL SET US FREE.
FREE FROM WHAT? FROM THE WITCH AGAIN?!
I DON'T EVEN KNOW HOW I'M SUPPOSED TO HELP YOU.
I DON'T KNOW, EITHER, BUT I BELIEVE YOU WILL.

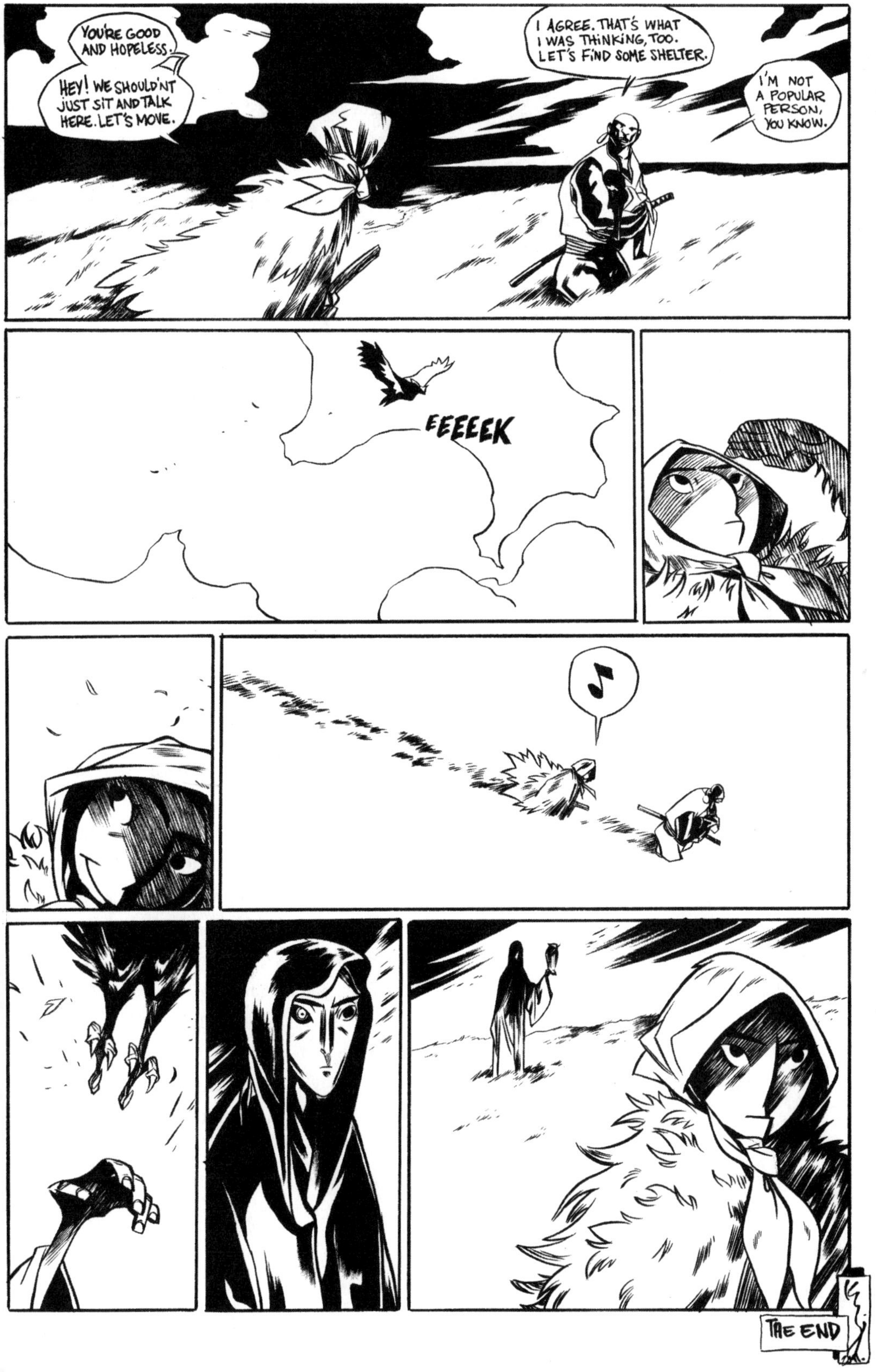
YOU'RE GOOD AND HOPELESS.
HEY! WE SHOULD'NT JUST SIT AND TALK HERE. LET'S MOVE.
I AGREE. THAT'S WHAT I WAS THINKING, TOO. LET'S FIND SOME SHELTER.
I'M NOT A POPULAR PERSON, YOU KNOW.
EEEEEK
♪
THE END

Thanks to Jesus Christ for giving me talent, time, faith, and strength—all day, every day. To my mother Mbuyi Tshinguta Monique, my brothers Alain and Yves, my sister Maryse. To Henri, Kaya, Félix, Basile, and Nola. To my aunt Madi and my great cousin Kwesi. To Maria and Amedeo, my family-in-law. To all my cousins in Belgium—endless love. To David Jean Alain Mutamba, his wife Ghislaine, to their children, Joyce-Bénédicte, Johanna-Isabelle, Olivianne-Léa. And to all the true Eagles from the CPP.

Thanks to my worldwide friends and their families: Ted Mabika Kumbu, Kai and Ginga, Ygal and Linda Bohbot, Orens, Jonah, my sweet Eli Anne, Nora Ghitescu, Geoffroy and Sandra Baud Pernes-Martin, Xavier Monjardin, Axelle Marais, Olivier Jouvray, Virginie Ollagnier Jouvray, Flavie, Jotaro Yoshida and Yukiko, Mike Asakawa, Kaori Ikeda, Issei Wada, Misaki Kido, Stéphane Capo-chichi, Melika Melstri, Claire Murigande, Valérie Roduit, Pierre Henri Beyrière, Charlotte Cochet, Anik Polo, Karim Ajlani, Giovanni Guida, Mark Johan Walder, Malick Silva, Xavier Ripolles, Stephane Pagani, Marc Villa, Ted Mathot, Daria Michel Scotti, Chhuy-Ing Ia, Nick Parry Jones, Ben Marchesini, Camille Eléonore Tellenbach, Olivier De Simone, Amalia Luyet and Trevor McMahan, little Jude, Léonie Cocquio and Jan Borgeaud, Franck and Valérie Juncker, Elsa Bernard, Yan Kem, Simon Loche, Joachim Meyer a.k.a. Grotesk, Lieve Vanleeuw, Andy Mason, Bryce Low, Atang Tshikare, Pete Woodbridge, Ophelie Loup, Ian Bonhote, Fabian Martinez, Christophe Clarey, Nicolas Nemiri, Cesarina Guida and Javier Valera, David Warner, Oren Haskins, Pierre Alary, Melissa Kassab, and Vincent Calmel.

Special thanks to my publisher Mike Richardson, my editor Philip Simon, the great Dan Jackson, David Scroggy, and all of the Dark Horse Comics crew. To all the fans and future readers—and to all the comic-book shops.

—J. P. Kalonji

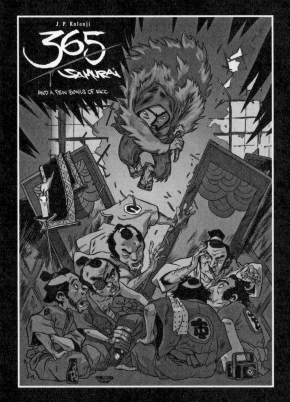

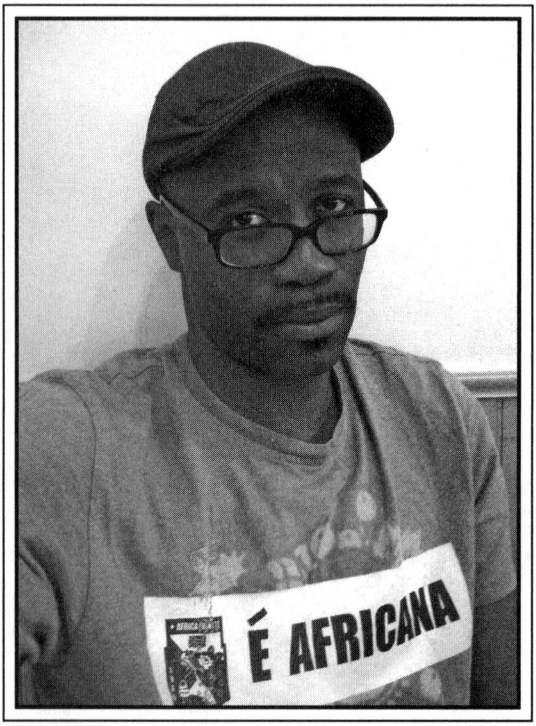
É AFRICANA

Jean-Philippe Kalonji was born in 1973 in Geneva, Switzerland. As he embarks on his second book with Dark Horse Comics, his work has continued to gain critical acclaim by fans the world over. Kalonji's previous graphic novel from Dark Horse, *365 Samurai and a Few Bowls of Rice,* was nominated for a "Great Graphic Novels for Teens" award by the Young Adult Library Services Association. Kalonji's rich and varied career has also led to work focusing on integration and xenophobia with organizations such as the Red Cross, *Art South Africa,* Pro Helvetia, and the Geneva Department of Education. For more information, please visit KalonjiArt.com